ALTERNATIVE APPROACHES TO SECOND LANGUAGE ACQUISITION

Edited by Dwight Atkinson

Routledge
Taylor & Francis Group

LONDON AND NEW YORK

First edition published 2011
by Routledge
2 Park Square, Milton Park, Abingdon, OX14 4RN

Simultaneously published in the USA and Canada
by Routledge
711 Third Ave, New York, NY 10017

Routledge is an imprint of the Taylor & Francis Group, an informa business

The right of Dwight Atkinson to be identified as author of the
editorial material and the authors for their individual chapters
has been asserted in accordance with sections 77 and 78 of
the Copyright, Designs and Patents Act 1988.

Typeset in Bembo and Stone Sans by
Florence Production Ltd, Stoodleigh, Devon
Printed and bound in Great Britain by
CPI Group (UK) Ltd, Croydon, CR0 4YY

British Library Cataloguing in Publication Data
A catalogue record for this book is available from the British Library

Library of Congress Cataloging in Publication Data
Alternative approaches to second language acquisition/edited by
    Dwight Atkinson.—1st ed.
        p. cm.
    Includes index.
    1. Second language acquisition—Study and teaching.   2. Language
and languages—Study and teaching.   I. Atkinson, Dwight.
    P118.2.A48 2011
    418.0071—dc22   2010034569

ISBN13: 978–0–415–54924–0 (hbk)
ISBN13: 978–0–415–54925–7 (pbk)
ISBN13: 978–0–203–83093–2 (ebk)

CONTENTS

CONTRIBUTORS

Dwight Atkinson Department of English, Purdue University, West Lafayette, Indiana, USA.

Patricia A. Duff Department of Language & Literacy Education, University of British Columbia, Vancouver, Canada.

Gabriele Kasper Department of Second Language Studies, University of Hawai'i, Honolulu, Hawai'i, USA.

James P. Lantolf Department of Applied Linguistics, The Pennsylvania State University, State College, Pennsylvania, USA.

Diane Larsen-Freeman School of Education, Department of Linguistics & English Language Institute, University of Michigan, Ann Arbor, Michigan, USA.

Carolyn McKinney School of Education, University of Cape Town, Cape Town, South Africa.

Bonny Norton Department of Language & Literacy Education, University of British Columbia, Vancouver, Canada.

Lourdes Ortega Department of Second Language Studies, University of Hawai'i, Honolulu, Hawai'i, USA.

Steven Talmy Department of Language & Literacy Education, University of British Columbia, Vancouver, Canada.

Johannes Wagner Department of Communication and Information Science, University of Southern Denmark, Kolding, Denmark

Since the appearance of the Firth and Wagner [1997] article, a variety of alternative perspectives have blossomed, extending the boundaries of SLA theory, adding to and enriching its constructs and methodologies.

(Swain & Deters, " 'New' Mainstream SLA Theory, Expanded and Enriched," *Modern Language Journal*, 2007, p. 821)

L2 acquisition is an enormously complex phenomenon and will benefit from a multiplicity of perspectives, theories, and research methodologies. Like other areas of the social sciences, it should and undoubtedly will remain open to a multiplicity of lines of enquiry and, as a result, will continue to be characterized by controversy and debate. Thus, whereas in the 1994 edition [of this volume] I expressed concern over whether SLA would survive as a coherent field of study, today I am more prepared to acknowledge that this may not be important and that diversity of approach and controversy constitute signs of the field's vigour and an inevitable consequence of the attempt to understand a complex phenomenon.

(Ellis, *The study of second language acquisition*, 2008, pp. xxii–xxiii)

Let all the flowers bloom . . . You never know which ones will catch the eye to become tomorrow's realities.

(Lantolf, "SLA theory building: 'Letting all the flowers bloom!' " *Language Learning*, 1996, p. 739)

One person is always wrong, but with two truth begins.

(Nietzsche, *The Gay Science*, 1887/1974, p. 218)

PREFACE

Over the last two decades, a variety of approaches to second language acquisition (SLA) have appeared that differ from the historically dominant one: cognitivism. Each of these approaches has contributed crucially to what, as a result, is now a conceptually richer field. Yet while these varied approaches have enriched SLA studies substantially, they have led, with a few exceptions, independent and even isolated existences.

If SLA were less complex, this might be an acceptable state of affairs. One approach might even rise to the top, eventually replacing cognitivism. It is increasingly apparent, however, that SLA is an extremely complex and multifaceted phenomenon. Exactly for this reason, it now appears that no single theoretical perspective will allow us to understand SLA adequately. It therefore becomes necessary for *all* the varied perspectives, and this includes cognitivism, to engage one another, to "talk" to each other, to discover how they relate, differ, complement, overlap, contradict, inform—in short, to show how they can, via comparison and contrast, lead us toward a richer, more multidimensional understanding of SLA. To put it differently: Although absolutely crucial for progress in the field, "letting all the flowers bloom" (Lantolf, 1996) alone is no longer enough. Having gathered the flowers, we must now lay them out in comparative perspective to see their possibilities for arrangement. Mere profusion will not suffice—sense must be made of the richness and profusion.

This is not an appeal to winnow theories—the famous "theory culling" of the 1990s. It is rather to see what can be done in the "Theory Proliferation Era" of SLA studies circa the second decade of the 21st century. Diversity is the ground, and now that the ground is established let us ask what to build on it. Certainly, we should proceed with caution, but efforts to bring the diverse approaches into engagement and interaction are crucial for progress to be made in the field.

I would like to thank the volume's contributors for their willingness to participate in this project and their hard work in bringing it to completion.

Squeezing diverse SLA approaches into a single comparative framework is no easy task, and efforts are just beginning, but whatever success this book will have is due to the authors' unstinting labor toward that goal. I would also like to thank my friends, students, and colleagues—and above all Eton Churchill, Diane Larsen-Freeman, Takako Nishino, Hanako Okada, Tetyana Smotrova, Yumi Takamiya, Beril Tezeller Arik, Jinju Nishino, and Jija Sohn—for their encouragement and participation in this endeavor. The editors at Routledge—initially the late Cathleen Petree, with whom I hatched the original idea, and then Louisa Semlyen—have also played crucial roles in bringing this project to fruition; the same holds true for Sophie Jacques, Julia Mitchell, and Sue Edwards. I end by thanking them all here.

Dwight Atkinson

INTRODUCTION

Cognitivism and second language acquisition

Dwight Atkinson

> [Language is] a genetic inheritance, a mathematical system, a social fact, an expression of individual identity, an expression of cultural identity, an outcome of dialogic interaction, a social semiotic, the intuitions of native speakers, a collection of memorized chunks, the sum of attested data, a rule-based discrete combinatory system, or an electrical activation in a distributed network . . . We do not have to choose. Language can be all of these things at once.
>
> (G. Cook & Seidlhofer, 1995, p. 4)

If language is many things, then so is its acquisition. It is therefore a curious fact that the study of second language acquisition (SLA) has historically been dominated by a single broad approach—that which goes by the name of "cognitive." From this perspective, language *may* be a "social semiotic," but above all it is a cognitive product. Its development is therefore first and foremost a cognitive process.

The dominance of this perspective has been widely acknowledged in SLA studies, as indicated by a sampling of influential statements:

> Theorists and researchers tend to view SLA as a mental process, that is, to believe that language acquisition resides mostly, if not solely, in the mind.
>
> (Davis, 1995, pp. 427–428)

> We may describe the central facts of SLA very simply in the following way: On the basis of experience with a particular language, L (that is, linguistic input from L), a learner possessing some capacity for language acquisition develops certain cognitive capacities to use L . . . There are thus three central cognitive or behavioral problems in the study of SLA: the problems of (a) the cognitive structures and abilities that underlie L2 use, (b) the relevant linguistic input, and (c) the capacity for language acquisition.
>
> (Ritchie & Bhatia, 1996, pp. 18–19)

SLA has been essentially a psycholinguistic enterprise, dominated by the computational metaphor of acquisition.

(R. Ellis, 1997, p. 87)

Most SLA researchers view the object of inquiry as in large part an internal, mental process: *the acquisition of new (linguistic) knowledge.* And I would say, with good reason. SLA is a process that (often) takes place in a social setting, of course, but then so do most internal processes—learning, thinking, remembering, sexual arousal, and digestion, for example—and that neither obviates the need for theories of those processes, nor shifts the goal of inquiry to a theory of the settings.

(Long, 1997, p. 319)

It is fair to say that the dominant theoretical influences [in SLA] have been linguistic and psycholinguistic . . . While more socially oriented views have been proposed from time to time, they have remained relatively marginal to the field overall.

(Mitchell & Myles, 1998, p. x)

The basic assumption in SLA research is that learners create a language system . . . What is important is that the learners themselves impose structure on the available linguistic data and formulate an internalized system.

(Gass & Selinker, 2001, p. 12)

Much current SLA research and theorizing shares a strongly cognitive orientation . . . The focus is firmly on identifying the nature and sources of the underlying L2 knowledge system, and on explaining developmental success and failure. Performance data are inevitably the researchers' mainstay, but understanding underlying competence, not the external verbal behavior that depends on that competence, is the ultimate goal. Researchers recognize that SLA takes place in a social context, of course, and accept that it can be influenced by that context, both micro and macro. However, they also recognize that language learning, like any other learning, is ultimately a matter of change in an individual's internal mental state. As such, research on SLA is increasingly viewed as a branch of cognitive science.

(Doughty & Long, 2003a, p. 4)

Even in those early days, we believed that we were witnessing the birth of a new field—one that did not see language as behavior, one that no longer ignored the mind, one that put cognitivism squarely at the forefront of its explanations. As it turns out, it was a powerful birthright. It is fair to say that a cognitivist view has dominated the field ever since.

(Larsen-Freeman, 2007, p. 775)

Specific interests and areas of expertise have led the authors [in the volume *Theories in Second Language Acquisition: An Introduction*] to the linguistic and cognitive aspects of SLA. Thus, the theories and perspectives taken in the present volume will reflect such orientations. To be sure, there are social perspectives that can be brought to bear on SLA. However, such perspectives tend to focus on the *use* of the second language and only minimally address issues of acquisition that are of concern here . . . Our intention is to gather those approaches that currently compete to explain the acquisition of a linguistic system.

(VanPatten & Williams, 2007, p. 13)

As these quotations indicate, the "strongly cognitive" (Doughty & Long, 2003a) or *cognitivist* (Larsen-Freeman, 2007) focus of mainstream SLA studies has resulted in a highly particular understanding, but one that is commonly accepted as natural, normal, and—for many—the only plausible explanation for SLA. The main aim of this book is to go beyond cognitivist approaches to SLA by exploring and comparing alternative perspectives, but before doing so cognitivism itself must be introduced and described. This chapter is therefore devoted to tracing the development of cognitivism in SLA studies and the fields that have influenced it. I conclude by briefly introducing the subsequent chapters in the volume, and why a volume like this is appearing at this time.

Defining Cognitivism[1]

The term *cognitivism* is typically used to denote the doctrine that: (1) the mind/brain is, for all intents and purposes, the necessary and sufficient locus of human thought and learning; and (2) such thought and learning is a form of *information processing*. Wallace (2007, p. 18) defined cognitivism as simply "the information processing view of human cognition," while Haugeland (1998, p. 9) defined it as "roughly the position that intelligent behavior can be explained (only) by appeal to internal 'cognitive processes'—that is, rational thought in a broad sense." Costall and Leudar (1996, p. 102) stated that:

For almost half a century, cognitivism has taken the form of functionalism (in the modern sense of that term), the idea that thought and action are to be explained exclusively in terms of self-sufficient rules and representations. Mental representations, formulated without reference to context, were supposed to explain (among many other things) how human beings and other animals manage to "go beyond" essentially impoverished perceptual information, imbue an essentially colorless and indifferent world with meaning, and "generalize" from one particular situation to another. The appeal to representations was an attempt to resolve the problems that arise from dualistic thinking rather than directly engage the underlying dualisms that constitute cognitivism itself, most notably the dualisms of mind and body, and of animal and environment.

Although cognitivism and related doctrines permeate modern thought and endeavor, all discussions I know of view mainstream cognitive science as its current intellectual base. In fact, cognitivism is enshrined in the founding documents of cognitive science, including Bruner, Goodnow, and Austin (1956), Chomsky (1959), Miller, Galanter, and Pribram (1960), Neisser (1976), and Sloan Foundation (1978). According to the last-mentioned, the "common research objective" of cognitive science is "to discover the representational and computational capacities of the mind and their structural and functional representation in the brain" (pp. 75–76). More recently, Boden (2006) has entitled her two-volume history of cognitive science *Mind as Machine*—a title that doubles as her definition of cognitive science.

The doctrine of cognitivism can be roughly represented as a linked set of features and assumptions. While only the first two or three can probably be regarded as criterial, the full set is widely shared by mainstream cognitive science, within which I also include connectionism (cf. Boden, 2006; Costall, 2007; Wheeler, 2005):

1. *Mind as computer*: Cognition is information processing—a dominantly uniform, mechanical set of operations that take in input, process it, and produce output on the model of a computer.

2. *Representationalism*: Symbolic or distributed internal representations are the primary units of cognition. Cognitive knowledge is stored as internal representations of the external (including socioculturally constructed) world, or as the stuff (e.g., nonactive neural connection patterns) of which they are formed.

3. *Learning as abstract knowledge acquisition*: Learning means extracting perceptual cues from the environment and processing them so that they become representations.[2] Knowledge must therefore be radically decontextualized and abstract: Internalized, it loses its concrete embedding in the environment. This view is crystallized in Chomsky's famous competence–performance distinction, in which real-world performance is a weak, indirect, and misleading indicator of actual knowledge. Actual knowledge—knowledge in its pure form—can only be found abstractly represented in the mind/brain.

4. *Centrality of language, and language as code*: Language has had a central place in cognitivist doctrine. This is partly because linguistic theory seems to provide the perfect model for how knowledge can be organized, stored, and activated in the cognitive apparatus—as a set of component units that are arrayed in production and processing in lawful combinations, i.e., as subject to syntactic rules. A cognitive "grammar" therefore consists of a set of symbols and a syntax for arranging them.[3]

Relatedly, the psycholinguistic study of language processing has been at the forefront of cognitive science. Following on point 1 above, the implicit theory of language undergirding cognitivism is that language is coded information, to be sent and received via "telementation" (Harris, 1991). Language production and comprehension therefore become, respectively, encoding and decoding processes wherein what are encoded/decoded are units (or at least vehicles) of thought. Likewise, language in this view becomes simply a tool for referring to/encoding the world.

5.   *Scientism*: Mainstream forms of cognitive science model themselves on the (often idealized) basis of the natural sciences and engineering, and especially their favored research methodologies. Other kinds of scientific inquiry, including natural history, some forms of ecology, and the various social science traditions emanating from Dilthey's (1883/1989) *Naturwissenshaft* (natural science) versus *Geistwissenshaft* (science of the spirit or mind, or, in modern terminology, human sciences) distinction are marginalized if not rejected.

6.   *Substance dualism and functionalism*: Starting with Descartes, an unbridgeable divide was posited between mind and everything else—the body and the material and sociocultural environment. In other words, mind was thought to be of a fundamentally different kind, or *substance*, than physical body and world. One result of substance dualism is *functionalism* (Clark, 2001)—the idea that cognition can (and, for some influential scholars, *must*) be understood apart from its concrete physical instantiations. Thus, classical cognitivists (and, more controversially, some connectionists—see Elman, 1998; Reeke & Edelman, 1988) see their object of study as having little if anything directly to do with neurology or biology. According to functionalism, a cognitive system can potentially be implemented in a wide variety of media, but implementation is not the cognitive scientist's concern.

7.   *Subject–object dualism*: As in other mainstream forms of science, cognitivism views the object of study—the mind—as "out there." As a scientific object, it has nothing directly to do with the researching subject—the human being "in here." The separation of the object from the subject studying it is a fundamental requirement of mainstream science and cognitive science.

8.   *Reductionism*: Even cognitive scientists who question whether cognition per se is the necessary and sufficient locus of thought and learning have often accepted the idea that they must focus on mind per se if they seriously hope to understand human thought and behavior (e.g., Gardner, 1985, p. 6). Fodor (1980) termed this position "methodological solipsism," and influentially recommended it to cognitive science researchers.

9.   *Aggregatism*: While cognitive science purports to account for individuals' cognition, it overwhelmingly studies aggregates of individuals, and then construes its results as representing "average human being[s]" (Block, 2003, p. 97). The assumption here—as noted in point 1 above—is that cognition is a mechanical process that does not vary meaningfully from person to person. It is therefore of the same general nature as other physical processes—e.g., gravity, motion, and electricity.

10. *Decompositionality*: Natural scientists have typically studied physical processes on the assumption that they are decomposable into parts, and that those parts, reassembled, amount to the whole phenomenon. Cognitive scientists dominantly assume that cognitive processes can be studied in the same way.

In what follows, I trace the historical development of the modern doctrine of cognitivism, with a special focus on its founding role in the field of SLA.

Before the Revolution

The systematic study of SLA was inspired by a "cognitive revolution" that began in North America in the 1950s. Although a comparatively recent event, its roots lead back to René Descartes (1596–1650), the main founder of modern Western philosophy.[4]

Before Descartes, the dominant Western philosophical tradition was neo-Aristotelian scholasticism (Dear, 1985). Scholasticism was also a religious tradition, with God at its center. Descartes remained true to scholasticism in some ways, but he put humans instead of God at the center. He did so by trying to *think* his way to the essence of human existence—to strip away, through setting to work his rational faculties, everything that could be doubted until he arrived at an essential core. Descartes' epoch-making words deserve to be quoted at length instead of in their usual sound-bite form:

> Inasmuch as I desired to devote myself wholly to the search for truth, I thought that I should . . . reject as absolutely false anything of which I could have the least doubt, in order to see whether anything would be left after this procedure which could be called wholly certain. Thus, as our senses deceive us at times, I was ready to suppose that nothing was at all the way our senses represented them to me. [Next,] as there are men who make mistakes in reasoning even on the simplest topics in geometry, I judged that I was as liable to error as any other, and rejected as false all reasoning which I had previously accepted as valid demonstration. Finally, as the same percepts which we have when awake may come to us when asleep without their being true, I decided to suppose that nothing that had ever entered my mind was more real than the illusions of my dreams. But I soon noticed that while I thus wished to think everything false, it was necessarily true that I who thought so was something. Since this truth, *I think, therefore I am, or exist*, was so firm and assured that all the most extravagant suppositions of the skeptics were unable to shake it, I judged that I could safely accept it as the first principle of the philosophy I was seeking.
>
> I then examined closely what I was, and saw that I could imagine that I had no body, and that there was no world nor any place that I occupied, but that I could not imagine for a moment that I did not exist. On the contrary, from the very fact that I doubted the truth of other things, or had

any other thought, it followed very evidently and very certainly that I existed. On the other hand, if I had ceased to think while my body and the world and all the rest of what I had ever imagined remained true, I would have had no reason to believe that I existed; therefore I concluded that I was a thing or substance whose whole essence or nature was only to think, and which, to exist, has no need of space nor of any material thing or body. Thus it follows that this ego, this mind, this soul, by which I am what I am, is entirely distinct from the body and is easier to know than the latter, and that even if the body were not, the soul would not cease to be all that it now is.

(1637/1960, pp. 24–25)

In this passage, Descartes placed the "I-as-thinker" at the center of existence; all else is incidental. The implications for understanding human life were profound. First, human mind was given the place formerly reserved for God—as the organizing principle of human existence, and in fact all life.[5] Second, the human body and the rest of the world were radically separated from the mind, assigned a subsidiary position, and thus took on a spectral character. Third, the human mind was viewed as a logical—even mathematical—device. Fourth and finally, cognition was reduced to what we now consider just one of its forms: consciousness. The portrait of mind entailed by these four principles—as logical, conscious, radically isolated, and virtually godlike in its powers—effected a "Copernican Revolution" in thinking about thinking, and thinking about being. The resulting worldview has sometimes been called *cognitivism* (e.g., Freeman & Núñez, 1999; Haugeland, 1998).

Cartesian-inspired cognitivism has dominated Western thought since the 17th century. With a few (notable) exceptions, the main trends in philosophy and human science have valorized mind per se: the notion of mental concepts/categories and how they are formed; mind-body dualism; the 19th-century birth of psychology; developments in logic and mind-as-machine; studies of "primitive thought"; Freudian psychology; and the ascent of cognitive psychology and cognitive science starting in the 1950s. Regarding this last development—the main outcome of the cognitive revolution described below—"the Cartesian picture remains over-whelmingly the dominant picture in cognitive science" (Brook, 2007, p. 6; cf. Wheeler, 2005).

Some have even argued that the term "cognitive revolution" may be a misnomer, given the continuing dominance of cognitivism in the West over the last 350 years. Thus, no less a cognitive revolutionary than Noam Chomsky has called Descartes' ideas "'the first cognitive revolution,' perhaps the only real one" (2007, p. 38), while another prominent revolutionary stated: "The so-called 'cognitive revolution' . . . was not so much a revolution as a return to an *ancien regime*" (Mandler, in Boden, 2006, p. 240). Such remarks fairly indicate the continued supremacy of cognitivism in Western intellectual history.

The Cognitive Revolution

Besides its long-term historical base, the cognitive revolution had more immediate roots as well. First, it was a direct response to American behaviorism, a radical psychology holding that humans acquired their behavioral habits through stimulus–response conditioning. Behaviorists effectively *banned* cognition as an unscientific explanatory variable, partly because mental activities couldn't be directly observed or measured, and partly because their theories gave it no place. The result was a vision of humans as more or less blank slates at birth, rote learners, and mechanical actors. B. F. Skinner's *Verbal Behavior* (1957) was considered the ultimate scientific statement of behaviorist views, at least concerning language.[6]

Chomsky's (1959) review of *Verbal Behavior* selectively dissected—and for many demolished—behaviorism, demonstrating how, taken to its logical extremes, it ended in absurdity. Chomsky's subsequent influence on the cognitive revolution was profound, even if his own innatist brand of cognitivism alienated many.

Yet well before Chomsky dissected Skinner, mid-20th-century psychologists had begun turning the tables on behaviorism—by trying, at base, to study the mind. They did so at first indirectly, by researching perception and certain "intervening variables" that complicated mechanical stimulus–response models. By the mid-1950s, however, psychologists such as Jerome Bruner were making a decisive break:

> The past few years have witnessed a notable increase in interest in and investigation of the cognitive processes . . . It has resulted from a recognition of the complex processes that mediate between the classical "stimuli" and "responses" out of which stimulus–response learning theories hoped to fashion a psychology that would by-pass anything smacking of the "mental." The impeccable peripheralism of such theories could not last . . . One might do well to have a closer look at these intervening "cognitive maps."
>
> (Bruner et al., 1956, p. vii)

More specifically, Bruner and his colleagues explored the cognitive categories and strategies used by experimental subjects in problem-solving—research that quickly gained a following. In 1960, Bruner co-founded the Harvard Center for Cognitive Studies with another cognitive revolutionary, the mathematical psychologist George Miller, and they used it to promote a vision of human beings as both "active, constructive problem solvers" (Gardner, 1985, p. 11) and limited-capacity information processors.

A second force behind the cognitive revolution—and one directly influencing the first—was the development of the digital computer. The first working digital computers resulted from theoretical breakthroughs in logic, cybernetics, and information theory, as well as more practical developments in electrical engineering —all driven by Allied efforts in World War II. Advances in artificial intelligence (AI)—computers designed to simulate human thought—followed. In 1956, Herbert Simon and Alan Newell produced a program that solved logic problems using thought-to-be-humanlike strategies, paving the way for more ambitious attempts to simulate human problem-solving. Although AI has since developed in a number of different directions, it has been an extremely active research area, and continues apace. Likewise, the computational view of the mind as a limited-capacity information processor—already described above—has been a central tenet of modern-day cognitivism.

Linguistics was the third force driving the cognitive revolution. At the same time (and in the same place) as Bruner and Miller were overturning behaviorist psychology, Chomsky was exposing the inadequacies of structuralist linguistics, the dominant North American approach to the scientific study of language. Chomsky showed that structuralism couldn't account for: (1) the nonlinear, hierarchical, and highly abstract organization of syntax; or (2) its "creativity," in the sense that any adequate grammar of a language had to account for the properties of infinite recursivity and generativity. Chomsky's own transformational approach to syntax, which he began to describe in his 1957 *Syntactic Structures*, was designed to address these shortcomings.

More exciting for the new cognitive psychologists, however, was the possibility that Chomsky's transformational syntax was "psychologically real." They assumed that syntactic transformations represented cognitive operations, and thus the more transformations required to produce a grammatical sentence, the more processing needed. This *derivational* approach to language processing (e.g., Miller & Chomsky, 1963) was highly influential for a time, and paved the way for cross-fertilization among psychology, artificial intelligence, and linguistics. Although eventually disproven, it left a lasting mark on the research agendas and research methods of psycholinguistics (Gardner, 1985).

Chomsky's greatest impact, however, came via his radical amputation of cognition from behavior—the famous competence–performance distinction. Chomsky argued that actual language use was so contaminated by human frailties that language-as-system became unavailable for scientific study. It was only, therefore, by excluding language in use that the scientific study of language could proceed. Through this bold rhetorical move, Chomsky: (1) revived an idealist Platonic worldview (see note 4) wherein true "reality" existed behind but was fundamentally separate from sense experience; (2) relocated the study of linguistics squarely and exclusively "in the head";[7] (3) made a powerful case for scientific reductionism—and a particularly *cognitivist* form of reductionism—which proved highly compelling to cognitive scientists; and (4) established a fundamental principle that has guided SLA since its birth.

Language Acquisition during the Revolution

Working at Harvard with Bruner and Miller was the developmental psychologist Roger Brown. Bruner and Miller had invited Brown to join them in founding the Center for Cognitive Studies, but he declined (Miller, 1977). Brown's research was primarily language-oriented, including pioneering work on first language (L1) acquisition.

In close collaboration with his students, Brown studied three young children acquiring L1 English over a five-year period.[8] By sampling naturalistic data at close intervals, Brown et al. were able to watch the children's morphology, syntax, and semantics develop. In the first published report on this research, Brown and Bellugi (1964/1970) described "three major phenomena which were evident almost at once" (p. 75) in the data: telegraphic speech, the "induction of the latent structure" (p. 89) of language on the part of the children, and their mothers' expansions of their telegraphic speech. Brown and Bellugi explained the first and third phenomena in quasi-behaviorist terms, but attributed far greater importance to the induction of latent structure:

> The processes of imitation and expansion are not sufficient to account for the degree of linguistic competence that children regularly acquire . . . All children are able to understand and construct sentences they have never heard but which are nevertheless well-formed, well-formed in terms of general rules that are implicit in the sentences the child has heard. Somehow, then, every child processes the speech to which he [*sic*] is exposed so as to induce from it a latent structure . . . The discovery of latent structure is the greatest of the processes involved in language acquisition and the most difficult to understand.
>
> (1964/1970, p. 91)

Brown's masterwork, *A First Language: The Early Stages* (1973), was a detailed analysis of the data collected in this project. His main conclusions were: (1) the frequency of forms in the input did not predict the order in which those forms were acquired; (2) the semantic and grammatical complexity of forms in the input (including the number of transformations involved in producing them) *did* predict acquisition order; and (3) the acquisition order of 14 grammatical morphemes was highly regular across all three children studied. Although Brown was extremely cautious in generalizing from these findings, his portrait of learners as active *hypothesis-testers* relying on complex and dynamic cognitive strategies was strong and clear. Equally important, he made available a rigorous but accessible methodology for studying acquisition—or, more precisely, grammatical morpheme acquisition.

Brown and colleagues were not the only researchers studying language acquisition during the cognitive revolution, but they were the most influential. They also helped establish the field of SLA, as described below.

A second major influence on language acquisition research at this time, although not primarily concerned with language acquisition per se, was Chomsky. As mentioned above, Chomsky's transformational syntax seemed to explain (for a while) why some linguistic structures were acquired before others. More generally and durably, it spawned the idea that linguistic knowledge was comprised of a discrete set of rules, making language acquisition a form of rule-learning. Most important of all, Chomsky's unvarying focus on the cognitively represented competence of (native) speakers, rather than their faulty real-world performance, again played a dominant role.

Second Language Acquisition: First Steps[9]

The systematic study of SLA grew directly out of the cognitive revolution. Theoretical developments were initiated by S. Pit Corder, whose 1967 paper, "The Significance of Learners' Errors" (1967/1981), is often cited as the founding manifesto of the field (Gass & Selinker, 2001; Thomas, 2004). There, Corder problematized the notion of error in second language (L2) teaching, arguing that, instead of treating errors as mere by-products of faulty instruction (the behaviorist position), they might rather be crucial evidence of SLA. Corder framed this proposal squarely in cognitive psychology's critique of behaviorism, Brown's L1 acquisition research, and Chomsky's linguistic theory:

> If then these [behaviorist] hypotheses about language learning are being questioned and new hypotheses being set up to account for the process of child language acquisition, it would seem reasonable to see how far they might also apply to the learning of a second language.
>
> Within this new context the study of errors takes on a new importance and will I believe contribute to a verification or rejection of the new hypothesis.
>
> This hypothesis states that a human infant is born with an innate predisposition to acquire language; that he [sic] must be exposed to language for the acquisition process to start; that he possesses an internal mechanism of unknown nature which enables him from the limited data available to him to construct a grammar of a particular language. How he does this is largely unknown and is the field of intensive study at the present time by linguists and psychologists. Miller (1964) has pointed out that if we wished to create an automaton to replicate a child's performance, the order in which it tested various aspects of the grammar could only be decided after careful analysis of the successive states of language acquisition by human children. The first steps therefore in such a study are seen to be longitudinal description of the child's language throughout the course of its development. From such a description it is eventually hoped to develop a picture of the procedures adopted by the child to acquire language.
>
> (1967/1981, p. 7)

Highlighting Brown and Fraser's (1964) point that errors tell us far more about language acquisition than does error-free language, because the latter may simply be memorized, Corder argued that research on L2 errors might reveal a "built-in syllabus" reflecting the cognitive rules, constraints, and hypothesis-testing capabilities of the language acquisition device. This information might then be used to design more "psychologically real" language teaching syllabi, such that "the learner's innate strategies dictate our practice and determine our syllabus . . . rather than impos[ing] upon him [sic] our preconception of how he ought to learn, what he ought to learn and when he ought to learn it" (p. 13).

If Corder's paper was the original theoretical impulse for organized SLA studies, then pioneering research by others furnished its empirical foundations. Several case studies (e.g., Huang, 1970; Ravem, 1968) started things off, but Heidi Dulay and Marina Burt soon established themselves as the most active and influential researchers. In a series of papers beginning in 1972, Dulay and Burt hypothesized that SLA was hardly a matter of transferring L1 structures to the L2, but rather a process of "active mental organization" (1972, p. 236) in which learners applied universal cognitive strategies to induce a grammar. They framed this hypothesis directly in the terms and issues of the cognitive revolution:

> The present focus of linguistic research is to formulate those principles that generate all and only grammatical sentences. The focus of psychological research is to discover those principles which a learner uses to arrive at the production of grammatical speech. Psycholinguistic language learning strategies appear to be a function of the interplay between linguistic complexity and learning complexity . . . We are all, in one way or another . . . searching for the rules of mental organization that limit the class of possible hypotheses a child uses when learning a language.
>
> (pp. 242–243)

To test their claim, Dulay and Burt first examined L2 learners' errors, based on Corder's suggestion that such errors provided a unique window on the learning process. Influenced by Brown's work, however, and using Brown's method of analysis, they began to study the grammatical morpheme acquisition of groups of young ESL learners from different L1 backgrounds. They found that these groups had highly similar "acquisition orders,"[10] which they interpreted as strong support for their "creative construction" hypothesis. According to this hypothesis, the *only* real reason children (at least) learned L2s was due to their innate programming—and they quoted Brown (1973) for support:

> We presently do not have evidence that there are selective social [environmental] pressures of any kind operating on children to impel them to bring their speech into line with adult models . . . Children work out rules for the speech they hear, passing from levels of lesser to greater complexity, simply because the human species is programmed at a certain period in its life to operate in this fashion on linguistic input.
>
> (Quoted in Dulay, Burt, & Krashen, 1982, p. 201)

Other researchers went on to demonstrate that adult L2 learners shared similar acquisition orders with Dulay and Burt's younger learners. Additional work on the L2 acquisition of syntactic subsystems such as negation and question-formation— especially by Brown's co-workers Courtney Cazden and Herlinda Cancino—filled out the emerging picture: Learners appeared to acquire complex structures in stages, sometimes over several years. This latter research was generally regarded less skeptically than the morpheme acquisition studies because it was longitudinal, thereby showing a real rather than virtual acquisition process (see note 10).

Cognitivist SLA: Later Developments

The main purpose of this chapter is to highlight the cognitivist basis of SLA, not to recap its full history. In this section, I therefore selectively review more recent historical developments that exemplify the field's strong and continuing cognitivist focus.

Despite the low opinion SLA researchers generally have of his work, Stephen Krashen was responsible for setting an important part of the field's current agenda: the emphasis on input. Current treatments of input, including the "Input-Interaction-Output" approach—regarded by some as *the* major school of mainstream SLA studies (e.g., Block, 2003)—can be traced back to Krashen.

Krashen rarely described his monitor model in cognitivist terms, but it was highly cognitivist. It featured the provision of input to a language acquisition device, which, depending on whether (1) the input was "comprehensible," and (2) an "affective filter" (a "mental block," as Krashen, 1985, p. 3 called it) was "up" or "down," gained access to that input for processing purposes. If it did, and there was enough input, language acquisition automatically ensued. Quite apart from Krashen's drawbacks and excesses, he clearly set the scene for what was to come.

Simultaneously with Krashen, and just as influentially in the long run, Richard Schmidt (1983) studied the English of "Wes," a Japanese immigrant to Hawai'i. Wes depended overwhelmingly on formulaic expressions—multi-word chunks that worked well in social situations but that, to Schmidt, did not constitute evidence of successful SLA. Schmidt hypothesized that missing from Wes's SLA process was "attention to form, which could be accomplished through . . . using conscious learning strategies such as . . . asking questions of native speakers, consulting available sources, and actively using deductive reasoning to look for general rules and exceptions" (p. 172). In other words, by being a "social" rather than "cognitive" learner—and despite his ability "to communicate well" (p. 172)—Wes's English was fundamentally deficient.

Schmidt followed up this research by studying his own learning of Portuguese during a five-month stay in Brazil (Schmidt & Frota, 1986). Keeping careful records of his exposure to Portuguese during classes and interactions with Portuguese speakers, Schmidt and his Brazilian collaborator found that, in almost all cases, he learned what he had noticed. That is, the forms Schmidt recorded being exposed to were largely those that subsequently appeared in his oral production. Schmidt and Frota therefore developed the hypothesis that consciously *noticing* linguistic forms was a necessary condition for SLA.

Schmidt (1990) was the first formal statement of this *noticing hypothesis*, and it has had a powerful influence on the field. In this paper, Schmidt discussed different definitions of consciousness and then reviewed theories of consciousness within a cognitivist information-processing framework—theories that strongly supported the idea that noticing is a necessary condition for learning. Then, after reviewing the SLA literature on related topics, Schmidt formally stated his hypothesis:

> I have claimed that subliminal language learning is impossible, and that intake is what learners consciously notice. This requirement of noticing is meant to apply equally to all aspects of language (lexicon, phonology, grammatical form, pragmatics), and can be incorporated into many different theories of second language acquisition.
>
> (p. 149)

Schmidt (2001) developed the concept of *attention*, arguing that it was the key cognitive concept underlying noticing. As one goal, he sought to:

> provide some of the details of the role of attention as that fits within a broader cognitive approach to understanding SLA, one that relies on the mental processes of language learners as the basic explanation of learning. I am particularly concerned with those mental processes that are conscious, under the working hypothesis that SLA is largely driven by what learners pay attention to and notice in target language input and what they understand the significance of noticed input to be.
>
> (pp. 3–4)

It would not be too much to say that Schmidt's concepts of noticing and attention hark back, via cognitivism's mind-as-computer metaphor, almost directly to Descartes' notion of human-constituting consciousness. The main difference seems to be that Schmidt's narrower interests convert "I think therefore I am" into "I notice therefore I learn." Returning to the present day, Schmidt's approach to SLA has powerfully influenced the field for the last 20 years, providing a solid theoretical framework for cognitivist SLA approaches. Input and interaction (e.g., Long, 1996), the closely related focus-on-form movement (e.g., Doughty & Williams, 1998), and discussions of implicit versus explicit language learning (e.g., N. Ellis, 1994) have all been strongly influenced by Schmidt's theory. Even parts of SLA studies closer to social psychology, such as individual differences research, have made efforts to incorporate noticing into their frameworks (e.g., Dörnyei & Skehan, 2003).

The final historical development in cognitivist SLA studies I will introduce is the 2003 publication of Catherine Doughty and Michael Long's landmark edited volume, *The Handbook of Second Language Acquisition* (2003b). Dominantly cognitivist in its approach (20 of the 24 chapters can reliably be classified as cognitivist, if cognitivist research methodologies are included), this volume constitutes a state-of-the-art account of mainstream SLA studies circa 2003. Its cognitivism is paradigmatically represented in its editors' statements on the goals and aims of SLA studies, as well as their repeatedly expressed desire that the field be viewed as a cognitive science. I quote at length to give a clear sense of Doughty and Long's influential position (the first quotation is repeated from the beginning of the present chapter):

> As reflected in the contributions of those in this volume . . ., much current SLA research and theorizing shares a strongly cognitive orientation . . . The focus is firmly on identifying the nature and sources of the underlying L2 knowledge system, and on explaining developmental success and failure. Performance data are inevitably the researchers' mainstay, but understanding underlying competence, not the external verbal behavior that depends on that competence, is the ultimate goal. Researchers recognize that SLA takes place in a social context, of course, and accept that it can be influenced by that context, both micro and macro. However, they also recognize that language learning, like any other learning, is ultimately a matter of change in an individual's internal mental state. As such, research on SLA is increasingly viewed as a branch of cognitive science.
>
> (Doughty & Long, 2003a, p. 4)

> A discernible trend [in SLA studies], therefore, especially in the 1980s and 1990s, has been for increasing numbers of researchers and theorists, rationalists all, to focus their attention on SLA as an internal, individual, in part innately specified, cognitive process—one that takes place in a social setting to be sure, and can be influenced by variation in that setting and by other interlocutors, but a psycholinguistic process, nonetheless, which ultimately resides in the mind-brain, where also lie its secrets.
>
> (Long & Doughty, 2003, p. 866)

> The second development [that cognitive science is generally accepted as dating from] was the dismantling of the behaviorist hegemony . . . and its replacement by a pre-eminently cognitive, information-processing approach that holds sway to this day.
>
> (Long & Doughty, 2003, p. 867)

> Underlying all [the authors in this volume's] work is a shared conception of SLA as a cognitive process involving representations and computations on those representations . . . But a common focus is not enough. For SLA to achieve the stability, stimulation and research funding to survive as a viable field of inquiry, it needs an intellectual and institutional home that is to some degree autonomous and separate from the disciplines and departments that currently offer shelter. Cognitive science is the logical choice.
>
> (Long & Doughty, 2003, p. 869)

I will leave it to the reader to decide whether these authoritative statements amount to a new cognitivist manifesto for the SLA field, but in my opinion they do. Such a strong cognitivist position provides a perfect backdrop for the current volume.

This Volume

Following Long and Doughty's second quotation given above, they wrote:

> There remain identifiable groups of scholars—socioculturalists, conversation analysts, and action theorists, for example—who persist in seeing external learner behavior, even group behavior, not mental states, as the proper domain of inquiry. More generally (and more vaguely) there are "critical theorists" and an often overlapping group of self-professed epistemological relativists, who express general angst with SLA's cognitive orientation and/or its growing accountability to one or more theories and to empirical findings while offering no alternative but the abyss.
>
> (2003, p. 866)

While aspects of this characterization might be questioned, the authors are clearly right on one count: There is a persistent (and growing—Larsen-Freeman, 2007; Long, 2007, chap. 6) body of scholars who do not follow mainstream SLA's dominant cognitivist orientation, including four major scholars who formerly took cognitivist positions.[11] Whether some or all of these "offer no alternative but the abyss" can be judged, in part, by reading the present volume.

The purpose of this volume is to collect under one cover SLA approaches that depart from the field's dominant cognitivist norms and assumptions, and to make those approaches directly comparable. I have chosen the term "alternative" to represent these approaches, understanding that it may have pejorative nuances for some—for example, that the approaches thus described are not central to SLA studies broadly conceived, or that "alternative" suggests an apocalyptic cognitivism-versus-anticognitivism battle. While Long and Doughty's just-quoted statement may encourage such views, my reasons for calling these approaches "alternative" are more modest and practical: I wished to collect together SLA approaches that seem to proceed differently than those of the historically dominant school, and then to get these approaches "talking to each other," or at least presented in directly comparable form.

To this end, I have asked the volume's authors to organize their chapters according to the same six topics and questions. These are:

1. *Overview* —What are the distinctive features of your approach?
2. *Theoretical principles*—What are the main theoretical concepts or principles underlying your approach?
3. *Research methods*—How is SLA studied in your approach?
4. *Supporting findings*—What research findings support your approach?
5. *Differences vis-à-vis other alternative approaches*—How does your approach differ from the other approaches described in this volume?[12]
6. *Future directions*—How do you envision your approach developing in the future?

A common plan is followed because, to this point, alternative approaches to SLA have been largely presented as isolated atoms—few if any systematic attempts have been made to bring them into mutual dialogue and engagement. Beyond simply highlighting a diversity of theoretical perspectives on SLA, then, the present volume seeks to initiate a process that will likely be crucial to the field's future: understanding how diverse approaches to SLA relate and differ.

The Chapters in this Volume

James Lantolf begins our exploration by providing a state-of-the-art description of the neo-Vygotskyan sociocultural approach to SLA. He describes *mediation* as its central focus—how language and other semiotic systems serve as tools by which learning/development/knowledge is appropriated. Lantolf further highlights the centrality of *praxis*—the unity of theory and practice—in sociocultural theory, reviewing recent research wherein classroom practice directly informs and is directly informed by theory.

Diane Larsen-Freeman offers a detailed portrait of a newer approach to SLA that is fast growing in popularity: *complexity theory*. Complexity theory emanates from the natural sciences, and holds that systematic behavior in nature is at least sometimes complex, dynamic, and self-organizing. A major consequence of this view is that variation and change are primary: Complex systems are ever-changing —as their behaviors change the environment, the system then adapts to the new environment by producing new behaviors. Larsen-Freeman explores the implications of complexity theory for SLA.

Bonny Norton and Carolyn McKinney provide a concrete and accessible introduction to *identity* perspectives on SLA. Adopting insights from poststructuralism and critical theory, they view SLA as a contingent process of identity construction rather than a mechanical act. Norton and McKinney highlight three aspects of identity: (1) its multiple, heterogeneous character—all human beings enact various, often conflicting identities at the same time; (2) its implications for power and opportunity in language learning; and (3) how identities change over time. In relation to these points Norton and McKinney discuss *investment*—what the learner envisions him- or herself putting into and gaining from learning/using the L2 in particular situations, and *imagined communities*—the various conceivable groups and communities the learner envisions him- or herself being able to join while doing so.

Patsy Duff and Steven Talmy give a comprehensive account of *language socialization* approaches to SLA. With foundations in linguistic anthropology, language socialization focuses on the engagement of "experts" and "novices" in constructing/responding to macro-level cultural-linguistic norms of conduct. Of special interest is the authors' account of the mutuality of socialization—experts and novices socialize *each other*, rather than socialization simply proceeding top-down. Duff and Talmy also describe the role of power and inequality in socialization, currently a major focus in this area.

Gabriele Kasper and Johannes Wagner provide a rich account of *conversation analysis* as an approach to studying SLA. They show how learning emerges in interaction, as social participants go about the daily activities of making sense of each other's talk both in and beyond classrooms. In the true CA tradition, Kasper and Wagner provide plentiful illustrative data from a variety of sources, and analyze those data in suggestive ways.

Dwight Atkinson describes the newest and least developed alternative SLA approach: *sociocognitive theory*. He argues that SLA is an adaptive process, so that what is being adapted to—environmental conditions—should also be included in conceptualizing SLA. Cognitivist accounts are thus problematized but cognition is in no sense ignored. Rather, it is viewed as an integrated part of the total mind–body–world environment, yielding an ecological view.

Finally, Lourdes Ortega provides a lively and informative discussion of the six alternative approaches to SLA described in this book, bringing to the task her special perspective as an outward-looking cognitivist. As with this introductory chapter, Ortega's participation in this project suggests that, while not focused mainly on cognitivist, mainstream SLA approaches as such, this volume by no means ignores or dismisses them.

Conclusion: Second Language Acquisition, Cognitivism, and Alternative Approaches to SLA

In this chapter, I have tried to suggest that SLA studies, under the influence of a cognitivist worldview and cognitivist cognitive science, has historically adopted a particular perspective on SLA—one that can accurately be called cognitivist. In fact, no SLA scholar I know of would disagree: By all accounts, the field has primarily adopted a view of learners as computational systems and of learning as information processing. Yet, while alternatives to this view are actively being explored, they have largely operated in isolation from one another. The current volume attempts to gather a cross-section of scholars together and to place their alternative SLA approaches in a common frame—one that promotes direct comparison across approaches. While it would be naive to assume equivalence or even commensurability among these approaches, it seems vital to put them "in play" together at the present time—to encourage active engagement among diverse understandings and forms of inquiry. It is by so doing, I believe, that our knowledge of SLA can best be moved forward. Surely, for such a complex and multifaceted phenomenon as SLA, nothing less will suffice.

Notes

1 The historical accounts in this chapter are based on the sources listed below, only some of which are cited in the body of the chapter. Doing so would have been impractical, as nearly every sentence would have required a citation. Likewise, since the main purpose of this chapter is not to make an original contribution to SLA history, but rather to set the scene for the current volume, I have chosen to list my sources here:

- *Defining Cognitivism*—Boden (2006); Clark (2001); Costall (2007); Costall & Leudar (1996); Gardner (1985); Harnish (2002); Harris (1991); Haugeland (1998); Suchman (2007); Wallace (2007); Wheeler (2005);
- *Before the Revolution*—Boden (2006); Brook (2007); Damasio (1994); Descartes (1637/1960); Gardner (1985); Wheeler (2005);
- *The Cognitive Revolution*—Bechtel, Abrahamsen, & Graham (1998); Boden (2006); Bruner (1983); Bruner et al. (1956); Chomsky (1959); Gardner (1985); Miller & Chomsky (1963); Skinner (1957);
- *Language Acquisition during the Revolution*—Boden (2006); Brown (1973); Brown & Bellugi (1964/1970); Bruner (1983); Gardner (1985); Miller (1977);
- *Second Language Acquisition: First Steps*—Brown & Fraser (1964); Corder (1967/1981); Dulay & Burt (1972, 1974); Dulay et al. (1982); Ellis (1994); Hakuta & Cancino (1977); Gass & Selinker (2001); Larsen-Freeman (1991); Larsen-Freeman & Long (1991); Mitchell & Myles (2004); Thomas (2004);
- *Cognitivist SLA: Later Developments*—Block (2003); Doughty & Long (2003a, 2003b); Doughty & Williams (1998); Gass & Mackey (2007); Krashen (1985); Long (1997); Long & Doughty (2003); Schmidt (1983, 1990, 2001); Schmidt & Frota (1986); Swain (2005).

2 *Nativist* theories of cognitive development, however—also important participants in the cognitivist enterprise—presuppose innate, preexisting knowledge structures that merely need to be "triggered" by input.

3 This is one assumption of classical cognitive science with which connectionists tend to disagree.

4 In fact, although Descartes is certainly the original *modern* champion of the view described here, its roots lead back at least to Plato:

> All these considerations, said Socrates, must surely prompt serious philosophers to review the position in some such way as this . . . The body fills us with loves and desires and fears and all sorts of nonsense, with the result that we literally never get an opportunity to think at all about anything . . . It seems so long as we are alive, we shall continue closest to knowledge if we avoid as much as we can all contact and association with the body, except when they are absolutely necessary, and instead of allowing ourselves to become infected with its nature, purify ourselves from it.
>
> (Plato, quoted in Gibbs, 2005, p. 3)

5 In fact, Descartes did give a (tricky) place to God in his system. But the implications of putting human cognition at the center of things were clear. For this reason Descartes spent much time and energy trying to avoid being sanctioned by religious authorities, as did many of his philosophical and scientific contemporaries.

6 The description in this paragraph applies far less to Britain and other parts of the world, where behaviorism had only a minor—although by no means insignificant—role (Boden, 2006).

7 One major problem with separating language from its use by relocating it "in the head" was that it made it almost impossible to study, in the sense that every linguistic product involves some form of language use. Thus, grammaticality judgments, possibly the (historically) most common form of research methodology in Chomskyan linguistics, are also linguistic performances (V. Cook, 1993). Simply put, a purely cognitive linguistics is an impossibility because, in the words of Halliday (1978, p. 33), "All language is language-in-use."

8 In fact, however, most of Brown and colleagues' subsequent publications focused on developments that took place in the first year of the study.

9 It is an unfortunate fact that no serious history of SLA studies exists (see Thomas (1998) for possible reasons, as well as Thomas (2004) for an important if preliminary step in this direction). In the meantime, given that the field is only about 40 years old, it seems reasonable to rely on the memories of its pioneers (e.g., Hakuta & Cancino, 1977; Larsen-Freeman, 1991; Larsen-Freeman & Long, 1991)—or if not to rely on them at least to take them seriously.

10 The concept of "acquisition order" was seriously critiqued at this time, due partly to the fact that it was based on "cross-sectional" instead of "longitudinal" data. That is, the original studies establishing SLA "acquisition orders" were not based on cross-time changes in research subjects' linguistic abilities, but were rather projected from one-shot studies of linguistic accuracy by L2 learners at different proficiency levels. For discussion, see Larsen-Freeman and Long (1991) and R. Ellis (2008).

11 These are Rod Ellis, Gabriele Kasper, Diane Larsen-Freeman, and Merrill Swain. Significantly, two of these scholars have chapters in this book.

12 Authors of two of the chapters declined to respond to this question. This is perhaps unsurprising in a field where rancor over mainstream versus other approaches has been prominent, and theories are now fast proliferating, making it difficult to stay abreast of the latest developments.

References

Bechtel, W., Abrahamsen, A., & Graham, G. (1998). The life of cognitive science. In W. Bechtel & G. Graham (Eds.), *A companion to cognitive science* (pp. 1–104). Malden, MA: Blackwell.

Block, D. (2003). *The social turn in second language acquisition*. Washington, DC: Georgetown University Press.

Boden, M. (2006). *Mind as machine: A history of cognitive science*. Oxford: Clarendon Press.

Brook, A. (2007). Introduction. In A. Brook (Ed.), *The prehistory of cognitive science* (pp. 1–14). Basingstoke: Palgrave Macmillan.

Brown, R. (1973). *A first language: The early stages*. Cambridge, MA: Harvard University Press.

Brown, R., & Bellugi, U. (1964/1970). Three processes in the child's acquisition of syntax. Reprinted in R. Brown, *Psycholinguistics: Selected papers by Roger Brown* (pp. 75–99). New York: Free Press.

Brown, R., & Fraser, C. (1964). The acquisition of syntax. *Monographs of the Society for Research on Child Development, 29*, 43–79.

Bruner, J. A. (1983). *In search of mind: Essays in autobiography*. New York: Harper & Row.

Bruner, J. A., Goodnow, J., & Austin, G. (1956). *A study of thinking*. New York: Wiley.

Chomsky, N. (1957). *Syntactic structures*. The Hague: Mouton.

Chomsky, N. (1959). A review of B. F. Skinner's *Verbal Behavior*. *Language, 35*, 26–58.

Chomsky, N. (2007). Language and thought: Descartes and some reflections on venerable themes. In A. Brook (Ed.), *The prehistory of cognitive science* (pp. 38–66). Basingstoke: Palgrave Macmillan.

Clark, A. (2001). *Mindware: An introduction to the philosophy of cognitive science*. Oxford: Oxford University Press.

Cook, G., & Seidlhofer, B. (1995). An applied linguist in principle and practice. In G. Cook & B. Seidlhofer (Eds.), *Principle and practice in applied linguistics: Essays in honour of H. G. Widdowson* (pp. 1–25). London: Oxford University Press.

Cook, V. (1993). *Linguistics and second language acquisition*. New York: St. Martin's.

Corder, H. P. (1967/1981). The significance of learners' errors. Reprinted in S. P. Corder, *Error analysis and interlanguage* (pp. 5–13). Oxford: Oxford University Press.

Costall, A. (2007). Bringing the body back to life: James Gibson's ecology of agency. In T. Ziemke, J. Zlatev, & R. M. Frank (Eds.), *Body, language and mind, Vol. 1: Embodiment* (pp. 55–83). Amsterdam: Mouton de Gruyter.

Costall, A., & Leudar, I. (1996). Situating action I: Truth in the situation. *Ecological Psychology, 8*, 101–110.

Damasio, A. R. (1994). *Descartes' error: Emotion, reason, and the human brain*. New York: Avon.

Davis, K. (1995). Qualitative theory and methods in applied linguistic research. *TESOL Quarterly, 29*, 427–454.

Dear, P. (1985). Totius in verba: Rhetoric and authority in the early Royal Society. *Isis, 76*, 144–161.

Descartes, R. (1637/1960). *Discourse on method and meditations*. Indianapolis, IN: Bobbs-Merrill.

Dilthey, W. (1883/1989). *Introduction to the human sciences*. Fort Wayne, IN: Wayne State University Press.

Dörnyei, Z., & Skehan, P. (2003). Individual differences in second language learning. In C. Doughty & M. H. Long (Eds.), *Handbook of second language acquisition* (pp. 589–630). Malden, MA: Blackwell.

Doughty, C. J., & Long, M. H. (2003a). The scope of inquiry and the goals of SLA. In C. J. Doughty & M. H. Long (Eds.), *Handbook of second language acquisition* (pp. 3–16). Malden, MA: Blackwell.

Doughty, C. J., & Long, M. H. (2003b). *Handbook of second language acquisition*. Malden, MA: Blackwell.

Doughty, C. J., & Williams, J. (Eds.) (1998). *Focus on form in classroom second language acquisition*. Cambridge: Cambridge University Press.

Dulay, H., & Burt, M. (1972). Goofing, an indicator of children's second language strategies. *Language Learning, 22*, 234–252.

Dulay, H., & Burt, M. (1974). Natural sequences in child second language acquisition. *Language Learning, 24*, 37–53.

Dulay, H., Burt, M., & Krashen, S. D. (1982). *Language two*. New York: Oxford University Press.

Ellis, N. (Ed.) (1994). *Implicit and explicit learning of languages*. San Diego, CA: Academic Press.

Ellis, R. (1997). SLA and language pedagogy: An educational perspective. *Studies in Second Language Acquisition, 19*, 93–116.

Ellis, R. (2008). *The study of second language acquisition* (2nd ed.) Oxford: Oxford University Press.

Elman, J. L. (1998). Connectionism, artificial life, and dynamical systems. In W. Bechtel & G. Graham (Eds.), *A companion to cognitive science* (pp. 488–505). London: Blackwell.

Fodor, J. A. (1980). Methodological solipsism considered as a research strategy in cognitive psychology. *Behavioral and Brain Sciences, 3*, 431–432.

Freeman, W. J., & Núñez, R. (1999). Introduction. In R. Núñez & W. J. Freeman (Eds.) *Reclaiming cognition: The primacy of action, intention, and emotion* (pp. ix–xix). Thorverton: Imprint Academic.

Gardner, H. (1985). *The mind's new science: A history of the cognitive revolution*. New York: Basic Books.

Gass, S. M., & Mackey, A. (2007). Input, interaction, and output in second language acquisition. In B. VanPatten & J. Williams (Eds.), *Theories of second language acquisition: An introduction* (pp. 175–200). Mahwah, NJ: Erlbaum.

Gass, S. M., & Selinker, L. (2001). *Second language acquisition: An introductory course*. Mahwah, NJ: Erlbaum.

Gibbs, R. W. (2005). *Embodiment and cognitive science*. Cambridge: Cambridge University Press.

Hakuta, K., & Cancino, H. (1977). Trends in second-language-acquisition research. *Harvard Educational Review, 47*, 294–316.

Halliday, M. A. K. (1978). *Language as social semiotic: The social interpretation of language and meaning*. London: Arnold.

Harnish, R. M. (2002). *Minds, brains, computers: An historical introduction to the foundations of cognitive science*. Malden, MA: Blackwell.

Harris, R. (1991). On redefining linguistics. In H. G. Davis & T. Taylor (Eds.), *Redefining linguistics* (pp. 18–52). London: Routledge.

Haugeland, J. (1998). *Having thought: Essays in the metaphysics of mind.* Cambridge, MA: Harvard University Press.

Huang, J. (1970). *A Chinese child's acquisition of English syntax.* Unpublished MA TESL thesis. University of California at Los Angeles.

Krashen, S. D. (1985). *The input hypothesis: Issues and implications.* Harlow: Longman.

Larsen-Freeman, D. (1991). Second language acquisition research: Staking out the territory. *TESOL Quarterly, 25*, 315–350.

Larsen-Freeman, D. (2007). Reflecting on the cognitive-social debate in second language acquisition. *Modern Language Journal, 91*, 773–787.

Larsen-Freeman, D., and Long, M. H. (1991). *An introduction to second language acquisition.* Harlow: Longman.

Long, M. H. (1996). The role of the linguistic environment in second language acquisition. In W. C. Ritchie & T. K. Bhatia (Eds.), *Handbook of second language acquisition* (pp. 413–468). London: Academic Press.

Long, M. H. (1997). Construct validity in SLA research: A response to Firth and Wagner. *Modern Language Journal, 81*, 318–323.

Long, M. H. (2007). *Problems in SLA.* Mahwah, NJ: Erlbaum.

Long, M. H., & Doughty, C. J. (2003). SLA and cognitive science. In C. J. Doughty & M. H. Long (Eds.), *Handbook of second language acquisition* (pp. 866–870). Malden, MA: Blackwell.

Miller, G. A. (1977). *Spontaneous apprentices: Children and language.* New York: Seabury Press.

Miller, G. A., & Chomsky, N. (1963). Finitary models of language users. In R. D. Luce, R. R. Bush, & E. Galanter (Eds.), *Handbook of mathematical psychology* (pp. 419–491). New York: Wiley.

Miller, G. A., Galanter, E., & Pribram, K. H. (1960). *Plans and the structure of behavior.* New York: Holt.

Mitchell, R., & Myles, F. (1998). *Second language learning theories.* London: Arnold.

Mitchell, R., & Myles, F. (2004). *Second language learning theories* (2nd ed.). London: Arnold.

Neisser, U. (1976). *Cognition and reality: Principles and implications of cognitive psychology.* San Francisco, CA: Freeman.

Ravem, R. (1968). Language acquisition in a second language environment. *International Review of Applied Linguistics, 6*, 165–185.

Reeke, G. N., & Edelman, G. M. (1988). Real brains and artificial intelligence. In S. R. Graubard (Ed.), *The artificial intelligence debate: False starts, real foundations* (pp. 144–173). Cambridge, MA: MIT Press.

Ritchie, C., & Bhatia, T. (Eds.). (1996). *Handbook of second language acquisition.* London: Academic Press.

Schmidt, R. W. (1983). Interaction, acculturation, and the acquisition of communicative competence: A case study of an adult. In N. Wolfson & E. Judd (Eds.), *Sociolinguistics and second language acquisition* (pp. 137–174). Rowley, MA: Newbury House.

Schmidt, R. W. (1990). The role of consciousness in second language learning. *Applied Linguistics, 11*, 129–157.

Schmidt, R. W. (2001). Attention. In P. Robinson (Ed.), *Cognition and second language instruction* (pp. 3–32). New York: Cambridge University Press.

Schmidt, R. W., & Frota, S. N. (1986). Developing basic conversational ability in a second language: A case study of an adult learner of Portuguese. In R. R. Day (Ed.), *Talking to learn: Conversation in second language acquisition* (pp. 237–319). Cambridge, MA: Newbury House.

Skinner, B. F. (1957). *Verbal behavior*. New York: Appleton Century Crofts.

Sloan Foundation (1978). *Cognitive science, 1978: Report of the State of the Art Committee*. New York: Sloan Foundation.

Suchman, L. A. (2007). *Human-machine reconfigurations: Plans and situated actions* (2nd ed.). Cambridge: Cambridge University Press.

Swain, M. (2005). The output hypothesis: Theory and research. In E. Hinkel (Ed.), *Handbook of research in second language teaching and learning* (pp. 471–484). Mahwah, NJ: Erlbaum.

Thomas, M. (1998). Programmatic ahistoricity in second language acquisition theory. *Studies in Second Language Acquisition, 20*, 387–405.

Thomas, M. (2004). *Universal grammar in second language acquisition: A history*. London: Routledge.

VanPatten, B., & Williams, J. (2007). Introduction: The nature of theories. In B. VanPatten & J. Williams (Eds.), *Theories in second language acquisition: An introduction* (pp. 1–16). Mahwah, NJ: Erlbaum.

Wallace, B. (2007). Introduction. In B. Wallace, A. Ross, J. Davies, & T. Anderson (Eds.), *The mind, the body and the world: Psychology after cognitivism?* (pp. 1–32). Exeter: Imprint Academic.

Wheeler, M. (2005). *Reconstructing the cognitive world: The next step*. Cambridge, MA: MIT Press.

1

THE SOCIOCULTURAL APPROACH TO SECOND LANGUAGE ACQUISITION

Sociocultural theory, second language acquisition, and artificial L2 development

James P. Lantolf

The sociocultural theory (SCT) approach to SLA (henceforth, SCT-L2) is grounded in the psychological theory of human consciousness proposed by L. S. Vygotsky. Although not developed specifically to explain SLA, SCT as a theory of human mental activity has much to offer regarding how individuals acquire and use languages beyond their first. Although some SCT researchers have examined bilingual acquisition, including issues relating to biliteracy, most SCT research within the field of SLA has concentrated on adult learners. Therefore the focus of the present chapter is on SCT-L2 research relating to adult SLA.

Overview

The central thread that runs through most SCT-L2 research since its inception (Frawley & Lantolf, 1985), and which marks it off from other SLA approaches, is its focus on if and how learners develop the ability to use the new language to *mediate* (i.e., regulate or control) their mental and communicative activity. To be sure, research concerning the Zone of Proximal Development (see below) has directly addressed acquisition, but even there development is understood not only in terms of target-like performance but also in terms of the quality and quantity of external mediation required. Seen as a whole, then, SCT-L2 research is distinguished from other SLA approaches by the fact that it places mediation, either by other or self, at the core of development and use.

Theoretical Principle(s)

SCT's foundational principle is that "all specifically human psychological processes (so-called higher mental processes) are mediated by psychological tools such as language, signs, and symbols" (Karpov & Hayward, 1998, p. 27). Mediation is the creation and use of artificial auxiliary means of acting—physically, socially, and mentally. In the physical world, auxiliary means, or *tools*, include shovels, hammers, bulldozers, dynamite, etc., all of which greatly enhance the human body's power to shape the environment: It is much easier to dig a hole with a shovel than one's hands. In the social and psychological worlds, our tools consist of symbols, e.g., numbers, graphs, models, drawings, and especially linguistic symbols. As with physical tools, the power of symbolic artifacts resides not in their structure but in their action potential. Thus, the physical structure of a shovel says little about its function. One must press it into service to discover its capacity to mediate digging action.

Similarly, the structure of language tells us little about its power to mediate our social/communicative and mental lives. Language's power resides instead in its use value—its meaning-making capacity. Early on, children start to appropriate the symbolic tools of their culture through joint goal-directed activity with adults. The process continues throughout the school years and into adolescence. According to Karpov and Hayward (1998), SCT distinguishes two types of symbolic mediation: *self-regulation*—the ability to plan, monitor, check, and evaluate self-performance (p. 27); and *concept-based regulation*—resulting from the appropriation and internalization of cognitive tools needed for mediation in specific "subject-domains" (p. 28). As Vygotsky stated:

> Man [*sic*] introduces artificial stimuli, signifies behavior, and with signs, acting externally, creates new connections in the brain. Together with assuming this, we shall tentatively introduce into our research a new regulatory principle of behavior, a new concept of determinacy of human reaction which consists of the fact that man creates connections in the brain from outside, controls the brain and through it, his own body.
>
> (1997, p. 55)

Children's early appropriation of language is implicit (i.e., beyond awareness) since the main function of interaction is not usually language learning but learning something else, including how to participate appropriately in social activities. Language serves as a symbolic artifact to facilitate such activities, but it is in and through these activities that language is appropriated (Wertsch, 2007, p. 185). Consequently, language remains largely invisible, at least if and until children enter school, where they are immersed in literacy activities. The effect of schooling is thus to make language highly visible and to enhance children's capacity to consciously shape it to meet their communicative needs.[1]

Crucially, there is a close relationship between the social and psychological uses of language. In its communicative function, language entails interaction between "I" and "You." Eventually, however, a new function emerges, in which the conversation becomes intrapsychological, i.e., between "I" and "Me", where "I" formulates plans and makes decisions and "Me" (the counterpart of "You" in social conversation) evaluates, critiques and revises these as necessary before the plan's external deployment (Vocate, 1994). The "I–Me" conversation is generally referred to as *private speech*, a termed coined by Flavell (1966) to replace Piaget's "egocentric speech."

To appreciate how the symbolic "I–Me" conversation serves to mediate behavior, consider Marx's example, borrowed by Vygotsky (1997, p. 68), of the architect, who first works out the design of the building symbolically in blueprint form before beginning to build. The blueprints comprise the plan of action on the ideal plane. The completed blueprint is actualized, or objectified, through physical activity that gives rise to the physical edifice. Vygotsky reasoned that all intentional human behavior, mental or physical, entails a transition from the ideal symbolic plane to the concrete objective plane. This includes acts of speaking, which are just as material as buildings. In other words, speaking entails the realization of an ideal symbolic plan of action that is realized in vocally emitted sound waves moving through space.

Research Methods

Because SCT focuses on the formation of mediational ability through appropriating and internalizing symbolic artifacts, it is not very useful to study this ability once formed, as with competent users of a language. That is, it is difficult to observe mediation once it has been internalized. In reaction-time research, for instance, when participants are asked to push a button in response to some stimulus, the thinking process that underlies the behavior is not observable and must instead be inferred by the researchers (Vygotsky, 1978).

Since SCT holds that development originates in the integration of biologically endowed abilities with culturally organized artifacts that mediate thinking, research concentrating on fully formed, "fossilized" (Vygotsky, 1978, p. 68) processes cannot differentiate behavior arising from one or the other source. The solution, according to Vygotsky (1978), is to trace the relevant processes *during their formation*—as they still operate on the external plane. This approach is known as the *genetic method*—"genetic" not as in found in genes, but because it is historical (i.e., tracks change over time). Thus, child development researchers study mediation by presenting children with tasks beyond their current developmental level while simultaneously offering them potential mediating artifacts and observing whether and how they integrate these artifacts into the problem-situation. Vygotsky (1978, p. 74) called this "the functional method of double stimulation" because, in essence, the children were presented with two tasks: to solve a difficult problem beyond their current ability and also to figure out a way to use an external auxiliary artifact to help them solve the problem. In L2 development, this means studying how learners deploy the new language to regulate their behavior when confronted with communicatively or cognitively challenging tasks.

Examples of how this methodology functions in L2 research are provided below. For present purposes, however, consider the forbidden-colors task (Vygotsky, 1986). Participants of different ages are asked questions and instructed to avoid using a specific color in their responses. Thus, participants might be asked to describe their home, with white being the forbidden color. Four-year-olds find it difficult to avoid using the forbidden term in such circumstances if their house is actually white. To help the children over this hurdle researchers provide pieces of differently colored paper as external mediational tools for thinking. However, four-year-olds cannot use the tool and continue producing the forbidden colors. But seven-year-olds use the paper, which they often place nearby to remind them of the forbidden color. Twelve-year-olds and adults have no need for external support since they can remind themselves on the internal plane which colors are forbidden. This experiment suggests that children gradually develop the ability, first, to use external mediation and, later, to internalize it.

Supporting Findings

SCT-L2 research reflects both ways of conceptualizing symbolic mediation: self-regulatory mediation and mediation provided by conceptual knowledge. It must be stressed that the distinction is only analytical—in normal activity the two aspects of mediation are inseparable. The first phase of SCT-L2 research focused on the self-regulatory function of L2 mediation, beginning with Frawley and Lantolf (1985). This line of research has been thoroughly reviewed (e.g., Lantolf & Beckett, 2009; Lantolf & Pavlenko, 1995; Lantolf & Thorne, 2006), so only its major findings will be treated here. The second phase of SCT-L2 research began with Negueruela (2003), when *concept-based instruction* (CBI) first attracted the attention of researchers. However, this does not mean that work on self-regulation has ceased: It continues unabated but with an expanded scope that now includes nonverbal components, in particular gesture. Since the latter research has not previously been reviewed in detail, it will be examined more closely here along with the CBI research. The first three subsections that follow address the research carried out on self-regulation, while the remainder of the chapter discusses the growing body of work on concept-based mediation and how this is developed through educational praxis.

Mediation as Self-Regulation

The focus of Frawley and Lantolf (1985), as with most research dealing with self-regulation, was not on the accuracy of learners' speech but on how their performance manifested their ability to maintain and regain self-regulation, in this case on picture-sequence narration tasks. Thus, the intermediate speakers in this study, unlike the advanced speakers, frequently used progressive aspect to describe events (e.g., "Here the little boy is eating the ice-cream cone"), much as one would describe action in a photograph. The researchers interpreted this usage as indicating that the speakers did not control the task and therefore could not create a coherent narrative. Instead, they opted to do what they were capable of—describe isolated pictures/events. Other speakers used the past tense to narrate some story events (e.g., "The man took the little boy's ice-cream cone.") rather than the historical present used by native speakers (NSs) and advanced L2 speakers. The researchers argued that this past-tense usage represented an attempt to regain self-regulation because past-tense morphology provides a kind of temporal distance from events, much like how standing back from a painting allows one to see the whole. Other studies (e.g., Appel & Lantolf, 1994; McCafferty, 1994) uncovered similar though by no means identical mediational L2 uses to carry out complex tasks.

Based on extensive research in Russia, Ushakova (1994) suggested that L2 learners are unlikely to develop the capacity to use the L2 to mediate mental functioning, even when they can use it in social interaction. She cast her conclusion in metaphorical terms: "[A] second language is looking into the windows cut out by the first language" (p. 154). A decade later, Centeno-Cortés and Jiménez-Jiménez (2004), using a more complex research design than in previous studies, again found that L2 speakers, including advanced speakers, were unable to use the language to mediate their online thinking during complex tasks. They reported that, even when able to sustain L2 private speech (i.e., self-speech as a mediational tool), speakers could not complete the tasks given. If, however, they switched to their L1 in its psychological function, they were much more likely to complete the tasks.

Coughlan and Duff's (1994) important study was the first to consider L2 self-regulation from an *activity-theory* perspective. Activity theory is considered by many SCT researchers as a sub-theory of SCT. It argues that human behavior is determined by its motive, goal, and the material circumstances in which it is enacted (Lantolf & Thorne, 2006). Coughlan and Duff showed that L2 performance need not be consistent across tasks for single learners or across different learners for single tasks. They argued that performance depends greatly on the specific goals individuals have for speaking. Similarly, Lantolf and Ahmed (1989) explained the variation in one L2 user's performance across three speaking tasks—picture story, interview, and free conversation—as shaped by the speaker's communicative goals. Specifically, the learner produced more accurate language when seeking to comply with the assumed interests of the researchers—to elicit evidence of his L2 ability. However, when conversing on a particular topic of interest to him, he produced much more speech and longer turns than in the previous tasks, but at the same time his speech became formally less accurate. The researchers concluded that the learner's accurate performance reflected other-regulation by the researchers, whereas his less accurate but more interesting and relevant performance exhibited his ability to self-regulate through the language. In other words, the learner's accurate performance in the first task reflected his attempt to comply with what he perceived as the interests of the researchers—to perform accurately in the L2 regardless of the content of the message. His performance in the second task reflected his personal interest in the topic and the only way for him to fully express this was through L2 speech that was not formally accurate.

Two studies have investigated using private speech to internalize L2 features in classrooms. Ohta (2001) studied the "vicarious" (p. 56) responses of learners when eavesdropping on interactions between the teacher and fellow students. Lantolf and Yáñez-Prieto (2003) conducted a smaller-scale study but similarly found that through private speech learners focused on those aspects of the target language they desired to learn. An especially interesting finding was that, through private speech, learners appeared to exhibit greater uptake of teacher recasts than reported elsewhere, where socially overt uptake was usually the focus.

Zone of Proximal Development

Earlier, I mentioned that children appropriate their community's cultural artifacts via socialization processes organized by caregivers. Vygotsky (1978) discovered that during socialization caregivers usually behave toward children as if they were able to carry out cultural activities, including those involving language, which they could not actually carry out by themselves. An especially important socialization activity for preschool children is play, which allows them to behave beyond their chronological age. Accordingly, "play contains all developmental tendencies in a condensed form and is itself a major source of development," because play "creates a zone of proximal development of the child" (p. 102). The *Zone of Proximal Development* (ZPD) is the activity in which instruction (i.e., socialization at home and formal teaching at school) and development "are interrelated from the child's very first day of life" (p. 84). Karpov (2005) pointed out that the optimal type of play for promoting development involves adults or older peers serving as models for imitation and providing mediation for children.

In the ZPD, mediators do things *with* rather than *for* children. A simple, though powerful, example of physical mediation in the ZPD is provided by Fogel (1993), wherein a mother undertakes to transfer her infant, who has only partial muscle control, from prone to upright position. One way of doing so is simply to reposition the infant from one posture to the other. A second way, however, is for the mother to mediate the infant by taking the infant's hands in her own and coaxing her to pull against them while pulling the infant up. This difference in options illustrates the ZPD concept: The infant cannot sit up on her own so, in the first case, the mother makes this the focal point of her own action. In the second case, the mother instead integrates the infant's behavior with her own mature capacity for bodily action. She collaboratively engages the infant in sitting-up action, instilling some sense of successful agency in her. This is how the ZPD works—by achieving through collaborative mediation what is unachievable alone. It is important to appreciate that the mediator needs to be aware of or discover those capacities that are in the ZPD of the other. Thus, if the infant in the example had no muscle control whatsoever, it would have been useless for her mother to try to move her into a sitting position.

Aljaafreh and Lantolf (1994) represents the initial study on L2 development in the ZPD. The researchers documented changes in learner control over specific L2 grammatical features resulting from mediation negotiated between three learners and an ESL tutor. The important findings of this study include: (1) different learners may require qualitatively different (i.e., more implicit or explicit) types of mediation for the same grammatical feature; (2) single learners may require different types of mediation for different features depending on their level of control over the feature; (3) mediation sometimes needs to be withheld to determine if learners have control over given features; and (4) development is determined not only by changes in learner performance but also shifts in mediation from more explicit to more implicit. A small-scale study by Nassaji and Swain (2000) showed that randomly provided mediation is less effective than mediation geared to a learner's ZPD.

Unfortunately, no further significant empirical research on L2 development in the ZPD was published for about a decade. However, Dunn and Lantolf (1998) dealt with the misconception that the ZPD and Krashen's i+1 were similar concepts. They argued that Krashen's concept is grounded in a Piagetian perspective that assumes a common internal syllabus for interlanguage development across all learners provided they receive sufficient comprehensible input, while development in the ZPD differs for different learners depending on the quality of mediation negotiated with others.

Dynamic Assessment

With the completion of Poehner's 2005 dissertation (published as a monograph in 2008), SCT-L2 researchers again began to investigate development in the ZPD. This time, however, a new concept, *dynamic assessment*, was introduced. Coined by Luria (1961), dynamic assessment (DA) is the systematic integration of the ZPD into educational praxis as the dialectical unity of instruction and assessment (Haywood & Lidz, 2007; Sternberg & Grigorenko, 2002). (For "educational praxis" and "dialectal unity of instruction," see subsection entitled "Educational Praxis and Concept-based Instruction" below). DA's underlying principle is that effective instruction requires not only assessment of what individuals or groups can accomplish alone, but also information on how learners react to instruction (i.e., mediation). The former only uncovers past development—it fails to consider potential future development. Because future development depends on mediation, responsiveness to instruction becomes an indispensable component of the assessment process.

Poehner (2008) described a four-month-long project on the oral ability of advanced university L2 French learners. Significantly, this project incorporated the important concept of *transcendence* (Poehner, 2007)—learners' ability to appropriate and generalize mediation to new, more complex activities. Through close micro-genetic (i.e., moment-to-moment) analysis of learners' speaking ability, Poehner documented how learners extended their gains from mediated interaction during recall of a scene from the movie, *Nine Months*, to recall of a more complex scene from *The Pianist*, to recall of a different genre—a passage from Voltaire's *Candide*. Poehner also corroborated two important findings from Aljaafreh and Lantolf (1994): (1) development manifests not only through changes in learner performance but also through changes in type of mediation supporting learner performance; and (2) development is not uniform for all learners. Thus, different learners need different types of mediation (from explicit to implicit) for the same L2 features, and single learners often require different forms of mediation for different L2 features.

In a four-month-long DA project on L2 listening comprehension, Ableeva (2010) asked intermediate university French students to recall authentic oral texts in which NSs compared American and French eating habits. Like Poehner, Ableeva included transcendence activities wherein learners recalled not just the original text but new and increasingly complex texts. She found statistically significant improvement in learner comprehension determined by number of propositions accurately recalled from NS texts. She also discovered an upper limit to text complexity even with extensive mediation: Although learners could extend their developing comprehension ability to more complex texts, including a French TV documentary on smoking in restaurants, they could not deal with a radio commercial for a restaurant chain delivered at an articulation rate typical of short radio ads and without the redundancy and pauses of the other texts. This is not surprising: Development is not a process whereby learners can master anything at any time. Even with effective mediation, development in the ZPD has an upper limit, but not one established a priori; rather it is determined through negotiated mediation between learners and others (Vygotsky, 1978). To be sure, most of the students had problems with the radio commercial even when receiving mediation, but this does not mean they can never comprehend such texts. Further focused instruction and experience with the language of commercial texts is likely to help. Similarly, we cannot expect someone who has mastered basic arithmetic to suddenly do calculus, regardless of how much mediation they receive. They must first receive explicit instruction in, and master, algebra. In both language and math, if the individual has no ZPD for the object of study, then mediation is useless.

Antón (2009) studied the use of DA in placement testing in an advanced university Spanish program. Her goal was to achieve more sensitive placement so that instruction was better attuned to student needs. Recall that the ZPD begins with actual ability based on independent performance but is oriented toward future development determined by learner responsiveness to mediation: Students with the same actual level of development do not necessarily project identical future development. Antón demonstrated this important feature of DA through analysis of mediation protocols from learners at the same ostensible proficiency level performing the same narrative task. For instance, in independent performance, two learners had similar problems sustaining coherent use of past-tense morphology, which in Spanish distinguishes perfective from imperfect aspect. Under mediation, however, their performance showed marked divergence: One learner not only improved his performance but also indicated his awareness of the precise nature of his difficulties during independent narration. The other learner showed little improvement under mediation, in fact requiring explicit mediation throughout the narration; nor did he indicate awareness of the nature of his problem. Clearly, such differential abilities require different types of instructional intervention. Antón argued that such ability differences are seldom manifested during independent performance on assessment tasks.

Lantolf and Poehner (2011) traced the integration of DA into a primary-level Spanish course. The instructor employed Lantolf and Poehner's (2006) teacher's guide on dynamic assessment, which explains its theoretical basis in the ZPD and presents case studies showing effective versus ineffective mediation. Based on this guide, the teacher adapted DA to her classroom environment, one in which DA-type instruction was possible for only 15 minutes per day.

More specifically, rather than follow the "interactionist" (Lantolf & Poehner, 2004) mediation-providing procedure employed by Poehner (2008) and Ableeva (2010), the instructor formulated a set of eight prompts arranged from most implicit ("Pause to give the student an opportunity to self-correct") to most explicit ("Provide the correct pattern with an explanation")—an approach labeled by Lantolf and Poehner (2004) "interventionist" DA. The latter's advantage is that it permits quantitative comparisons across learners on single tasks, and within learners across tasks at different times. Its disadvantage is that it restricts mediation to predetermined prompts and therefore risks missing opportunities to maximally help students.

Analyzing instructional conversations from this classroom, Lantolf and Poehner (2011) traced the cross-time development of Spanish nominal concord in the performance of one student. They argued that the student's struggle with nominal concord resulted in development deemed unlikely had the teacher provided immediate recasts instead of calibrated mediation promoting his struggle. Another interesting aspect of this study, as argued by Poehner (2009), was that the other students appeared to benefit from observing this student–teacher interaction. This indicates that instructors and students can operate within a group ZPD (cf. Guk & Kellogg, 2007).

Concept-based Mediation

So far, I have discussed mediation as a self-regulating process growing out of other-regulation in the ZPD. The second form of mediation central to SCT is mediation through concepts. Concepts are here understood as the meanings that cultures construct to make sense of the world. The most pervasive concepts are found in language, including lexical, figurative (as in metaphor, metonymy, and other tropes), and grammatical meanings, such as tense, aspect, mood, voice, and anaphora.

Vygotsky (1986, chaps. 5 & 6) distinguished two kinds of concepts: *spontaneous* (i.e., everyday) *concepts* and *scientific concepts*. The latter will be treated more fully below—suffice it to say here that, while spontaneous knowledge is usually appropriated indirectly during socialization, scientific knowledge is appropriated through "the intentional introduction of signs . . . designed and introduced by an external agent" such as a teacher, resulting in an often marked reorganization of activity (Wertsch, 2007, p. 185).

According to Vygotsky, spontaneous knowledge is derived through observing entities and events as they appear to our senses. As a result, some types of spontaneous knowledge are superficial and therefore incomplete or even erroneous. For example, children often consider whales fish since they have fins and live in water. Even adult language betrays empirical origins—e.g., in English, the sun "rises," "sets," and "moves" through the sky, although such words depart from our scientific understanding of celestial motion. Vygotsky considered the language of children prior to schooling part of spontaneous knowledge. As mentioned earlier, Vygotsky argued that schooled literacy brings spontaneously acquired linguistic knowledge into consciousness, but there are limits to what learners can be reasonably expected to figure out of the complex features of a language in the amount of time normally allocated to organized language study—and this is where scientific knowledge makes its distinctive contribution. This is an important point, as will become clear later in discussing concept-based instruction.

Paradis (2009) and Ullman (2005) have recently proposed models of SLA that distinguish between declarative and procedural (or implicit) knowledge. In L1 acquisition, grammatical knowledge is internalized (i.e., proceduralized) non-consciously through socialization processes similar to those posited by Vygotsky. Lexical knowledge, on the other hand, although also acquired during socialization, is accessible to consciousness. The distinction between the two types of knowledge in both Paradis's and Ullman's models is captured by the distinction between procedural and declarative knowledge.[2] One line of research within SCT-L2 has focused on the ability of L2 users to appropriate declarative knowledge of L2 lexical concepts. This research has also been framed within Slobin's (2003) *thinking-for-speaking* model, as discussed in the following subsection.

Thinking for Speaking

SCT-L2 research informed by Slobin's (2003) thinking-for-speaking (TFS) model has investigated whether learners can develop the ability to appropriate and think through meanings available in the L2, especially within the semantic domain of motion in event narratives. In particular, the research has considered the interface between speech and gesture as verbal and imagistic carriers of meaning, respectively. This research is premised on the assumption that, when speakers encode their thinking in language for communicative purposes, language shapes (or *completes*—Vygotsky, 1986) the thinking process itself. Borrowing Vygotsky's (1986) concept of inner speech, McNeill (2005) argued that not only speech but also gesture shapes thinking. He maintained that speech and gesture form a dialectical unity, or *growth point*, where gesture is the imagistic and synthetic co-expression of what is represented symbolically and analytically in speech. Specifically, the growth point is the focus of a speaker's attention, as made manifest in the synchronization of the stroke (or movement) of the gesture with a particular segment of speech.

The main semantic domain in which L2 TFS gesture research has been conducted is motion events. Talmy (2000) proposed a typological distinction among languages according to how they encode such events. Some languages pattern like English and highlight *manner of motion* encoded in verbs (e.g., *skip, trudge, sidle, scamper, creep*), with *path of motion* marked in a satellite phrase (e.g., *through the swamp, up the ladder, down the stairs*). Other languages pattern like Spanish and highlight path of motion encoded in verbs (e.g., *salir* "to exit," *entrar* "to enter," *subir* "to get into"—as with a car), with manner encoded (if at all) in an adverb or participle (e.g., *El barril salió del sótano flotando* "The barrel left the basement floating"). This does not mean that languages like Spanish lack manner of motion verbs, but their inventory is restricted compared to English-like languages. Thus, while Spanish has the equivalent of *jump*, *walk*, or *run*, it has nothing like *sidle*, *scamper*, or *trudge*.

McNeill (2005) showed that, along with expressing motion events through speech, speakers simultaneously gesture to co-express movement. Thus, English speakers often express manner of motion with complex manner verbs while producing a synchronized gesture. In Spanish-like languages, on the other hand, gestures used in such contexts synchronize with path verbs. In addition, speakers can express manner through gesture even when not expressed in speech, an option not generally found in English-like languages. Thus, a Spanish speaker might say, "The barrel left from the basement," and mark the manner of motion with a gesture. It should be noted that, unlike self-regulation and concept-based instruction, motion-event lexical knowledge is not (as far as I know) intentionally taught in classrooms. Thus, if learners acquire this knowledge it is likely through indirect processes.

The question regarding L2 development is whether learners can adopt L2 TFS patterns as manifested in speech–gesture growth points. If so, it would provide evidence of the formation of a new inner order whereby learners internalize and use completely new conceptual meanings—at least as regards motion events—to mediate their thinking process. Some research (e.g., Özyürek, 2002; Stam, 2006) shows that L1 Spanish and L1 Turkish learners of English shift to the English gesture–speech pattern for encoding path of motion in verb satellites. However, there is little evidence of pattern shifts for manner of motion. Negueruela, Lantolf, Jordan, and Gelabert (2004) found no evidence of such shifts in advanced L2 speakers of Spanish (L1 = English) or English (L1 = Spanish).

Choi and Lantolf (2008) encountered one highly experienced immigrant L2 English (L1 Korean) speaker who used one English manner verb synchronized with an appropriate manner gesture in narrating a cartoon story. None of their advanced Korean L2 (L1 English) immigrant speakers showed evidence of moving to a Korean pattern for marking manner. Korean is similar to Spanish in that it marks path of motion on verbs (although in Korean they are compound constructions) and manner of motion with an adverb, or a gesture in the absence of verbal co-expressivity. The L1 English speakers in both this study and Negueruela et al. (2004) tended to display lexical search difficulties when expressing manner in their L2s. The problem was that the languages in question (Korean, Spanish) do not have the complex manner verbs the speakers were searching for. In both studies, this behavior indicates that L2 speakers continue to rely on their L1 to mediate TFS activity.

Gullberg (in press) showed that L1 Dutch French learners are able to shift from Dutch to French patterns of gesture–speech integration when describing object placement. The Dutch lexicon has verbs that mark placement of objects in space (e.g., Dutch equivalents of *put*, *set*, *place*, *stand*, *lie*). French, on the other hand, has few such verbs, preferring *mettre* ("put") to describe such actions. In addition, Dutch speakers use a co-expressive gesture depicting the shape of the object (e.g., bowl, bottle, dish) moved, while French speakers use a co-expressive deictic gesture to indicate the landing site of the object (e.g., extended index finger pointing to the target site). The L2 French speakers in Gullberg's study not only used the appropriate French verb but also shifted from the gesture shape of their L1 to the indexical gesture of the L2, thus manifesting a concomitant shift in TFS. Although Gullberg's research adds to the evidence provided by Stam (2006) of a shift in TFS, the jury is still out with regard to a shift in manner of motion.

Educational Praxis and Concept-Based Instruction

Although symbolic mediation is the core concept of SCT, in laying the groundwork for his new psychology Vygotsky insisted that theory could no longer be separated from practice, as stated in the 11th Thesis of Marx's *Theses on Feuerbach*: "The philosophers have only *interpreted* the world, in various ways; the point, however, is to *change* it" (1845/1978, p. 145, italics in original). Vygotsky explained as follows:

> Previously theory was not dependent on practice; instead practice was the conclusion, the application, an excursion beyond the boundaries of science, an operation which lay outside science and came after science, which began after the scientific operation was considered completed. Success or failure had practically no effect on the fate of the theory . . . Now the situation is the opposite. Practice pervades the deepest foundations of the scientific operation and reforms it from beginning to end. Practice sets the tasks and serves as the supreme judge of theory, as its truth criterion. It dictates how to construct the concepts and how to formulate the laws.
>
> (1926/2004, p. 304)

The dialectical unity of theory–practice reflected in this quote is referred to as *praxis*—material activity adapted to specific goals and informed by theory, while simultaneously testing those same theoretical principles (Sanchez Vasquez, 1977, p. 95). For Vygotsky, the highest test of a theory (in the theory–practice dialectic that is praxis) is practice. In this spirit, Stetsenko and Arievitch (2004, p. 78) have suggested that Kurt Lewin's famous comment that "there is nothing more practical than a good theory" should be expanded to include the "mirror expression—that there is nothing more theoretically rich than a good practice" (p. 77). The challenge of a praxis-based approach was to create a psychology that would promote the development of new processes rather than continuing to focus on observing existing ones.

A praxis-based approach to SCT has been applied to a wide array of social domains, including workplaces (e.g., Engeström & Middleton, 2008), medical settings (e.g., Luria, 1973), economic and political domains (e.g., Ratner, 2006), and above all education (e.g., Moll, 1990). One might plausibly argue that Aljaafreh and Lantolf's (1994) work on L2 learning in the ZPD signaled the beginning of a praxis-based approach to L2 education, especially given Vygotsky's (1978, p. 85) proposal that mediation in the ZPD is an important part of what school learning brings to developmental processes. However, there is another component of educational praxis that is just as important—mediation through scientific concepts. Both components are necessary for a full commitment to educational praxis. Therefore, in my view, the pedagogical project reported in Negueruela (2003) marks the true beginning of L2 praxis, in which the theory is not just a lens for observing learning processes but a means for making them happen. Following Negueruela, several completed or in-progress studies on L2 instruction bring scientific concepts to center stage as the unit of L2 instruction. Before looking at this research, however, it is necessary to discuss the nature of scientific concepts themselves and how they differ from knowledge created in the everyday world.

Scientific versus Everyday Knowledge

I have already introduced the notion of everyday/spontaneous knowledge in my discussion of concept-based mediation. While this knowledge generally operates below the level of full consciousness, and in the case of native-language grammatical knowledge remains inaccessible to conscious inspection, scientific knowledge is highly explicit and completely open to conscious analysis. Setting aside implicit grammatical knowledge for the moment, declarative everyday knowledge not only of vocabulary but also other types of encyclopedic knowledge can be superficial and is often erroneous or incomplete. Scientific knowledge (sometimes referred to as theoretical knowledge), on the other hand, represents "the generalizations of the experience of humankind that is fixed in science, understood in the broadest sense of the term to include both natural and social science as well as the humanities" (Karpov, 2003, p. 66). Scientific concepts are not only explicit, they are also domain-specific, and "aimed at selecting the essential characteristics of objects or events of a certain class and presenting these characteristics in the form of symbolic and graphic models" (p. 71). The power of scientific knowledge resides in its "generative" capacity to the extent that it is generalizable across diverse situations (Kozulin, 1998, p. 55).

To illustrate the distinction between everyday and scientific knowledge, consider Ratner's (2006) example: Everyday knowledge is reflected in such utterances as, "The clothes dried *because* I hung them out in the sunshine." According to Ratner, the relationship between sunshine and drying clothes here is "associative" rather than causal in a scientific sense given that one can replace "because" with "the descriptive term *when* with no change in meaning" (p. 161). Legitimate scientific explanation, on the other hand, provides specific reasons for a process along with its underlying mechanisms: "The clothes absorb the light, which increases the kinetic energy of the water molecules in the wet clothing to the point that they overcome the adhesive forces that bound them to the clothes" (p. 161). This account explains why clothes dry in the presence of any source that increases the kinetic energy of water molecules; it likewise accounts for the failure of clothes to dry.

A general assumption of SLA research is that the acquisition process is psychologically uniform no matter where it occurs. Long, for example, asserted the following:

> Change the social setting altogether (e.g., from street to classroom), or from a foreign to a second language environment and, as far as we know, the way the learner acquires does not change much either (as suggested, e.g., by comparisons of error types, developmental sequences, processing constraints, and other aspects of the acquisition process in and out of classrooms).
>
> (2007, p. 145)

The Universal Acquisition Hypothesis (UAH)—my term—is grounded in the assumption that the basic mechanisms of acquisition are situated inside learners' heads. As Long explained: "An eight-hour flight from a foreign to a second language environment does not alter a learner's brain after all, so why should one *expect* any basic differences?" (2007, p. 145, italics in original). To my knowledge, the UAH has been challenged by only one SLA researcher, Tarone (2007), who presented evidence of a learner manifesting different acquisition sequences for English questions in the school versus home environment.

SCT agrees with Tarone. This is because a central mechanism of mental development is the mediation available in different sociocultural environments. As already mentioned, mediation is realized through social, largely communicative, interaction and the cultural concepts individuals have access to in different environments. Of course, concepts and social interaction are interdependent—social mediation employs culturally constructed concepts, either the everyday variety or the scientific type encountered in educational settings.

Paradis's (2009) model of declarative and procedural knowledge (see above) makes an important claim regarding SLA that resonates deeply with L2 educational praxis. His essential claim is that, in the absence of intensive and extensive immersion, L2 learners are unlikely to develop implicit automatized competence (i.e., procedural knowledge) to anything like the degree of L1 learners. Instead, L2 learners, in particular those with primary and unique classroom L2 exposure, build up explicit/declarative knowledge, which through practice can result in "speeded-up controlled use" (p. 8).[3] Through speeded-up declarative knowledge, learners can become quite fluent and proficient in meeting their communicative needs. In the following two subsections, I discuss SCT-L2 research that focuses on the intentional—or as Vygotsky put it, "artificial"—development of communicatively functional declarative knowledge.

Concept-based Instruction

As mentioned above, concept-based instruction (CBI) has as its centerpiece, or unit of instruction, systematic, explicit knowledge of the relevant features of the L2. Several studies have been conducted within this framework on L2 praxis, beginning with Negueruela (2003). As Negueruela's work has already been discussed in the research literature, however, I will present an overview of a nearly completed dissertation that deals with Chinese (Mandarin) as a foreign language (Lai, 2011). To be sure, examples from Negueruela's work—as well as Yáñez-Prieto's (2008), also framed within CBI—will be included where relevant. Before discussing Lai's research, however, it is necessary to consider in concrete terms CBI's implementation in language classrooms.

The specific procedures followed in most L2 CBI to date were stipulated by the best-known pedagogical theorist of Vygotsky's school, Piotr Gal'perin (see Haenen, 1996; Talyzina, 1981). Gal'perin's program, known as Systemic-Theoretical Instruction, follows a specific sequence of instructional phases, which, as implemented in most recent L2 studies, are: systematic verbal explanation of the concept in the target language, including comparison with the L1 whenever feasible —> materialization of the concept —> communicative activities —> verbalization —> internalization.

The first phase, *explanation*, must be based on scientific knowledge of the concept under study. In my view, cognitive linguistics provides a potentially useful source of such knowledge for language instruction (Lantolf, in press). This is because cognitive linguistics foregrounds meaning and seeks to develop theoretical concepts that generalize across language domains. A second reason I believe cognitive linguistics is compatible with SCT is its robust use of visual models to depict linguistic concepts. This links the theory closely with Gal'perin's (1970) first two phases of instruction—explanation and materialization, with the latter concept being based on the premise that the former alone is often problematic for learners. Thus, Gal'perin argued that students tend to memorize explanations as rules rather than understanding concepts well enough for them to inform and guide practical activity. He therefore proposed the second phase—*materialization*—in which the concept is represented visually as a model, graph, or other synthetic depiction. Gal'perin called the materialization of a concept a *schema for the orienting basis of action* (SCOBA). SCOBAs provide learners with resources that are then formulated as a plan of action in the third, or *communication*, phase of instruction. In language instruction, communication can involve a wide array of activities, ranging from tasks to scenarios (Di Pietro, 1987) to literature-based conversations and writing activities (Yáñez-Prieto, 2008) to service learning (Grabois, 2008), where language is used as a tool for accomplishing specific goals. The fourth phase, *verbalization*, is the point at which learners use language (i.e., engage in *languaging*—Swain, 2006) to both explain the concept to themselves and explain to themselves how they use it in specific communicative activities. In essence, this phase calls for production of speech in its psychological function with the intention of giving rise to the final, or *internalization* phase of the developmental process.

Learners' reactions regarding the value of SCOBAs and their verbalization have been quite revealing, given that the procedures are not commonly employed in language programs. One student from Negueruela's (2003) study made the following comment:

> The charts are a grammar-figuring-out-guide that work better than the rules (like the rules for preterit and imperfect) that we had learned in Spanish 100. It was very helpful to see the concepts in a visual structure because the concept of grammar is a very structural concept, and being able to visualize it made it make much more sense.
>
> (p. 453)

A student from Yáñez-Prieto's (2008) study offered the following remarks on how SCOBAs impacted his thinking:

> It's kind of funny how you can have a grammar . . . grammatical structure actually tell a story. I'd not really noticed that or seen that before. I mean, the words are telling the story and the grammar is telling the story, which is kind of weird. Yeah, I'd never seen that before. Interesting.
>
> (p. 267)

The SCOBAs not only made the language feature visible for this student, they also compelled him to think deeply about the connection between structure and meaning-making.

With regard to verbalization, the comment of a student from Negueruela's (2003) study revealed that talking to himself contributed to his understanding, at the same time helping him gain confidence in speaking the new language:

> Although sometimes recording myself speak was a bit awkward, I think it was overall extremely helpful. It made me more comfortable speaking and improvising, and it forced me to truly think about the grammar.
>
> (p. 438)

A second student from the same course corroborated this perspective:

> The activities that have helped me the most are the verbalization ones with the cassette tape player. I feel as though with verbalization exercises I not only improved my speaking, but also learned a lot of information about the indicative and subjunctive.
>
> (p. 434)

Swain, Lapkin, Knouzi, Suzuki, and Brooks (2009) contended that verbalization is also effective in a collaborative format where students explain to each other rather than themselves a concept and the implementation of its SCOBA. Swain et al.'s reasoning is based on Vygotsky's argument that speech is reflexive and therefore can simultaneously serve to mediate others and self. It remains to be seen if private verbalization or social languaging is more effective in promoting internalization, or if they are equally effective.

CBI in Chinese Temporal Grammar

Lai (2011) analyzed the effects of a CBI program designed to develop the ability of L2 learners of Chinese to use temporal grammar. Without going into detail, Chinese does not mark tense morphologically but instead relies either on context or adverbial particles. One set of particles marks time on a horizontal dimension and another marks it vertically. Taking the horizontal dimension first, whereas English conceptualizes past time as behind and future time as in front of the speaker, Chinese does the opposite—the particle *qian*, "front," designates past, while *hou*, "back," designates future. Thus, the Chinese *lian tian qian*, "two days front," is expressed in English as "two days ago," while *san nian hou*, "three years back," is rendered "after three years." As regards the vertical dimension, Chinese also uses it to designate past and future. Thus, the particle *shang*, "up," indicates immediate past, while *xia*, "down," marks immediate future, with *shang* functioning similarly to English "last" and *xia* similarly to "next." *Sang xinqi*, "up week," translates into English as "last week" and *Xia yi nian*, "down one year," is "next year." Thus, the language distinguishes between distal and immediate past and future in accordance with the two different spatial dimensions.[4]

Lai (2011) pointed out that, traditionally, Chinese-language pedagogy has not focused heavily on teaching temporal particles as tense markers. In some textbooks the particles are introduced as part of compound lexical items without indicating their tense-marking function. In other cases, brief rules of thumb for marking tense are given, accompanied by illustrative examples. As argued by myself and others (e.g., Lantolf, 2007; Negueruela, 2003), rules of thumb are much like everyday knowledge—incomplete, superficial, and/or erroneous, and as such they do not explicate the essence of the concept under study. Using cognitive linguistics as her theoretical foundation, Lai presented her students with a sophisticated yet useable explanation of particle-based tense-marking in Chinese using the SCOBA given in Figure 1.1. For present purposes I leave out the details and focus instead on the most important aspects of the explanation.

Lai (2011) implemented her instructional program over a five-day period in a first-year/beginning-level university Chinese course. Except for the special instruction on temporal grammar, the students followed the regular course syllabus. After instruction, the students were given a post-test in which they were asked to write a narrative based on a picture story. The same test was given to two other classes: a beginning-level class, which received temporal instruction according to the course textbook; and an intermediate-level class, which had received instruction on temporal grammar in their first and second years of study. The class receiving Systemic Theoretical Instruction performed significantly better ($p < .05$) than the

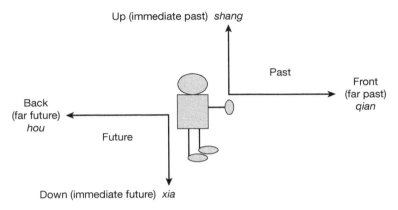

FIGURE 1.1 SCOBA visualizing temporal particles in Chinese (from Lai, 2011).

other first-year class, and no differently (in terms of statistical significance) from the intermediate class.

Future Directions

The current SCT-L2 research program clearly suggests fruitful areas for future research. In my view, four are particularly important. The first is research that implements dynamic assessment within group-wide ZPDs. The SCT-L2 work carried out so far on this topic, although limited in scope, has generated interesting results. In educational domains such as L1 literacy development, the classroom itself has been construed as a ZPD where instruction is organized according to principles of activity theory, especially by using a division of labor whereby texts are read collectively with specific tasks (e.g., preparing lists of potentially problematic words, reading between the lines) parceled out based on teacher assessment of student strengths and weaknesses (Cole, 1996). The notion of division of labor is a powerful one that should be fully exploited in future L2 educational praxis.

A second area for future research is extending concept-based instruction beyond grammar—to pragmatics, figurative language (a form of language much under-appreciated in L2 pedagogy), and especially the interface of language and culture (see Agar, 1994). Thorne, Reinhardt, and Golombek (2008) conducted a pilot study implementing a CBI approach to teaching international teaching assistants at a U.S. university how to deploy directive constructions with appropriate mitigators and intensifiers when interacting with American students. This study is just a first step in exploring CBI's potential for pragmatics instruction. In theory, any conceptual domain can be taught through CBI, but it requires a clear and systematic statement of the concept, an imaginative approach to formulating a coherent SCOBA, and the implementation of appropriate communicative activities.

A third area for future research focuses on the central claim of educational praxis, which, as pointed out above, restructures developmental processes. The approach to education advocated by Vygotsky contrasts with Piagetian perspectives whereby processes of development unfold smoothly and consistently for all learners regardless of the learning environment, including intentionally and systematically organized educational praxis. Piagetian models of SLA (e.g., Krashen, 1981; Pienemann, 1998) support common and invariant acquisition sequences based on an internal natural syllabus that operates across all learners and across all learning circumstances. Given that Vygotskian theory views the environment as a central mechanism in development, it challenges the existence of a natural syllabus. Thus, an interesting test of the two theoretical stances would be to conduct an instructional study designed to interfere with the natural syllabus. In my view, the research conducted within Pienemann's (1998) processability model has produced the most robust and consistent results supporting a natural syllabus based on processing constraints. It has also assessed negatively the impact of instruction on the syllabus; however, in my view this research has not taken sufficient account of quality of instruction. A praxis approach to instruction as discussed in this chapter should be brought to bear on the theory of natural development. To this end, we are in the process of conducting an instructional project on word order in Chinese topicalized constructions, including temporal and locative adverbs as well as direct objects. Zhang (2008), conducted within Pienemann's framework, found no instructional influence on the developmental sequence predicted by the processability model. The goal of our project is to test Zhang's findings through CBI.

A final area where I believe fruitful SCT-L2 research can be carried out is within Slobin's thinking-for-speaking framework, especially if speech–gesture synchronization, as defined by McNeill (2005), is included. The question of whether L2 users can employ their new language to mediate their thinking processes continues to be intriguing, and approaching the topic from the perspective of McNeill's growth-point hypothesis has exceptional promise.

Conclusion

In a recent paper, VanPatten (2010), a proponent of an influential SLA theory, addressed the relationship between SLA research and practice. He pointed out that teachers often assume a direct relationship between research and teaching, and as a consequence expect that "research should somehow *improve* instruction" (p. 30). VanPatten's response was that such expectations may be inappropriate. He stated that, while SLA research "cannot speak to the day-to-day issues that confront" teachers (p. 29), it can help them "*understand* acquisition and thus *inform* instruction" by offering "insight into what the learning problems are" (p. 30), and that this in turn "might also lead to a better set of expectations regarding the interface between teaching and acquisition" (p. 36). Because of its commitment to educational praxis, SCT-L2 adopts a very different stance on the relationship between theory and practice. A particular divergence between VanPatten's position and what has been advocated here concerns the explicit teaching of scientific knowledge of L2 linguistic features. In VanPatten's view, "it would be absurd to expect learners to grasp issues related to theoretical linguistics as part of their language learning experience" (p. 36). Instead, he believes that adjustments should be made to the input to help learners infer the appropriate uses of the features to be internalized. The approach espoused by not only SCT-L2 but also applied cognitive linguistics (De Knop & De Rycker, 2008) dictates that learners should indeed be presented with explicit and theoretically sophisticated explanations of L2 features, visualized in a pedagogically relevant SCOBA. That is, features should be presented in a form students can use to guide their thinking and performance.

As indicated throughout this chapter, SCT-L2 is very much concerned with concrete classroom activity and its impact on learning. It argues for the pedagogical relevance of explicit and rigorous linguistic explanation, especially that derived from cognitive linguistics, and is devoted to discovering how to make learning happen through direct instruction. It is different from other theories of SLA in that it does not assume that acquisition is a universal process. On the contrary, because mediation is different in different sociocultural domains, development in these domains is expected to be psychologically different.

Notes

1 Tarone, Bigelow, and Hansen (2009) demonstrated how low levels of literacy impact L2 learning. One of their interesting findings is that such learners have reduced levels of awareness of L2 input.
2 The declarative/procedural model will become relevant later in my discussion of scientific knowledge and concept-based instruction.
3 Following Hulstijn (2003), Paradis allows for the possibility that in some circumstances L2 learners can use explicit knowledge to indirectly benefit the formation of implicit, automatized knowledge. I have argued elsewhere (e.g., Lantolf, 2007, 2008) that explicit knowledge can also become automatic procedural knowledge as a result of internalization, with internalization in SCT being the process whereby individuals appropriate and integrate cultural artifacts, making them their own (Wertsch, 1998). Paradis's understanding of internalization differs from SCT's in that he sees it as relevant to the formation of implicit knowledge only; in turn, only implicit knowledge, according to Paradis, is automatized. Hence, he distinguishes between automatized (i.e., implicit) knowledge and speeded-up explicit knowledge. To avoid terminological confusion, I will use Paradis's "speeded-up" rather than "automatized explicit" knowledge in the following discussion. But because internalization is central to Vygotsky's theory, I will continue to use this concept to refer to the process whereby *any* type of knowledge is appropriated and used for mediation of social or psychological behavior.
4 Proximal and distal time depends on the temporal framework in which one operates. Within the time frame of "weeks," for example, proximal time would be either "last week" or "next week," while distal time would be either "the week before last" or "the week after next."

References

Ableeva, R. (2010). *Dynamic assessment of listening comprehension in L2 French*. Unpublished doctoral disseration, The Pennsylvania State University.

Agar, M. (1994). *Language shock: Understanding the culture of conversation*. New York: Quill.

Aljaafreh, A., & Lantolf, J. P. (1994). Negative feedback as regulation and second language learning in the zone of proximal development. *Modern Language Journal, 78,* 465–483.

Antón, M. (2009). Dynamic assessment of advanced second language learners. *Foreign Language Annals, 42,* 576–598.

Appel, G., & Lantolf, J. P. (1994). Speaking as mediation: A study of L1 and L2 text recall tasks. *Modern Language Journal, 78,* 437–452.

Centeno-Cortés, B., & Jiménez-Jiménez, A. (2004). Problem-solving tasks in a foreign language: The importance of the L1 in private verbal thinking. *International Journal of Applied Linguistics, 14,* 7–35.

Choi, S.-J., & Lantolf, J. P. (2008). The representation and embodiment of meaning in L2 communication: Motion events in speech and gesture in L2 Korean and L2 English speakers. *Studies in Second Language Acquisition, 30,* 191–224.

Cole, M. (1996). *Cultural psychology: A once and future discipline*. Cambridge, MA: Belknap Books.

Coughlan, P., & Duff, P. (1994). Same task different activities: Analysis of a SLA task from an activity theory perspective. In J. P. Lantolf & G. Appel (Eds.), *Vygotskian approaches to second language research* (pp. 173–194). Norwood, NJ: Ablex.

De Knop, S., & De Rycker, T. (Eds.) (2008). *Cognitive approaches to pedagogical grammar. A volume in honor of René Dirven*. Berlin: Mouton de Gruyter.

Di Pietro, R. J. (1987). *Strategic interaction*. Cambridge: Cambridge University Press.

Dunn, W., & Lantolf, J. P. (1998) Vygotsky's zone of proximal development and Krashen's i+1: Incommensurable constructs; incommensurble theories. *Language Learning, 48,* 411–442.

Engeström, Y., & Middleton, D. (Eds.) (1998). *Cognition and communication at work*. Cambridge: Cambridge University Press.

Flavell, J. (1966). *La language privé* [Private speech]. *Bulletin de Psychologie, 19,* 698–701.

Fogel, A. (1993). *Developing through relationships: Origins of communication, self, and culture*. Chicago. IL: University of Chicago Press.

Frawley, W., & Lantolf, J. P. (1985). Second language discourse: A Vygotskyan perspective. *Applied Linguistics, 6,* 19–44.

Gal'perin, P. Ia. (1970). An experimental study in the formation of mental actions. In E. Stones (Ed.), *Readings in educational psychology: Learning and teaching* (pp. 142–154). London: Methuen.

Grabois, H. (2008). Contribution and language learning: Service–learning from a sociocultural perspective. In J. P. Lantolf & M. E. Poehner (Eds.), *Sociocultural theory and the teaching of second languages* (pp. 380–406). London: Equinox.

Guk, I., & Kellogg, D. (2007). The ZPD and whole class teaching: Teacher-led and student-led interactional mediation of tasks. *Language Teaching Research, 11,* 281–299.

Gullberg, M. (in press). Language-specific encoding of placement events in gestures. In E. Pedersen & J. Bohnemeyer (Eds.), *Event representations in language and cognition*. Cambridge: Cambridge University Press.

Haenen, J. (1996). *Piotr Gal'perin: Psychologist in Vygotsky's footsteps*. New York: Nova Science Publishers.

Haywood, H. C., & Lidz, C. S. (2007). *Dynamic assessment in practice. Clinical and educational applications*. New York: Cambridge University Press.

Hulstijn, J. H. (2003). Incidental and intentional learning. In C. J. Doughty & M. H. Long (Eds.) *The handbook of second language acquisition* (pp. 349–381). Oxford: Blackwell.

Karpov, Y. V. (2003). Vygotsky's doctrine of scientific concepts: Its role for contemporary education. In A. Kozulin, B. Gindis, V. S. Ageyev, & S. Miller (Eds.), *Vygotsky's educational theory in cultural context* (pp. 39–64). Cambridge: Cambridge University Press.

Karpov, Y. V. (2005). *The neo-Vygotskian approach to child education.* Cambridge: Cambridge University Press.

Karpov, Y. V., & Hayward, C. (1998). Two ways to elaborate Vygotsky's concept of mediation. *American Psychologist, 53,* 27–36.

Kozulin, A. (1998). *Psychological tools: A sociocultural approach to education.* Cambridge, MA: Harvard University Press.

Krashen, S. D. (1981). *Second language acquisition and second language learning.* Oxford: Pergamon.

Lai, W. (2011). *Concept-based foreign language pedagogy: Teaching the Chinese temporal system.* Unpublished doctoral dissertation, The Pennsylvania State University. Manuscript in preparation.

Lantolf, J. P. (2007). Conceptual knowledge and instructed second language learning: A sociocultural perspective. In S. Fotos & H. Nassaji (Eds.), *Form focused instruction and teacher education: Studies in honour of Rod Ellis* (pp. 35–54). Oxford: Oxford University Press.

Lantolf, J. P. (2008). Praxis and L2 classroom development. *ELIA: Estudios de Linguistica Inglesa Aplicada, 8,* 13–44.

Lantolf, J. P. (in press). Integrating sociocultural theory and cognitive linguistics in the second language classroom. In E. Hinkel (Ed.), *Handbook of research on second language teaching and learning, Vol. II.* (2nd ed.). New York: Routledge.

Lantolf, J. P., & A. K. Ahmed. (1989). Psycholinguistic perspectives on interlanguage variation: A Vygotskyan analysis. In S. Gass, C. Madden, D. Preston, & L Selinker (Eds.), *Variation in second language acquisition, Vol. II: Psycholinguistic issues* (pp. 93–109). Clevedon: Multilingual Matters.

Lantolf, J. P., & Beckett, T. (2009). Research timeline for sociocultural theory and second language acquisition. *Language Teaching, 42,* 459–475.

Lantolf, J. P., & Pavlenko, A. (1995). Sociocultural theory and second language acquisition. *Annual Review of Applied Linguistics, 15,* 38–53.

Lantolf, J. P., & Poehner, M. E. (2004). Dynamic assessment: Bringing the past into the future. *Journal of Applied Linguistics, 1,* 49–74.

Lantolf, J. P., & Poehner, M. E. (2006). *Dynamic assessment in the foreign language classroom: A teacher's guide* [149pp. and Video DVD: Version 1.0]. University Park, PA: CALPER.

Lantolf, J. P., & Poehner, M. E. (2011). Dynamic assessment in the classroom: Vygotskian praxis for L2 development. *Language Teaching Research, 15,* 1–23.

Lantolf, J. P., & Thorne, S. L. (2006). *Sociocultural theory and the genesis of second language development.* Oxford: Oxford University Press.

Lantolf, J. P., & Yáñez-Prieto, C. (2003). Talking yourself into Spanish: Intrapersonal communication and second language learning. *Hispania, 86,* 97–108.

Long, M. (2007). *Problems in SLA.* Mahwah, NJ: Erlbaum.

Luria, A. R. (1961). Study of the abnormal child. *American Journal of Orthopsychiatry: A Journal of Human Behavior, 31,* 1–16.

Luria, A. R. (1973). *The working brain.* New York: Basic Books.

Marx, K. (1845/1978). Theses on Feuerbach. In R. C. Tucker (Ed.), *The Marx-Engels reader* (2nd ed., pp. 143–146). New York: W. W. Norton.

McCafferty, S. G. (1994). The use of private speech by adult ESL learners at different levels of proficiency. In J. P. Lantolf & G. Appel (Eds.), *Vygotskian approaches to second language research* (pp. 117–134). Norwood, NJ: Ablex.

McNeill, D. (2005). *Gesture and thought.* Chicago, IL: University of Chicago Press.

Moll, L. (Ed.) (1990). *Vygotsky and education: Instructional implications and applications of sociohistorical psychology*. Cambridge: Cambridge University Press.

Nassaji, H., & Swain, M. (2000). A Vygotskian perspective on corrective feedback in L2: The effect of random versus negotiated help on the learning of English articles. *Language Awareness, 9*, 34–51.

Negueruela, E. (2003). *A sociocultural approach to the teaching-learning of second languages: Systemic-theoretical instruction and L2 development*. Unpublished doctoral dissertation, The Pennsylvania State University.

Negueruela, E., Lantolf, J. P., Jordan, S. R., & Gelabert, J. (2004). The "private function" of gesture in second language communicative activity: A study on motion verbs and gesturing in English and Spanish. *International Journal of Applied Linguistics, 14*, 113–147.

Ohta, A. (2001). *Second language acquisition processes in the classroom: Learning Japanese*. Mahwah, NJ: Erlbaum.

Özyürek, A. (2002). Speech-gesture relationship across languages and in second language learners: Implications for spatial thinking and speaking. *Proceedings of the Annual Boston University Conference on Language Development, 26*, 500–509.

Paradis, M. (2009). *Declarative and procedural determinants of second language*. Amsterdam: Benjamins.

Pienemann, M. (1998). *Language processing and second language development: Processability theory*. Amsterdam: Benjamins.

Poehner, M. E. (2007). Beyond the test: L2 Dynamic Assessment and the transcendence of mediated learning. *Modern Language Journal, 91*, 323–340.

Poehner, M. E. (2008). *Dynamic assessment: A Vygotskian approach to understanding and promoting L2 development*. Berlin: Springer.

Poehner, M. E. (2009). Group dynamic assessment: Mediation for the L2 classroom. *TESOL Quarterly, 43*, 471–492.

Ratner, C. (2006). *Cultural psychology. A perspective on psychological functioning and social reform*. Mahwah, NJ: Erlbaum.

Sanchez Vasquez, A. (1977). *The philosophy of praxis*. London: Merlin Press.

Slobin, D. I. (2003). Language and thought online: Cognitive consequences of linguistic relativity. In D. Gentner & S. Goldin-Meadow (Eds.), *Language in mind: Advances in the study of language and thought* (pp. 157–192). Cambridge, MA: MIT Press.

Stam, G. (2006). Thinking for speaking about motion: L1 and L2 speech and gesture. *International Review of Applied Linguistics, 44*, 143–169.

Sternberg, R. J., & Grigorenko, E. L. (2002). *Dynamic testing: The nature and measurement of learning potential*. Cambridge: Cambridge University Press.

Stetskenko, A., & Arievitch, I. (2004). Vygotskian collaborative project of social transformation: History, politics and practice in knowledge construction. *International Journal of Critical Psychology, 12*, 58–80.

Swain, M. (2006). Languaging, agency and collaboration in advanced second language proficiency. In H. Byrnes (Ed.), *Advanced language learning: The contribution of Halliday and Vygotsky* (pp. 95–108). Washington, DC: Georgetown University Press.

Swain, M., Lapkin, S., Knouzi, I., Suzuki, W., & Brooks, L. (2009). Languaging: University students learn the grammatical concept of voice in French. *Modern Language Journal, 93*, 5–29.

Talmy, L. (2000). *Toward cognitive semantics, Vol. II: Typology and process in concept structuring*. Cambridge, MA: MIT Press.

Talyzina, N. F. (1981). *The psychology of learning*. Moscow: Progress Press.

Tarone, E. (2007). Sociolinguistic approaches to second language acquisition research—1997–2007. *Modern Language Journal, 91*, 837–848.

Tarone, E., Bigelow, M., & Hansen, K. (2009). *Literacy and second language oracy*. Oxford: Oxford University Press.

Thorne, S. L. Reinhardt, J., and Golombek, P. (2008). Mediation as objectification in the development of professional academic discourse: A corpus-informed curricular innovation. In J. P. Lantolf & M. E. Poehner (Eds.), *Sociocultural theory and the teaching of second languages* (pp. 256-284). London: Equinox.

Ullman, M. T. (2005). A cognitive neuroscience perspective on second language acquisition: The declarative/procedural model. In C. Sanz (Ed.), *Mind and context in adult second language acquisition: Methods, theory, and practice* (pp. 141–178). Washington, DC: Georgetown University Press.

Ushakova, T. N. (1994). Inner speech and second language acquisition: An experimental-theoretical approach. In J. P. Lantolf & G. Appel (Eds.), *Vygotskian approaches to second language research* (pp. 135–156). Norwood, NJ: Ablex.

VanPatten, B. (2010). Some verbs are more perfect than others: Why learners have difficulty with *ser* and *estar* and what it means for instruction. *Hispania, 93*, 29–38.

Vocate, D. R. (1994). Self-talk and inner speech: Understanding the uniquely human aspects of intrapersonal communication. In D. R. Vocate (Ed.), *Intrapersonal communication: Different voices, different minds* (pp. 3–32). Hillsdale, NJ: Erlbaum.

Vygotsky. L. S. (1926/2004). The historical meaning of the crisis in psychology: A methodological investigation. In R. W. Rieber & D. K. Robinson (Eds.), *The essential Vygotsky* (pp. 227–344). New York: Kluwer/Plenum.

Vygotsky, L. S. (1978). *Mind in society. The development of higher psychological processes*. Cambridge, MA: Harvard University Press.

Vygotsky, L. S. (1986). *Thought and language*. Cambridge, MA: MIT Press.

Vygotsky, L. S. (1997). *The collected works of L.S. Vygotsky, Vol. III: Problems of the theory and history of psychology*. New York: Plenum.

Wertsch, J. V. (1998). *Mind as action*. Oxford: Oxford University Press.

Wertsch, J. V. (2007). Mediation. In H. Daniels, M. Cole, & J. V. Wertsch (Eds.), *The Cambridge companion to Vygotsky* (pp. 178–192). New York: Cambridge University Press.

Yáñez-Prieto, C. M. (2008). *On literature and the secret art of invisible words: Teaching literature through language*. Unpublished doctoral dissertation, The Pennsylvania State University.

Zhang, Y. (2008). Testing the topic hypothesis: The L2 acquisition of Chinese syntax. In F. Mansouri (Ed.), *Second language acquisition research: Theory-construction and testing* (pp. 173–198). Newcastle upon Tyne: Cambridge Scholars Publishing.

2

A COMPLEXITY THEORY APPROACH TO SECOND LANGUAGE DEVELOPMENT/ ACQUISITION

Diane Larsen-Freeman

As noted in the introduction to this volume, my original orientation to second language acquisition (SLA) was cognitive. This should not be surprising: I came of academic age in the early 1970s, when language acquisition was just starting to be studied scientifically. I was intrigued by Corder's (1967) hypothesis, itself inspired by Chomsky's universal grammar, of a "built-in" syllabus in learners. My interest mounted when Selinker (1972) added the interlanguage construct—a transitional linguistic system activated by a "psychological structure . . . latent in the brain" (p. 211). I saw in both ideas the potential to facilitate the SLA process. Instructional syllabi could be aligned with the built-in syllabus, and second language (L2) instruction could follow natural acquisition processes. This thinking was encouraged by Brown's (1973) discovery of a highly regular acquisition order of English grammatical morphemes for three first language (L1) acquirers. SLA researchers subsequently proposed an acquisition order common to all learners of English as a second language (Dulay & Burt, 1973). This was a revolutionary claim at the time because most L2 behavior was thought to be shaped by the L1.

I, too, undertook early L2 morpheme acquisition studies (Larsen-Freeman, 1976). Although many have since faulted such studies, they inspired researchers to move beyond contrastive analysis and consider the L2 learning process in its own right,[1] as well as to understand that SLA is psycholinguistic rather than purely linguistic (Larsen-Freeman & Long, 1991). These important shifts spawned research into learning strategies, interlanguage processes, and interaction effects, all seeking to account for how learners acquire mental grammars. This effort endured: Four decades later, many still regard SLA as centrally a cognitive process (Doughty & Long, 2003).

While I certainly endorse a role for cognition in SLA, over time I became disenchanted with the limitation of this focus. Although the factors thought to influence SLA kept multiplying, no greater understanding seemed to result. Experimental designs attempted to control for all factors except the one hypothesized as causal. Not only was such research of suspect ecological validity, it also rested on the questionable assumption that a single factor caused some effect. To me this denied the commonsense understanding that SLA processes were complex, situated, and likely multivariate. Then, too, aggregating findings across studies seemed impossible, given differences in how and where data were collected.[2] Ubiquitous variability was also evident in SLA, both intra- and interindividually. Some of this variability was due to the social contexts in which learners lived and studied, but such contexts could not be treated as static backdrops. Moreover, language teaching clearly did not involve transferring mental systems from head to head. It was clear that SLA was no simple process of accretion and that stage views had to address the fact that development was neither unidirectional nor linear.

Thus, I was ready to think anew about SLA when I serendipitously encountered James Gleick's (1987) writing on chaos/complexity theory. Gleick wrote: "The act of playing the game has a way of changing the rules" (p. 24), and, though he was writing about naturally occurring dynamic systems rather than linguistic rules, I perceived deep parallelism with language and its acquisition. In contrast to my own (generative) training in linguistics, I came to understand language as a complex adaptive system, which emerges bottom-up from interactions of multiple agents in speech communities (Larsen-Freeman, 1997; Ellis with Larsen-Freeman, 2009), rather than a static system composed of top-down grammatical rules or principles. The system is adaptive because it changes to fit new circumstances, which are also themselves continually changing.

This view of language had implications for understanding SLA. There is no built-in syllabus and, while general, innate cognitive processes and social drives may exist, it is more accurate to say that interlanguage systems emerge from use. This was consistent with my earlier finding that morpheme accuracy order and the frequency of these same morphemes in the input correlated significantly (Larsen-Freeman, 1976). Learners interact locally, and in so doing tune to and imitate frequently occurring patterns, especially those that are salient and semantically transparent. However, the imitation is not exact. It might be better to think in terms of "adaptive imitation," wherein learners adapt patterns—sometimes amalgams of old and new—to suit their communicative needs (Macqueen, 2009). These patterns subsequently become part of learners' language resources, available for further use and modification.

In sum, I concluded that language, its use, and its acquisition are mutually constitutive, simply occurring at different levels of ecological scale—individual through speech community—and timescale. I turn next to introduce the theory that inspired me to think this way.

Overview

Organized Complexity

As indicated earlier, complexity theory originated in the natural sciences. It has a particular place, described by Weaver (1948) as occupied with problems of organized complexity. In contrast, Weaver characterized 17th–19th-century science as dealing with problems of *simplicity*—situations having small numbers of measurable and controllable variables. Problems of simplicity abound in science. Thus, high school physics courses often feature the simple problem of predicting the motion of a billiard ball on a pool table. When two or more billiard balls are introduced, however, the problem becomes surprisingly difficult. With 10 billiard balls, it becomes unmanageable. Problems that involve many elements in this way are not simple; instead, they reflect the class of problems Weaver called *disorganized complexity*. Each of the many individual variables may exhibit erratic behavior; however, one can still talk about the average properties of the collective system. Indeed, this is the basis of actuarial science. How long any individual will live is not known, but life insurance companies remain in business because someone has calculated the average age of death. According to Weaver, problems of disorganized complexity are numerous, and the spectacular success of recent science has been largely in dealing with such problems, e.g., the fundamental laws of heredity and the motion of atoms.

However, even these scientific developments have ignored a third set of problems—those of *organized complexity*. These problems arise in systems where the number of variables is not the defining factor. Although complex systems usually have many components, either inert elements such as gas molecules or living agents such as schooling fish, what is different from problems of disorganized complexity, to which statistical methods hold the key, is that problems of organized complexity deal simultaneously with sizeable numbers of factors interrelated into an organic whole. Weaver (1948, p. 539) offered the following examples: "What is a gene and how does the original genetic constitution of a living organism express itself in the developed characteristics of the adult?" On what does the price of wheat depend? How to explain the collective behavior of organized groups like labor unions? And especially relevant today: "To what extent must systems of economic control be employed to prevent the wide swings from prosperity to depression?" These and many other problems involve a substantial number of relevant and interdependent variables coming together in organic wholes. Organized complexity, I believe, challenges us to understand language and SLA anew.

Relational Systems, Dynamism, and Self-organization

Von Bertalanffy (1950) proposed General Systems Theory to account for how complex order arises. He opposed reductionism in explaining entities as the sum of their parts, advocating instead a systems approach—understanding the relationships among parts that connect them to the whole. It is important to note that these relationships keep changing, with some parts playing more central roles at times, and at other times playing minor or no obvious roles at all. Complexity theory has benefited from this core perspective because it advocates a systems view of complex phenomena, one that centers on the relations among a system's elements or agents. Just as a bird flock emerges out of the interaction of individual birds, complex systems self-organize via the interaction of their parts. Self-organization is the creation of more complex order spontaneously, without outside influence or internal plan (Mitchell, 2003). That is, stabilities in a dynamic system *emerge*. This dynamic process is responsible for the patterns and orderly arrangement of both the natural world and the realms of mind, society, and culture (Heylighen, 2008).

The stabilities of complex systems are based in their autopoietic (Maturana & Varela, 1972) nature, which means that they continually change and build new structures while maintaining their identity. This can easily be seen by the fact that the body's cells are constantly being transformed, as some die and are replaced by new cells, all the while preserving the organism's identity. The same quality also applies to language, which is perpetually changing, while staying sufficiently robust to keep its name, e.g., Swahili.

Complex Systems are Open and Adaptive

In the 1970s chemist Ilya Prigogine studied systems open to energy from outside themselves. Open systems continue to change and adapt as their dynamics are "fed" by energy coming into the system, whereas closed systems reach a static state or equilibrium. Energy taken into an open system leads to self-organization. The resulting more complex structure is planned or managed by no outside source or central authority. Instead, each developmental step sets the conditions for the next step, just as with epigenesis, where "the form of the [human] body is literally constructed by the construction process itself—and is not specified in some pre-existing full instruction set, design or building plan" (van Geert, 2003, pp. 648–649).

Because the system is open, self-organization is not a once-and-for-all process. According to Heylighen:

> A system is never optimally adapted to an environment since the process of evolution of the system will itself change the environment so that a new adaptation is needed, and so on . . .
>
> Another difference between . . . [a] simple model and more complex evolution is that evolution is in general *parallel* or *distributed*: there is not just one system and its environment, there is a multitude of systems evolving simultaneously, partially autonomously, partially in interaction. This "network" structure of evolutionary processes entails that no absolute distinction can be made between internal and external, i.e. between system and environment. What is "system" for one process is "environment" for another one.
>
> (1989, p. 26)

This perspective is also central to cybernetics, where action by an environmentally situated system causes change in the environment, and that change then manifests itself to the system as information, or feedback, that causes the system to adapt to new conditions: The system changes its behavior.

Change in Complex Systems

Complexity theory is fundamentally about change. Behavioral change in complex systems takes two forms. The first is gradual and linear. The second is sudden and dramatic, in which the system undergoes a *phase transition* or *phase shift in state space* in which a new order self-organizes, generating new, emergent behaviors. The sudden rise of new orders is characteristic of nonlinear systems—changes that are not proportionate to their causes. Unpredictable behavior in a nonlinear system is known as *chaos* and is the primary focus of chaos theory.[3] Even in chaotic systems, however, there are patterns.

Nonlinearity in chaotic systems is due to their sensitivity to initial conditions. Working on the problem of weather prediction, meteorologist Edward Lorenz (1972) discovered that small differences in initial conditions of weather systems could have big effects later on, a phenomenon he named "the butterfly effect." A small difference, such as a butterfly flapping its wings in one part of the world, can affect weather patterns elsewhere, making it impossible to predict weather beyond short-term forecasts. The point here is that even the smallest detail in a complex system can have profound effects.

In sum, complexity theory seeks to explain complex, dynamic, open, adaptive, self-organizing, nonlinear systems. It focuses on the close interplay between the emergence of structure on one hand and process or change on the other. Language, its use, its evolution, its development,[4] its learning, and its teaching are arguably complex systems. Thus, complexity theory offers a way to unite all these phenomena. Complexity theory can therefore be tapped for its useful perspective on dynamic phenomena such as L2 development. No longer must we decontextualize, segregate, idealize, and atemporalize language (Larsen-Freeman, 2008). One of complexity theory's innovations is that in acknowledging the complexity of natural systems, it avoids reductionist solutions. It sees complex behavior as arising from interactions among many components—a bottom-up process based on the contributions of each, which are subject to change over time.

Theoretical Principles

Language is a Dynamic Set of Graded Patterns Emerging from Use

Complexity theory sees language as a dynamic set of patterns emerging from use. Over time, those that frequently, saliently, and reliably occur become emergent stabilities in a complex system: "Sequences of elements come to be automatized as neuromotor routines" in individuals (Beckner et al., 2009, p. 11), sedimented out of discourse, with grammar seen not as the source of understanding and communication, but rather a by-product of communication (Hopper, 1998). The patterns or routines themselves are variegated in form—not necessarily linguists' units, which may not have psychological reality for speakers. Usage-based linguists (e.g., Tomasello, 2003) call these patterns "constructions"—form–meaning–use composites ranging from single morphemes to idioms to partially filled lexical patterns to complex clauses. The borders of constructions are graded, not discrete.

Invoking the closely related dynamic systems theory, Spivey (2007) spoke exactly like this about cognition itself. Rejecting a symbolic-computational approach to cognition inspired by the serial-processing computer, Spivey argued that the "external discreteness of actions and utterances is commonly misinterpreted as evidence for the internal discreteness of the mental representations that led to them" (p. 3). Instead, Spivey proposed "a perspective on mental life in which the human mind/brain typically construes the world via partially overlapping fuzzy areas that are drawn out over time," a thesis he referred to as "continuity of mind." This view entails a synchronic account of a language involving "graded probabilistic contingencies (not logical rules) governing the relationships between syntactic categories" (p. 171).

The gradedness applies to pronunciation, too: The same word is pronounced differently by the same speaker with every use (Milroy & Milroy, 1999). The variation may not be perceptible, although over time it results in grammaticization processes such as phonological reduction in high-frequency words, semantic shift, faster processing, fusion ("I am going to" shortening to /aimənə/), and the promotion of a stochastic grammar (Bybee & Hopper, 2001, p. 10). The language system is in constant flux. Stability is possible only through constant change—just as we remain erect only by making constant microadjustments in distributing our weight to our two feet. Even when not undergoing obvious qualitative change, the system changes every time a form is used, if only to increase the probability of the form's use in the future.

Language-using Patterns are Heterochronic and Adapted to their Context of Use

Because of its link to the environment, "complexity theory challenges the nomothetic programme of universally applicable knowledge at its very heart—it asserts that knowledge must be contextual" (Byrne, 2005, in Haggis, 2008, p. 169). Language is adapted to its contexts of use. In complexity theory "reciprocal causality" (Thompson & Varela, 2001) is invoked: "Upwards" emergence of patterns from individuals interacting is nonetheless "downwardly" entrained due to both the historic trajectory of the system and by its present-day sociocultural norms. Indeed, as Semetsky (2008, p. 91) stated, "The dynamical process comprises the 'past that is carried into the present.'" Thus, dynamical systems theorists give special attention to the historicity of a system as well. As with other complex systems, language-using patterns are heterochronous: Language events on some local timescale may simultaneously be part of language change on longer timescales (Lemke, 2002, p. 80).

Language Development Proceeds through Soft-assembly and Co-adaptation

This same dynamic view applies to language development, a term I prefer these days to acquisition because open systems are never fully acquired (Larsen-Freeman, 2010). As with speech communities, interlanguage emerges bottom-up through use. As such, no innate language faculty is posited, though, as indicated earlier, innate domain-general cognitive abilities and social drives may exist. Instead, learners' language resources are thought to develop from interactions they experience. This takes place through processes of *co-adaptation* (Larsen-Freeman & Cameron, 2008a) and *soft-assembly* (Thelen & Smith, 1994).

Language development itself occurs in social context. From a complexity theory perspective, such context contributes significantly to language development by affording possibilities for co-adaptation between interlocutors. As a learner interacts with another individual, their language resources are dynamically altered, as each adapts to the other—a mimetic process. Dynamic systems theorists term this the "coupling" of complex systems, which concerns neither rule acquisition nor "conformity to uniformity" (Larsen-Freeman, 2003). Nor does it concern the acquisition of a priori grammatical structures, which cannot be known separately from our perception of their emergence in the ongoing flow of experience (Kramsch, 2002). Co-adaptation is an iterative process; indeed, language development itself can be described as an iterative process, with learners visiting the same or similar territory repeatedly.

With each visit, learners soft-assemble their language resources. Thelen and Smith (1994) coined the term "soft-assembly" to refer to processes involving articulation of multiple components of a system, where "each action is a response to the variable features of the particular task" (p. 64). In other words, the assembly is said to be "soft" because the elements being assembled, as well as the specific ways they are assembled, can change at any point during the task or from one task to another.

Larsen-Freeman and Cameron (2008a) appropriated the term "soft-assembly" to signify how learners use their language resources to respond intentionally to the communicative pressures presented by their interlocutors, including classmates and teachers. For L2 learners, these language resources include not only what they know and can do in the L2, but their L1 patterns (e.g., manifest in relexification), patterns from other languages/language varieties they control, and nonverbal behavior. They cobble these together—a real-time response—considering options and constraints, their intrinsic embodied dynamics, their language-using identities and history, who their interlocutors are, the ongoing activities they are engaged in, and the affordances of the context.

Stable Patterns Emerge Bottom-up from Frequent Soft-assemblies in Co-adapted Interactions

From repeated soft-assemblies in co-adapted interactions, stable language-using patterns emerge. "Stable" does not mean "static"—the learner's system is best considered a "statistical ensemble" of interacting elements (Cooper, 1999). It has a historicity because it is a cumulative, though selective,[5] record of one's linguistic experience (Bakhtin, 1981). Using the patterns leads them to become entrenched in the user's mind and, at another scale-level, to be taken up collectively, although not usually intentionally, by the speech community. Thus, usage-based views of L1 acquisition (e.g.,Tomasello, 2003) and emergentist views of SLA (Ellis & Larsen-Freeman, 2006) align well with complexity theory.

Such views hold that humans are sensitive to frequency of perceptually salient and semantically transparent linguistic features in the language to which they are exposed. Thus, language development is a probabilistic process, with learners extracting probabilities of particular forms occurring in particular contexts with particular frequencies. Because language is a fractal[6] (Larsen-Freeman, 1997), the distribution of its forms obeys a scale-free power law. A language's most frequently occurring words are therefore used a geometrically greater number of times (Zipf, 1935) than the rest. The data learners are exposed to are thus *skewed* (perhaps intentionally in co-adaptation), making language easier to learn.

Goldberg, Casenhiser, and Sethuraman (2004) demonstrated the effect of Zipf's Law in L1 acquisition. For each English verb-argument construction in children's speech they examined, there was a strong tendency for a single verb to occur very frequently, a profile that notably mirrored mothers' speech to these children. It was argued that this promotes acquisition: Tokens of one particular verb account for the greatest share of instances of each particular argument frame, and this pathbreaking verb provides the prototypical meaning for the construction (Ellis, 2002). In learning categories from exemplars, acquisition is thus optimized by introducing an initial, low-variance sample centered upon prototypical exemplars (Elio & Anderson, 1981, 1984), allowing learners to get a "fix" on what will account for most category members. The category's boundaries can then later be defined by experience of the full breadth of tokens and a semantic/pragmatic bootstrapping process. Importantly, the categories do not exist a priori, but are "temporal, emergent, and disputed" (Hopper, 1998, p. 156).

Learners Play an Active Role in Language Development

Not only is "positive evidence" available and involved in the process, so is negative evidence. As Spivey (2007, p. 202) observed, learners can learn from the conspicuous absence of positive evidence. That is, learners may note when a particular form occurs less frequently than they expected. Or, as Spivey puts it, "Negative evidence from the environment is not needed in such a situation because the predictive learner generates his or her own negative evidence" (p. 202).

Thus, it is not necessary to posit a central, rule-governed, mental grammar functioning in a top-down manner. The knowledge underlying fluent, systematic, apparently rule-governed language use is the learner's entire collection of memories of previously experienced utterances, both the learner's own and those attended to in co-adapting to interlocutors. This socially situated perspective includes an active view of the learner—someone learning from positive evidence while generating his or her own negative evidence by actively noticing and exploring the boundaries of the system. However, before continuing, three caveats to this account need to be acknowledged. The first concerns frequency, the second the critical role of individual variability, and the third L1 influence. I will discuss these in order.

Frequency is Important, but not Sufficient

Although I have made much of frequency effects in L2 development, I do not wish to exaggerate their role unduly. The failings of operant conditioning as an explanation for language acquisition are well known. Therefore, it is not only frequency—development of particular language patterns also depends on the degree to which their salience captures learners' attention, and their *cue contingency*, the reliability with which learners can ascribe meaning or function to the language patterns flowing around them. Having ascribed meaning/function to frequently occurring forms, learners can begin to categorize them, often doing so around prototypes. The social associations, social value, and role of particular forms in organizing discourse are also important (Celce-Murcia & Larsen-Freeman, 1999; Larsen-Freeman, 2002a, 2003). Indeed, L2 learners assume a high degree of agency in what they take from communicative exchanges for further use. All these factors conspire in the development and use of any pattern and suggest why learners' developmental trajectories can be similar, but not identical.

Neither does saying that frequency is important mean that learners merely reproduce what they hear, or else, as Chomsky (1959) argued, linguistic creativity would not exist. However, unlike Chomsky's claim that rule-governed processes are required for novel forms to arise, a complexity theory perspective highlights morphogenesis, or new pattern development, through analogy (Larsen-Freeman, 2003). Indeed, connectionists subscribing to emergentist accounts show that generalizations form from increasing experience of usage and develop longitudinally (Christiansen & Chater, 2001; Elman et al., 1996). Furthermore, connectionist simulations demonstrate that novel forms (i.e., forms not present in the input data) can arise through overgeneralization (Rumelhart & McClelland, 1986), just as they presumably do from social interaction in contexts of natural language acquisition.

Variability is Pervasive

The second caveat concerns the uniqueness of the paths trod by individual learners. Because people's experience with the language and identities they adopt with different co-adaptors is not static, along with commonalities in the learning process, there will also be variation. Indeed, a basic tenet of dynamic systems theory is that, for change to occur, stable patterns must become unstable in the endogenous environment—or what I have referred to as the intrinsic dynamics of the learner—in order for the learner's system to self-organize in new ways. Variability pervades language production, its presence too profound to be relegated to noise and random performance factors (de Bot, Lowie, & Verspoor, 2007). This is due partly to the fact that humans bring with them unique starting points. Even our brains are different. Humans then shape their own contexts in a unique manner. The dynamism of different factors—the fact that their contribution to the learning process waxes and wanes in interaction with others—also explains why correlations between individual difference factors vary across studies.

Dörnyei (2009a) has recently suggested that the seemingly straightforward picture of individual differences based on stable and monolithic learner traits is part of an idealized narrative. He noted that a situated and process-oriented perspective on SLA reveals that learner attributes vary considerably from time to time and situation to situation. As a result, seeking explanations of individual differences in cause-and-effect and generalizable findings does not fit a complexity theory perspective. Thus, it "is no longer sufficient to talk about individual differences in SLA against a backdrop of a universal learner . . . variation becomes the primary given; categorization becomes an artificial construct of institutionalization and scientific inquiry" (Kramsch, 2002, p. 4) such that it may not be possible to "tell the dancer from the dance" (p. 1, paraphrasing William Butler Yeats). In Ushioda's (2009, p. 218) terms, "The unique local particularities of the person as self-reflective [embodied] intentional agent, inherently part of and shaping his or her own context, seem to have no place in this [earlier] kind of [individual differences] research."

As learners shape their contexts, development can be radically affected. While development can often seem to be gradual and incremental, it also evidences sudden changes in performance, suggesting a fundamental *restructuring* of learners' language resources (McLaughlin, 1990). In short, language learning is not just about adding knowledge to an unchanging system. It is about changing the system (Feldman, 2006).

Cross-linguistic Influence Manifests Itself in Numerous Ways

The third caveat relates to the major influence on L2 development of the learners' knowledge of other languages. L2 learners come to L2 development with a lifetime of L1 experience and, given the world norm of multilingualism, likely of other languages too (Herdina & Jessner, 2002). Neural commitment to these patterns (MacWhinney, 2006), and to those of other languages, results in cross-linguistic influence, which manifests itself in numerous ways from a target-centered perspective: relexification, overgeneralization, avoidance, overproduction, and hypercorrection. The other languages also tune learners' perceptual mechanisms advantageously, but can sometimes also block them from perceiving L2 differences (Ellis, 2006). But it is not only in producing and perceiving L2 forms that cross-linguistic influence is evident. Cross-linguistic research shows that different languages shape how constructions are put together, leading to nonnative categorization and "thinking for speaking" (Slobin, 1996), with patterns of even very advanced learners reflecting underlying construals of the L1.

These various factors interact dynamically (de Bot et al., 2007; Ellis & Larsen-Freeman, 2006), such that even the most diligent older L2 learner does not develop the linguistic facility of L1 users. To assist L2 learners who wish to achieve target proficiency, their consciousness must be recruited and their attention directed through explicit instruction, which needs to be complemented by opportunities for these learners to use their language resources in psychologically authentic activities (Larsen-Freeman, 2003). Without explicit instruction, language use by most adult language learners results in developing limited language resources. By the same token, development is never complete: "There is no end and there is no state"—a title I gave to a book chapter (Larsen-Freeman, 2006a). Learners' language resources are always dynamic ensembles, expanding and contracting with time, place, and circumstance. Yet, rather than promoting a deficit view of second language development, adult learners are seen as multicompetent (Cook, 1991), attaining different levels of mastery, accomplishing what they intend, and using different languages, each appropriate to its particular time and place.

Intentionality and Agency are Important

Some have criticized the extension of complexity theory—a theory originating in the natural sciences—to human endeavors such as language acquisition. They have pointed out that self-organization may not be inevitable in human processes due to agency and volition, which can override any inevitability characteristic of naturally occurring complex systems. However, the fact that complexity theory originated in the natural sciences does not detract from its usefulness to applied linguists. Indeed, complexity theory gives applied linguists a new transdisciplinary theme, highlighting dynamism and complexity, thereby offering an alternative to the earlier transdisciplinary theme of structuralism (Larsen-Freeman, Lowie & Schmid, in press). I do think, however, that the charge of neglect of human agency deserves to be addressed.

To address the charge, I should first note that complexity theory has been widely applied to human activities, and agency or intentionality are not ignored in these applications. That humans make choices in the moment is certain, and it would be at a researcher's peril to ignore their agency. In language interactions, for instance, speakers make decisions to deploy language resources to realize transactional, interpersonal, educative, self-expressive, etc. goals and the multiple dimensions of self and identity, affective states, and social face. However, it is not contradictory that, at the same time as individuals are operating in intentional ways in the moment, their personal language resources and those of their speech communities are being transformed beyond their conscious intentions. It is not that we plan to change language; language changes. As Keller (1985, p. 211) observed: "Language is thus a consequence of human actions, albeit actions which are only unintentionally transformative." Similarly, due to the ways humans register and process information (e.g., construction frequencies), the self-organization of individuals' language resources is inevitable, provided the learner's system remains open.

Nothing is Foreclosed in Open, Dynamic Systems

Having claimed that self-organization in complex systems is inevitable, I must hasten to add that a system is not simply fated to go on reproducing itself. In an open system—the type studied by complexity researchers—anything can change. The openness of complex systems speaks to critical applied linguists' mission to challenge power imbalances in the world. From a complexity theory perspective, such imbalances are always potentially rectifiable. Complexity theory may not tell us how to do so, but understanding how systems operate is crucial to transforming them.

Speaking to this point, Osberg (2007) claimed that enlightenment understandings of causality are guided by "a logic of determinism." This logic is based on a linear and individual conception of cause and effect, in which self-determined causes yield predictable consequences; causality is based on processes that are fully determined. As such, there is no freedom within the process for anything else to occur. However, complexity theory provides a nondeterministic logic, suggesting that complex dynamic systems are free to develop along alternative trajectories—what Osberg called "a logic of freedom":

> This is a logic in which choice is an *operator* in the process itself—part of its internal "mechanics"—not something that happens *to* a process, something applied from the outside. Since emergent processes are not fully determined— they contain within themselves the possibility of freedom—the logic of emergence could therefore also be characterized as a *logic of freedom* (rather than a logic of determination).
>
> (2007, p. 10)

Thus, while a complex system's potential might be constrained by its history, it is never fully determined by it: "Knowing how to negotiate our way through a world that is not fixed and pre-given but . . . continually shaped by the types of actions in which we engage" (Varela, Thompson, & Rosch, 1991, p. 144) is one challenge of being human.

Research Methods

Complexity Theory Requires Several Departures from Typical Research Procedures

The challenge presented by researching dynamic, nonlinear, open complex systems, together with their tendency toward self-organization and interaction across levels and timescales, compels us to rethink traditional research designs (Larsen-Freeman & Cameron, 2008b). Having made this point, I should immediately add that many extant research methods, both quantitative and qualitative, can be used to study complex systems.

However, several departures from normal procedures and assumptions must be acknowledged up front. For instance, in the context of quantitative research, Byrne (2002, p. 9) explained that conventional statistical reasoning in the social sciences is incapable of dealing with relationships among levels—or relating individuals to social collectivities—other than by regarding social collectivities as mere aggregates of individuals with no emergent properties. Moreover, although many extant research methods can be used with complexity theory, an exception may be that of the classical pre-test/post-test experimental design. Conventional experiments are problematic from a complexity theory perspective because of their lack of ecological validity. Further, they can only, at best, lead to claims about proximate, linear causes, while not allowing for multiple or reciprocally interacting factors that change over time. In addition, they ignore nonlinearity (Larsen-Freeman, 1997). Who can say, for example, based on a pre-test/post-test design that a particular experimental treatment did not work? If the results are non-significant, the effects of the treatment may simply not yet be manifest. While having control groups avoids some unwarranted inferences, there can be no expectation that the experimental group and the control group are equivalent, even if pre-test scores are not different at a statistically significant level. A further limitation of conventional experiments occurs when researchers attempt to control context and situation, rather than investigating adaptation to the unique particularities of context: "They try to ensure that an intervention is implemented uniformly despite different circumstances; and they focus on post intervention outcomes instead of what happens while the intervention is implemented" (Reinking & Watkins, 2000, p. 384). Indeed, it is processes—not outcomes per se—that are of most interest to complexity researchers.

A major challenge in studying complex systems is how to limit the focal point of interest. Because everything is interconnected, it is problematic to sever one component from the whole and single it out for examination. By doing so, one is likely to get findings that do not hold up when the whole is considered. Since the system is open to the environment, the challenge is even greater because clearly specifying the boundaries of a complex system is by no means intuitive (Cilliers, 2001) and, even if done with deliberation, "an overemphasis on closure will . . . lead to an understanding of the system that may underplay the role of the environment" (p. 141). This may not be a unique burden of complexity theory, however—perhaps we have been deluding ourselves in thinking that we can segregate *any* subsystem/component and still get meaningful results from its study. Because everything is always interacting and interfacing in human and nonhuman environments organically, notions of what are "inside" and "outside" a system are never simple or uncontested (p. 142).

Of course, it is humanly impossible to study everything at once: "Boundaries are still required if we want to talk about complex systems in a meaningful way— they are in fact necessary" (Cilliers, 2005, p. 612); however, strategic considerations are at stake when drawing them. Therefore, we must at least recognize the challenge in defining a focal point for our investigations. As Atkinson, Churchill,

Nishino, and Okada (2007) stated, we must "seek to view mind, body, and world relationally and integratively, as constituting a continuous ecological circuit" (p. 170). Gregory Bateson (1972, p. 465) put it this way: "The way to delineate the system is to draw the limiting line in such a way that you do not cut any of these pathways in ways which leave things inexplicable."

The biologist Richard Lewontin offered a functional solution to the boundary-drawing problem:

> [We] cannot escape from the dialectical relation between parts and wholes. Before we can recognise meaningful parts we must define the functional whole of which they are the constituents. We will then recognize quite different ways of breaking up the organism depending on what we are trying to explain. The hand is the appropriate unit for investigation if we are concerned with the physical act of holding, but the hand and eye together are an irreducible unit for understanding how we come to seize the object that is held.
>
> (1998, pp. 81–82)

Componential Explanations are not Appropriate when Studying Functional Wholes

Settling upon what the functional whole is, then, is key. Since the focus of complexity theory is relationships, a "componential" explanation (Clark, 1997, p. 104), which centrally assumes that one can best understand an object of inquiry by taking it apart and examining its pieces, will not do. Moreover, even if it were possible to understand the behavior of the individual parts and their interactions, the individual parts do not make the same contributions to interactions over time: One factor will be more influential at one time, but less so at another. This leads to the conclusion that researchers have to find new, functional ways of viewing our "objects of concern," reconceptualizing them in terms of processes, change, and continuities.

Complexity Theory Calls for Retrodiction instead of Prediction

Recall the butterfly effect, mentioned earlier, and the sensitivity of complex systems to initial conditions. Initial conditions are often unknowable at a particular point in time. This means that the usual scientific method, which calls for making predictions and then testing them, is fraught with problems from a complexity theory perspective. Systems and behavior can of course be described retrospectively—once change has happened; in fact, this is the central work of complexity theory. What we can observe in language development is what has already changed—the trajectory of the system. This is a "trace" of the real system, from which we try to reconstruct the elements, interactions, and developmental processes of the system (Byrne, 2002). Such an approach calls for *retrodiction* (or retrocasting) rather than prediction (or forecasting), i.e., explaining the next state by the preceding one.

This may not be as radical as it sounds at first blush. After all, many scientists have viable theories regarding phenomena but are unable to predict their behavior—think of meteorologists, seismologists, or evolutionary biologists. For instance, evolutionary biologists have an explanation for speciation, but they cannot even predict which flu strain will arise next year, or how virulent it will be. Of course, we may have expectations of how a process will unfold, or even its outcomes, based on prior experience, but essentially a complex systems perspective separates explanation and prediction.

Three Methods for Studying Complex, Dynamic Systems

Van Gelder and Port (1995) proposed three methods for studying dynamic systems: quantitative modeling, qualitative modeling, and dynamical description. *Quantitative modeling* is not possible when studying human beings because it involves assigning numerical values to everything in a system. Due to this intrinsic difficulty with mathematical models, complexity researchers typically prefer computer simulations, which, while of course being approximations, are easier to manipulate so that more different factors and variations influencing the phenomenon can be explored. *Qualitative modeling*, or computer simulation, has been employed in applied linguistics from a complexity theory perspective (e.g., Meara, 2006). It has several strengths. First, it forces the researcher to make explicit the assumptions about the complex system under investigation—computers can only be programmed on the basis of explicit assumptions. Second, models can be taken through multiple iterations, replicating temporal change in short order. Agent-based computer models have been used successfully in social science to model the emergence of large-scale regularities from individual agents interacting locally, such as epidemic dynamics, wealth distributions, and even the reconstruction of ancient civilizations. Of course, the computer model is an analogy vis-à-vis the real-world system, inevitably involving complexity reduction and approximation.

However, qualitative modeling need not involve computers. Larsen-Freeman and Cameron (2008a) have suggested procedures for "complexity thought modeling." Indeed, as Epstein (2008) pointed out, the choice is not really whether or not to model, because anytime you imagine a dynamic system unfolding, you are modeling. However, Cilliers (2001) warned that, "Our models have to 'frame' the problem in a certain way, and this framing will inevitably introduce distortions." He added:

> This is not an argument against the construction of models. We have no choice but to make models if we want to understand the world. It is just an argument that models of complex systems will always be flawed in principle, and that we have to acknowledge these limitations.
>
> (p. 138)

The third way to study complex systems—*dynamical description*—"provides a general conceptual apparatus for understanding the way systems, including, in particular, nonlinear systems, change over time" (van Gelder & Port, 1995, p. 17). *Ethnography* offers a viable method for dynamical descriptions, which "attempt to honor the profound wholeness and situatedness of social scenes and individuals-in-the-world" (Atkinson, 2002, p. 539). Dynamical descriptions can also be generated by *formative experiments*, which focus on the dynamics of pedagogy. In a formative experiment, "the researcher sets a pedagogical goal and finds out what it takes in terms of materials, organization, or changes in the intervention in order to reach the goal" (Newman, 1990, in Reinking & Watkins, 2000, p. 388). Formative experiments attempt to investigate the potential of a system rather than its state. The researcher accepts the fact that change in one system can produce change in other connected systems, attempts to describe the interconnected web of factors influencing change, and investigates processes of co-adaptation in response to changed pedagogic goals.

Design experiments, too, work with a complexity approach. Barab (2006) explained that, in complex learning environments, it is difficult to test the causal impact of particular variables with experimental designs. Design-based research "deals with complexity by iteratively changing the learning environment over time— collecting evidence of the effect of these variations and feeding it recursively into future design" (p. 155). Then, too, *microdevelopment*, which permits the study of "motors of change" (Thelen & Corbetta, 2002, p. 59) using dense longitudinal corpora, as well as other longitudinal designs that yield rich descriptions, are compatible with a complexity theory approach.

Complexity theory increases our understanding of complex systems, but it does not present us with tools to predict or control behavior accurately. We may thus learn a lot about the dynamics involved in the functioning of such systems, but we will not be able to use these general principles to make accurate predictions in individual cases. Complexity theory underscores the importance of contingent factors, of considering the specific conditions in a specific context at a specific time. No general model can capture such singularities.

Supporting Findings

Although complexity theory is in its infancy vis-à-vis L2 development, input and interaction have long been central to accounts of SLA, and therefore some earlier findings support a complex systems perspective. For instance, as mentioned earlier, restructuring (McLaughlin, 1990) of learners' grammatical systems is compatible with complexity theory. In complexity theory terms, restructuring is a phase shift in language development that comes about through self-organization. Whereas development is often gradual and incremental, sudden shifts in performance can also occur. Such appears to be the case when English learners go from using regular and irregular verbs correctly in the past tense to overgeneralizing the regular to irregular forms, saying such things as "eated." The irregulars eventually reappear, their acquisition thus following a "U-shaped" pattern overall. The stage at which irregulars disappear and are replaced by regularized forms is sudden, suggesting a fundamental restructuring or self-organization of the underlying grammar.

More recent support for complexity theory in L2 development comes from research inspired by usage-based theories of child language acquisition (Tomasello, 2003). These theories have turned upside down generative assumptions of innate language acquisition devices and top-down, rule-governed processing, replacing them with data-driven, emergent accounts of linguistic systematicities (Beckner et al., 2009). This perspective, which complexity theory encourages, has just begun to be applied to L2 development. For instance, Ellis and Ferreira-Junior (2009) investigated the L2 emergence of verb-argument structure in English. Their corpus linguistic analysis of naturalistic and elicited NS and NNS speech showed that the language NNSs are exposed to and subsequently use adheres to a Zipfian profile— that is, several verbs occur far more frequently than others in particular verb-argument constructions, facilitating the acquisition of such constructions. This Zipfian profile is scale-free, which means that it occurs despite the size of the corpus. In this way it could be said that language is a fractal—a pattern of self-similarity characterizing dynamic systems (Larsen-Freeman, 1997).

Larsen-Freeman (2006b) offered a dynamical description of the interlanguage of five Chinese learners of English over time. Traditional measures of complexity, accuracy, and fluency demonstrated the nonlinearity of the development process at the individual level and trade-offs individuals made among them. Data analysis also revealed the existence of dynamic language-using patterns, some stable and some shaped by learners for each context of use.

For instance, one of the learners was explaining in writing how she ran into an ex-teacher at a social function in another city: "When I was taking my food, a lady past by me, and I had a feeling that I knew her, but her name just was on my tongue I could say it." Here, a Chinese expression is relexified into English— "taking my food"; "passed" is spelled like its more frequent homophone (and as many proficient L1 English speakers might spell it); the likely formula "I had a feeling that" is used; a Chinese idiom, "her name was on my tongue," which is slightly different from English "on the tip of my tongue," is adopted; the two final clauses are not linked; and the final clause is missing a negative.

Now, here is the same idea unit, written by the student six weeks later: "When I was picking up my food, a lady past by me, and I had a strong felling I knew her. I could not mention who she was." "Taking my food" is now replaced by "picking up," no longer relexified from Chinese; "passed" is still misspelled; "strong" is added to the formula; "feeling" is now misspelled as "felling"; the complementizer "that" is dropped; the final two clauses are connected; and the negative appears in the final clause. While this idea unit is still not accurate from a target-language perspective, it is closer. These two brief examples suggest that the learner was adapting her language resources in the moment. She was making use of L1 patterns, formulaic utterances, and competing forms, some target-like and some not, in order to communicate her intended meaning. How the variability and specific adaptation of "make-do" solutions at one time lead to instability and stability in cross-time development is of course a central question, and is not answerable from this study, which would have benefited from a denser corpus collected over a longer time period. However, it is plausible that the repeated application of the procedure led to changes in the system (Verspoor, Lowie, & de Bot, 2008). As Hopper (1998) put it, forms are constantly being adapted to the needs of the hearer or audience—speech is performed in a context of adjustment to others. Thus, learners are not engaged in learning sentences, but rather in learning to adapt their behavior to increasingly complex surroundings.

Macqueen (2009) added to this finding by tracing the development of language-using patterns in the writing of four L2 learners. One learner, Catalina, appeared to be working on the pattern "have a/an . . . impact on. . . ." On May 5, 2005, she wrote, "it can *have a* negative psychological *impact above* some people," where the preposition was non-target-like.

From the beginning, Catalina used the verb *have* primed to collocate with *a* (adjective) *impact* and followed by a preposition. She also appeared to understand that it needed to be preceded by a negative adjective. However, Catalina needed to work out which preposition to use, especially since, as she told Macqueen, *on* and *above* are the same word in Spanish and so she was confused as to which one to use. Between May and October, Catalina noticed the combination of *impact* and *on*. Catalina could even remember the occasion when she first heard these words used together.

Later, she produced the general pattern as follows:

- "by *having a* negative emotional *impact on* their workers" (October 28, 2005);
- "Violence on TV and video games can *have a* negative psychological *impact on* teenagers" (February 23, 2006);
- "tax policy *has an* unsure *impact on* private saving incentives" (May 5, 2006).

Discussing all four participants in her study, Macqueen wrote:

> Tracing the geneses of these patterns revealed that their university patterning was an amalgam of old (pre-university) patterns and new imitations that had been freshly adapted from the disciplinary discourse. These pattern histories demonstrate firstly that the imitation of expert texts is a very significant feature of the participants' L2 use at university, and secondly that changes in imitated patterns are the result of a dynamic and interrelated combination of factors including new language experiences and subsequent encounters with patterns, perception, memory, attention, intention, experimentation, message, co-text constraints, task requirements, and identity forging.
>
> (2009, pp. 234–235)

Macqueen went on to endorse a complexity theory perspective in which both stability and variability in co-textual patterning emerged through an iterative process she referred to as adaptive imitation. In the two studies mentioned so far and Verspoor, Lowie, and van Dijk (2008), variability is clearly a central element, an intrinsic property of a self-organizing developing system.

Finally, Caspi (2010), in a recently completed doctoral thesis, has used the mathematical tools provided by dynamic systems theory, particularly those connected with Paul van Geert's (2003) precursor model. From her modeling, Caspi concluded that the receptive–productive gap in lexical knowledge is a temporal and developmental phenomenon. In addition, in L2 writing, she found support for a hierarchical order among the four dimensions of lexical complexity, lexical accuracy, syntactic complexity, and syntactic accuracy, and importantly demonstrated that these four categories can arise without postulating separate developmental mechanisms for each.

Differences vis-á-vis Other Alternative Approaches

Complexity theory shares features with other approaches discussed in this volume, such as the unified view of the social and cognitive of the sociocognitive and sociocultural approaches and the groundedness in data and attention to detail of conversation analysis. However, while complexity theory shares with the Vygotskyan perspective the view that cognition (or higher mental functions) emerges from ongoing social interaction, it is also interested in how minds affect the social contexts they operate in. Complexity theory thus supports ecological accounts of learning that place its locus exclusively neither in the brain/body nor social interaction, but in their intersection.

Complexity theory may also differ from other approaches in this volume in that complex systems display behavior over a wide range of timescales. It may further differ in rejecting the subjective/objective dichotomy—complexity theorists understand that they are part of the system they are attempting to explain. There is no standing outside and viewing it with objectivity. Cilliers is worth quoting at length in this regard:

> An understanding of knowledge as constituted within a complex system of interactions would, on the one hand, deny that knowledge can be seen as atomized "facts" that have objective meaning. Knowledge comes to be in a dynamic network of interactions, a network that does not have distinctive borders. On the other hand, this perspective would also deny that knowledge is something purely subjective, mainly because one cannot conceive of the subject as something *prior* to the "network of knowledge," but rather as something constituted *within* that network. The argument from complexity thus wants to move beyond the objective/subjective dichotomy, as Morin (2007) also argues. The dialectical relationship between knowledge and the system within which it is constituted has to be acknowledged. The two do not exist independently, thus making it impossible to first sort out the system (or context), and then to identify the knowledge within the system. This co-determination also means that knowledge and the system within which it is constituted is in constant transformation.
>
> (2008, p. 48)

One other obvious difference from the alternative approaches featured here is that complexity theory is transdisciplinary (Larsen-Freeman, forthcoming). It has informed such disparate fields as physics, biology, the social sciences, engineering, management, economics, medicine, education, literature, etc. Its power comes not only from its application to many different disciplines, but also from its application at many different levels: neurons in the human brain, cells and microbes in the human body, and flora and fauna in an ecosystem, as well as more social activities such as information flow in social or computer networks, infectious disease transmission, the economic behavior of consumers and firms, and now language and language development. Each of these phenomena works as a "complex system."

Kramsch summarized complexity theory's uniqueness in theorizing language behavior in SLA in particular:

> Complexity theory, which originated in the physical sciences, has been used as a productive metaphor in SLA to stress the relativity of self and other, the need to consider events on more than one timescale and to take into account the fractal nature and unfinalizability of events.
>
> (2009, p. 247)

Future Directions

Whiteside (in press) observed that, with increasing global communication and migration, speakers of the world's languages are encountering each other in ways never before imagined. Given the current reality of transnational flows of language and people, it is not surprising that the holistic view provided by complex, dynamic systems would attract multilingualism researchers (de Bot et al., 2007; Herdina & Jessner, 2002; Kramsch & Whiteside, 2008; Leather & van Dam, 2003; van Lier, 2004). As Jessner (2008) pointed out, it makes little sense to look at linguistic systems in isolation when studying multilingualism, because the behavior of each system largely depends on the behavior of previous and subsequent systems. Thus, Kramsch and Whiteside encouraged researchers "to see interactions in multilingual environments as complex dynamic systems where the usual axes of space and time are reordered along the lines of various historicities and subjectivities among the participants" (2008, p. 667).

Of course, there is still much yet to be learned about L2 development from a complexity theory perspective. A few examples must suffice:

1. As is well-documented, individual variation pervades L2 development. However, to what extent, if any, is this variation patterned? Researchers are obliged to account for regularities as well as uniqueness.
2. How best to adopt a complexity theory perspective that "allows us to consider simultaneously the ongoing multiple influences between environmental and learner factors in all their componential complexity and the emerging changes in both the learner *and* the environment as a result of this development" (Dörnyei, 2009b, p. 251), a process referred to above as co-adaptation?

3. Co-adaptation appears to skew language use in accordance with Zipf's Law. What happens if the skewing is even more exaggerated, e.g., by the teacher in the classroom? Can adaptive imitation of language-use patterns be promoted, thereby accelerating L2 development?

Above all, complexity theory argues for epistemological modesty. To understand L2 development more completely, we must resist the arrogance of certainty and premature closure (Larsen-Freeman, 2002b). Indeed, complexity theory "should . . . be seen not as aiming at a new 'synthetic theory' of complexity of any kind, but a cross-disciplinary field of research and a meeting place for dialogue" (Emmeche, 1997, in Cilliers, 2001, p. 137).

Notes

1 See Leopold (1939–1949) for an earlier example.
2 However, recent meta-analyses show some promise in this regard (e.g., Norris & Ortega, 2000).
3 Chaos theory and dynamic systems theory share a great deal with complexity theory, but have more of a mathematical lineage than a scientific one.
4 These days, I prefer "development" to "acquisition." While I note that the latter is well established, it suggests to me a commodification of language—a static entity that once taken in, remains in a static state (Larsen-Freeman, 2010). See a further comment on this distinction later in the main body of the text.
5 This depends on what one attends to and the limits of one's memory.
6 A fractal is a pattern that is self-similar at all levels of scale.

References

Atkinson, D. (2002). Toward a sociocognitive approach to second language acquisition. *Modern Language Journal, 86,* 525–545.

Atkinson, D., Churchill, E., Nishino, T., & Okada, H. (2007). Alignment and interaction in a sociocognitive approach to second language acquisition. *Modern Language Journal, 91,* 169–188.

Bakhtin, M. (1981). *The dialogic imagination: Four essays.* Austin, TX: University of Texas Press.

Barab, S. (2006). Design-based research: A methodological toolkit for the learning scientist. In R. K. Sawyer (Ed.), *The Cambridge handbook of the learning sciences* (pp. 153–170). Cambridge: Cambridge University Press.

Bateson, G. (1972). *Steps to an ecology of mind.* New York: Ballantine.

Beckner, C., Blythe, R., Bybee, J., Christiansen, M. H., Croft, W., Ellis, N. C., Holland, J., Ke, J., Larsen-Freeman, D., & Schonemann, T. (2009). Language is a complex adaptive system: Position paper. *Language Learning, 59,* Supplement 1, 1–27.

Brown, R. (1973). *A first language.* Cambridge, MA: Harvard University Press.

Bybee, J., & Hopper, P. (Eds.) (2001). *Frequency and the emergence of linguistic structure.* Amsterdam: Benjamins.

Byrne, D. (2002). *Interpreting quantitative data.* London: Sage.

Caspi, T. (2010). *A dynamic perspective on second language acquisition.* Unpublished doctoral dissertation, University of Groningen, Netherlands.

Celce-Murcia, M., & Larsen-Freeman, D. (1999). *The grammar book*. Boston, MA: Heinle/Cengage.

Chomsky, N. (1959). A review of B. F. Skinner's *Verbal Behavior*. *Language, 35*, 26–58.

Christiansen, M. H., & Chater, N. (Eds.) (2001). *Connectionist psycholinguistics*. Westport, CO: Ablex.

Cilliers, P. (2001). Boundaries, hierarchies and networks in complex systems. *International Journal of Innovation Management, 5*, 135–147.

Cilliers, P. (2005). Knowledge, limits and boundaries. *Futures, 37*, 605–613.

Cilliers, P. (2008). Knowing complex systems: The limits of understanding. In F. Darbellay, M. Cockell, J. Billotte, & F. Waldvogel (Eds.), *A vision of transdiciplinarity* (pp. 43–50). Lausanne: EPFL Press & CRC Press.

Clark, A. (1997). *Being there*. Cambridge, MA: MIT Press.

Cook, V. (1991). The poverty-of-the-stimulus argument and multi-competence. *Second Language Research, 7*, 103–117.

Cooper, D. (1999). *Linguistic attractors: The cognitive dynamics of language acquisition and change*. Amsterdam/Philadelphia: Benjamins.

Corder, S.P. (1967). The significance of learners' errors. *International Review of Applied Linguistics, 5*, 161–170.

de Bot, K., Lowie, W., & Verspoor, M. (2007). A dynamic systems theory to second language acquisition. *Bilingualism: Language and Cognition, 10*, 7–21.

Dörnyei, Z. (2009a). *The psychology of second language acquisition*. Oxford: Oxford University Press.

Dörnyei, Z. (2009b). Individual differences: Interplay of learner characteristics and learning environment. *Language Learning, 59*, Supplement 1, 237–255.

Doughty, C., & Long, M. (Eds.) (2003). *Handbook of second language acquisition*. Malden, MA: Blackwell.

Dulay, H., & Burt, M. (1973). Should we teach children syntax? *Language Learning, 23*, 245–258.

Elio, R., & Anderson, J. R. (1981). The effects of category generalizations and instance similarity on schema abstraction. *Journal of Experimental Psychology: Human Learning & Memory, 7*, 397–417.

Elio, R., & Anderson, J. R. (1984). The effects of information order and learning mode on schema abstraction. *Memory & Cognition, 12*, 20–30.

Ellis, N. C. (2002). Frequency effects in language processing: A review with implications for theories of implicit and explicit language acquisition. *Studies in Second Language Acquisition, 24*, 143–188.

Ellis, N. C. (2006). Selective attention and transfer phenomena in SLA: Contingency, cue competition, salience, interference, overshadowing, blocking, and perceptual learning. *Applied Linguistics, 27*, 1–31.

Ellis, N. C. (with Larsen-Freeman, D.) (2009). Constructing a second language: Analyses and computational simulations of the emergence of linguistic constructions from usage. *Language Learning, 59*, Supplement 1, 93–128.

Ellis, N. C., & Ferreira-Junior, F. (2009). Construction learning as a function of frequency, frequency distribution, and function. *Modern Language Journal, 93*, 370–386.

Ellis, N. C., & Larsen-Freeman, D. (2006). Language emergence: Implications for applied linguistics. *Applied Linguistics, 27*, 558–589.

Elman, J., Bates, E., Johnson, M., Karmiloff-Smith, A., Parisi, D., & Plunkett, K. (1996). *Rethinking innateness: A connectionist perspective on development*. Cambridge, MA: MIT Press.

Epstein, J. (2008, July). Why model? Keynote address to the Second World Congress on Social Simulation, George Mason University, Washington, DC.

Feldman, J. (2006). *From molecule to metaphor*. Cambridge, MA: Bradford/MIT Books.

Gleick, J. (1987). *Chaos: Making a new science*. New York: Penguin Books.

Goldberg, A. E., Casenhiser, D. M., & Sethuraman, N. (2004). Learning argument structure generalizations. *Cognitive Linguistics, 15*, 289–316.

Haggis, T. (2008). Knowledge must be contextual: Exploring some possible implications of complexity and dynamic systems theories for educational research. *Educational Philosophy & Theory, 40*, 159–176.

Herdina, P., & Jessner, U. (2002). *A dynamic model of multilingualism*. Clevedon: Multilingual Matters.

Heylighen, F. (1989). Self-organization, emergence and the architecture of complexity. *Proceedings of the 1st European Conference on System Science* (AFCET, Paris), 23–32.

Heylighen, F. (2008). Complexity and self-organization. In M. J. Bates & M. N. Maack (Eds.), *Encyclopedia of library and information sciences, Vol. 2* (pp. 1215–1224). Oxford: Taylor & Francis.

Hopper, P. (1998). Emergent grammar. In M. Tomasello (Ed.), *The new psychology of language* (pp. 155–175). Mahwah, NJ: Lawrence Erlbaum Associates.

Jessner, U. (2008). A DST model of multilingualism and the role of metalinguistic awareness. *Modern Language Journal, 92*, 270–283.

Keller, R. (1985). Toward a theory of linguistic change. In T. Ballmer (Ed.), *Linguistics dynamics: Discourses, procedures and evolution*. (pp. 212–237). Berlin: Walter de Gruyter.

Kramsch, C. (Ed.). (2002). *Language acquisition and language socialization*. London: Continuum.

Kramsch, C. (2008). Ecological perspectives on foreign language education. *Language Teacher, 41*, 389–408.

Kramsch, C. (2009). Third culture and language education. In L. Wei & V. Cook (Eds.), *Continuum contemporary applied linguistics* (233–254). London: Continuum.

Kramsch, C., & Whiteside, A. (2008). Language ecology in multilingual settings: Towards a theory of symbolic competence. *Applied Linguistics, 29*, 645–671.

Larsen-Freeman, D. (1976). An explanation for the morpheme acquisition order of second language learners. *Language Learning, 26*, 125–134.

Larsen-Freeman, D. (1997). Chaos/complexity science and second language acquisition. *Applied Linguistics, 18*, 141–165.

Larsen-Freeman, D. (2002a). The grammar of choice. In E. Hinkel & S. Fotos (Eds.), *New perspectives on grammar teaching* (pp. 105–120). Mahwah, NJ: Lawrence Erlbaum Associates.

Larsen-Freeman, D. (2002b). Language acquisition and language use from a chaos/complexity theory perspective. In C. Kramsch (Ed.), *Language acquisition and language socialization* (pp. 36–44). London: Continuum.

Larsen-Freeman, D. (2003). *Teaching language: From grammar to grammaring*. Boston, MA: Heinle/Cengage.

Larsen-Freeman, D. (2006a). Second language acquisition and the issue of fossilization: There is no end, and there is no state. In Z.-H. Han & T. Odlin (Eds.), *Studies of fossilization in second language acquisition* (pp. 189–200). Clevedon: Multilingual Matters.

Larsen-Freeman, D. (2006b). The emergence of complexity, fluency, and accuracy in the oral and written production of five Chinese learners of English. *Applied Linguistics, 27*, 590–619.

Larsen-Freeman, D. (2008). On the need for a new understanding of language and its development. *Journal of Applied Linguistics, 3*, 281–304.

Larsen-Freeman, D. (2010). Having and doing: Learning from a complexity theory perspective. In P. Seedhouse, S. Walsh, & C. Jenks (Eds.), *Conceptualising learning in applied linguistics* (pp. 52–68). Basingstoke: Palgrave Macmillan.

Larsen-Freeman, D. (forthcoming). Complex, dynamic systems: A new transdisciplinary theme for applied linguistics? *Language Teaching*.

Larsen-Freeman, D., & Cameron, L. (2008a). *Complex systems and applied linguistics*. Oxford: Oxford University Press.

Larsen-Freeman, D., & Cameron, L. (2008b). Research methodology on language development from a complex systems perspective. *Modern Language Journal*, *92*, 200–213.

Larsen-Freeman, D., & Long, M. (1991). *An introduction to second language acquisition research*. London: Longman.

Larsen-Freeman, D., Lowie, W., & Schmid, M. (in press). Introduction. In M. Schmid & W. Lowie (Eds.), *Modelling bilingualism: From structure to chaos*. Amsterdam: John Benjamins.

Leather, J., & van Dam, J. (Eds.) (2003). *Ecology of language acquisition*. Dordrecht: Kluwer.

Lemke, J. (2002). Language development and identity: Multiple timescales in the social ecology of learning. In C. Kramsch (Ed.), *Language acquisition and language socialization* (pp. 68–87). London: Continuum.

Leopold, W. (1939–1949). *Speech development of a bilingual child*. Northwestern University Studies in the Humanities, Evanston, IL.

Lewontin R. (1998). The evolution of cognition: Questions we will never answer. In D. Scarborough & S. Sternberg (Eds.), *An invitation to cognitive science, Vol. 4: Methods, models, and conceptual Issues* (pp. 107–132). Cambridge, MA: MIT Press.

Lorenz, E. (1972, December). Predictability: Does the flap of a butterfly's wings in Brazil set off a tornado in Texas? Paper presented at The American Association for the Advancement of Sciences, Washington, DC.

Macqueen, S. M. (2009). *The emergence of patterns in second language writing: A sociocognitive exploration of lexical trails*. Unpublished doctoral dissertation, University of Melbourne.

MacWhinney, B. (2006). Emergentism: Use often and with care. *Applied Linguistics*, *27*, 729–740.

Maturana, H., & Varela, F. (1972). *Autopoiesis and cognition*. Boston, MA: Reidel.

McLaughlin, B. (1990). Restructuring. *Applied Linguistics*, *11*, 113–128.

Meara, P. (2006). Emergent properties of multilingual lexicons. *Applied Linguistics*, *27*, 620–644.

Milroy, J., & Milroy, L. (1999). *Authority in language* (3rd ed.). New York: Routledge.

Mitchell, S. (2003). *Biological complexity and integrative pluralism*. Cambridge: Cambridge University Press.

Norris, J. M., & Ortega, L. (2000). Effectiveness of L2 instruction: A research synthesis and quantitative meta-analysis. *Language Learning*, *50*, 417–528.

Osberg, D. (2007, April). *Emergence: A complexity-based critical logic for education?* Paper presented at the Complex Criticality in Educational Research colloquium of the American Educational Research Association, Chicago, IL.

Reinking, D., & Watkins, J. (2000). A formative experiment investigating the use of multimedia book reviews to increase elementary students' independent reading. *Reading Research Quarterly*, *35*, 384–419.

Rumelhart, D. & McClelland, J. (1986). On learning the past tenses of English verbs. In J. McClelland, D. Rumelhart, & the PDP Research Group (Eds.), *Parallel distributed processing: Explorations in the microstructure of cognition, Vol. 2: Psychological and biological models* (pp. 216–271). Cambridge, MA: MIT Press.

Selinker, L. (1972). Interlanguage. *International Review of Applied Linguistics*, *10*, 209–231.

Semetsky, I. (2008). On the creative logic of education, or re-reading Dewey through the lens of complexity science. *Educational Philosophy & Theory*, *40*, 83–95.

Slobin, D. (1996). From "thought and language" to "thinking for speaking." In J. Gumperz & S. Levinson (Eds.), *Rethinking linguistic relativity* (pp. 70–96). New York: Cambridge University Press.

Spivey, M. (2007). *The continuity of mind*. Oxford: Oxford University Press.

Thelen, E., & Corbetta, D. (2002). Microdevelopment and dynamic systems: Applications to infant motor development. In N. Granott & J. Parziale (Eds.), *Microdevelopment* (pp. 59–79). Cambridge: Cambridge University Press.

Thelen, E., & Smith, L. (1994). *A dynamic systems approach to the development of cognition and action*. Cambridge, MA: MIT Press.

Thompson, E., & Varela, F. (2001). Radical embodiment: Neural dynamics and consciousness. *Trends in Cognitive Science, 5*, 418–425.

Tomasello, M. (2003). *Constructing a language*. Cambridge, MA: Harvard University Press.

Ushioda, E. (2009). A person-in-context relational view of emergent motivation, self and identity. In Z. Dörnyei & E. Ushioda (Eds.), *Motivation, language identity and the L2 self* (pp. 215–228). Bristol: Multilingual Matters.

van Geert, P. (2003). Dynamic systems approaches and modeling of developmental processes. In J. Valsiner & K. Connolly (Eds.), *Handbook of developmental psychology* (pp. 640–672). London: Sage.

van Gelder, T., & Port, R. (1995). It's about time: An overview of the dynamical approach to cognition. In R. Port & T. van Gelder (Eds.), *Mind as motion: Explorations in the dynamics of cognition* (pp. 1–44). Cambridge, MA: MIT Press.

van Lier, L. (2004). *The ecology and semiotics of language learning: A sociocultural perspective*. Boston, MA: Kluwer.

Varela, F., Thompson, E., & Rosch, E. (1991). *The embodied mind: Cognitive science and human experience*. Cambridge, MA: MIT Press.

Verspoor, M., Lowie, W., & de Bot, K. (2008). Input and second language development from a dynamic perspective. In T. Piske & M. Young-Scholten (Eds.), *Input matters in SLA* (pp. 77–88). Bristol: Multilingual Matters.

Verspoor, M., Lowie, W., & van Dijk, M. (2008). Variability in second language development from a dynamic systems perspective. *Modern Language Journal, 92*, 214–231.

von Bertalanffy, L. (1950). An outline for general systems theory. *British Journal for the Philosophy of Science, 12*, 134–165.

Weaver, W. (1948). Science and complexity. *American Scientist, 36*, 536–544.

Whiteside, A. (in press). Using dynamic systems/complexity theory in linguistic data analysis: A language ecology approach to the study of individual and social process. In L. Cooker & P. Benson (Eds.), *The applied linguistic individual: Sociocultural approaches to autonomy, agency, and identity*. London: Equinox.

Zipf, G. K. (1935). *The Psycho-biology of language*. Boston, MA: Houghton Mifflin.

3

AN IDENTITY APPROACH TO SECOND LANGUAGE ACQUISITION

Bonny Norton and Carolyn McKinney

Overview

The central argument of the identity approach to second language acquisition (SLA) is twofold: First, SLA theorists need a comprehensive theory of identity that integrates the individual language learner and the larger social world; second, SLA theorists need to address how relations of power in the social world affect learners' access to the target language community. In relation to the former, a fully developed theory of identity highlights the multiple positions from which language learners can speak, and how sometimes marginalized learners can appropriate more desirable identities with respect to the target language community. In relation to the latter, identity theorists are concerned about the ways in which opportunities to practice speaking, reading, and writing, acknowledged as central to the SLA process (cf. Spolsky, 1989), are socially structured in both formal and informal sites of language learning. Identity theorists thus question the view that learners can be defined in binary terms as motivated or unmotivated, introverted or extroverted, inhibited or uninhibited, without considering that such affective factors are frequently socially constructed in inequitable relations of power, changing over time and space, and possibly coexisting in contradictory ways within a single individual.

Norton first published these key arguments in the mid-1990s (Norton, 1997; Norton Peirce, 1995), supporting this theory with a comprehensive study of language learners (Norton, 2000). She then followed up these findings in subsequent research, often conducted collaboratively (Kanno & Norton, 2003; McKinney & Norton, 2008; Norton, 2001; Norton & Gao, 2008; Norton & Pavlenko, 2004; Norton & Toohey, 2001, 2004; Pavlenko & Norton, 2007). Norton uses the term identity "to reference how a person understands his or her relationship to the world, how that relationship is constructed across time and space, and how the person understands possibilities for the future" (2000, p. 5). In this view, every time learners speak, they are negotiating and renegotiating a sense of self in relation to the larger social world, and reorganizing that relationship in multiple dimensions of their lives.

Drawing on poststructuralist theory, Norton argues that three characteristics of identity are particularly relevant to SLA: the multiple, non-unitary nature of identity; identity as a site of struggle; and identity as changing over time. The construct of identity as multiple is particularly powerful because learners who struggle to speak from one identity position can reframe their relationship with their interlocutors and reclaim alternative, more powerful identities from which to speak. This has profound implications for SLA.

There is now a wealth of research that explores the relationship between identity and language learning, testament to the fact that issues of identity and power are being recognized as central to SLA (see, for example, volumes by Blackledge & Creese, 2010; Block, 2003, 2007b; Clarke, 2008; Day, 2002; Heller, 2007; Higgins, 2009; Kanno, 2003, 2008; Kubota & Lin, 2009; Lin, 2007; Miller, 2003; Nelson, 2009; Norton, 2000; Norton & Toohey, 2004; Pavlenko & Blackledge, 2004; Potowski, 2007; Toohey, 2000; Tsui & Tollefson, 2007). Further, while much of this research explores the multiple and intersecting dimensions of language learners' identities, there is also a growing body of research that seeks to investigate the ways in which particular relations of race, gender, class, and sexual orientation may impact the process of SLA. Identity research does not regard such identity categories as psychometric variables, but rather as sets of relationships that are socially and historically constructed within particular relations of power (cf. Davis & Skilton-Sylvester, 2004; Ibrahim, 1999; King, 2008; Kubota & Lin, 2006; Nelson, 2009). Further, the key concepts of a learner's *investment* in the target language (Norton, 2000; Norton Peirce, 1995; Norton & Gao, 2008), as well as their identification with *imagined communities* (Anderson, 1991; Kanno & Norton, 2003; Norton, 2001; Pavlenko & Norton, 2007), have been developed to broaden our understanding of processes of SLA.

Motivation and Investment

Drawing on identity theory, as well as the micro-level workings of power in everyday social encounters (cf. Foucault, 1980), Norton and Toohey (2001) have argued that many theories of the good language learner have been developed on the premise that language learners can choose under what conditions they will interact with members of the target language community and that the language learner's access to the target language community is a function of the learner's motivation. The concept of motivation is drawn primarily from social psychology, where attempts have been made to quantify a learner's commitment to learning the target language. The pioneering work of Gardner and Lambert (e.g., 1972) has been particularly influential in introducing the notions of instrumental and integrative motivation into the field of SLA. In their work, *instrumental motivation* references the desire of language learners to learn an L2 for utilitarian purposes, such as employment, while *integrative motivation* references the desire to learn a language to successfully integrate with the target language community. While researchers such as Crookes and Schmidt (1991), Dörnyei (1994, 1997), and

Oxford and Shearin (1994) have sought to extend the theoretical framework proposed by Gardner and Lambert, such debates often do not do justice to the complex relationship between power, identity, and SLA.

The construct of *investment*, first introduced by Norton (Norton Peirce, 1995), signals the socially and historically constructed relationship of learners to the target language, and their often ambivalent desire to learn and practice it. It is best understood with reference to the economic metaphors that Bourdieu used in his work – in particular the notion of cultural capital. Bourdieu and Passeron (1977) used the term "cultural capital" to reference the knowledge and modes of thought that characterize different classes and groups in relation to specific sets of social forms, with differential exchange values. Norton argued that, if learners invest in a second language, they do so with the understanding that they will acquire a wider range of symbolic and material resources, which will in turn increase the value of their cultural capital. Learners expect or hope to have a good return on that investment—a return that will give them access to hitherto unattainable resources.

By way of example, consider a recent classroom-based study conducted by Duff (2002) in a multilingual secondary school in Canada that included native English speakers and English language learners. Drawing on macro-level and micro-level contexts of communication in one content course, Duff found that the teacher's attempts to foster respect for cultural diversity in the classroom had mixed results. In essence, the English language learners in the class were afraid of being criticized or laughed at because of their limited command of English. As Duff noted, "Silence protected them from humiliation" (p. 312). This silence, however, was perceived by the native English speakers as representing "a lack of initiative, agency, or desire to improve one's English or to offer interesting material for the sake of the class" (p. 312). It is clear from the classroom data, however, that the English language learners in the class were not unmotivated; rather, it could be argued that they were not *invested* in the language practices of their classroom, where there were unequal relations of power between the English language learners and native speakers, with differential cultural capital.

Significantly, this notion of investment is not equivalent to instrumental motivation. The concept of instrumental motivation often presupposes a unitary, fixed, and ahistorical language learner who desires access to material resources that are the privilege of target language speakers. The notion of investment, on the other hand, conceives of the language learner as having a complex identity and multiple desires. The notion presupposes that, when language learners speak, they are not only exchanging information with target language speakers, but they are constantly organizing and reorganizing a sense of who they are and how they relate to the social world. Thus an investment in the target language is also an investment in a learner's own identity, an identity that is constantly changing across time and space.

The construct of investment provides for a different set of questions associated with a learner's commitment to learning the target language. Instead of asking, for example, "To what extent is the learner motivated to learn the target language?" the researcher asks, "What is the learner's investment in the target language practices of this classroom or community?" A learner may be a highly motivated language learner, but may nevertheless have little investment in the language practices of a given classroom, which may, for example, be racist, sexist, elitist, or homophobic. Thus, despite being highly motivated, a learner could be excluded from the language practices of a classroom, and in time positioned as a "poor" or unmotivated language learner.

Imagined Communities and Imagined Identities

An extension of interest in identity and investment concerns the *imagined communities* that language learners aspire to when they learn a language (Anderson, 1991; Kanno & Norton, 2003; Norton, 2001; Pavlenko & Norton, 2007). Imagined communities refer to groups of people, not immediately tangible and accessible, with whom we connect through the power of the imagination. In our daily lives we interact with many communities whose existence can be felt concretely and directly. These include our neighborhood communities, our workplaces, our educational institutions, and our religious groups. However, these are not the only communities with which we are affiliated. As Wenger (1998) suggested, direct involvement in community practices and concrete relationships—what he calls *engagement*—is not the only way in which we belong to a community; for Wenger, imagination is another important source of community. Norton (2001) extended Wenger's work by proposing the construct of imagined communities with respect to L2 learning, arguing that it serves, in part, to explain non-participation and resistance in the language classroom. Imagined communities provide insight into imagined identities.

Imagined ties extend both spatially and temporally. Benedict Anderson (1991), who first coined the term "imagined communities," argued that what we think of as nations are imagined communities, "because the members of even the smallest nation will never know most of their fellow-members, meet them, or even hear of them, yet in the minds of each lives the image of their communion" (p. 6). Thus, in imagining ourselves bonded with our fellow compatriots across time and space, we can feel a sense of community with people we have not yet met, and perhaps may never meet. A focus on imagined communities in SLA enables us to explore how learners' affiliation with such communities might affect their learning trajectories. Such communities include future relationships that exist only in the learner's imagination as well as affiliations—such as nationhood or even transnational communities—that extend beyond local sets of relationships. These imagined communities are no less real than the ones in which learners have daily engagement and might even have a stronger impact on their identities and investments.

Theoretical Principles

The theoretical assumptions that underlie the identity approach to SLA are best understood with reference to poststructuralist theories of language and subjectivity, respectively, and sociocultural theories of learning. We examine each of these in turn.

Poststructuralist Theories of Language

Language learning engages the identities of learners because language itself is not only a linguistic system of signs and symbols, but also a complex social practice through which relationships are defined, negotiated, and resisted. This view draws on poststructuralist theories of language, which have achieved prominence in the late 20th century and are associated, for many scholars, with the work of Bakhtin (1981), Bourdieu (1977), Derrida (1980), Kramsch (2010), Kress (1989) and Luke (2004). These theories build on, but are distinct from, structuralist theories of language, associated predominantly with the work of Saussure. Saussure's (1966) distinction between speech (*parole*) and language (*langue*) was an attempt to provide a way of recognizing that, despite geographical, interpersonal, and social variations, languages have shared patterns and structure. For structuralists, the building blocks of language structure are signs that comprise the signifier (or sound-image) and the signified (the concept or meaning). Saussure asserted that neither the signifier nor the signified preexists the other and that the link between them is arbitrary. He noted that it is the linguistic system that guarantees the meaning of signs and that each linguistic community has its own set of signifying practices that give value to the signs in a language.

One of the criticisms poststructuralists have levelled at this notion of language is that structuralism cannot account for struggles over the social meanings that can be attributed to signs within a given language. The signs /research/, /SLA/, and /poststructuralism/, for example, can have different meanings for different people within the same linguistic community. Witness, for example, debates over the meaning of "SLA theory" in the field of applied linguistics, which have given rise to contrasts between cognitivist and social approaches to language learning (Atkinson, 2002; Block, 2007a; Larsen-Freeman, 2007; Swain & Deters, 2007; Zuengler & Miller, 2006). This edited collection itself contributes to this debate. Thus, while structuralists conceive of signs as having idealized meanings and linguistic communities as being relatively homogeneous and consensual, post-structuralists take the position that the signifying practices of societies are sites of struggle, and that linguistic communities are heterogeneous arenas characterized by conflicting claims to truth and power. The poststructuralist theories of Bakhtin (1981) and Bourdieu (1977), discussed next, foreground struggles over meaning and legitimacy, which are particularly relevant to the identity approach to SLA.

Mikhail Bakhtin (1981, 1984), a Russian philosopher and literary scholar, took the position that language needs to be investigated as situated utterances in which speakers, in dialogue with others, struggle to create meanings. In this view, the notion of the individual speaker is a fiction as all speakers construct their utterances jointly on the basis of their interaction with listeners, both in historical and contemporary, actual and assumed communities. Any one utterance for Bakhtin is thus a link in the chain of speech communication, as the context of any one utterance is past, present, and future utterances on the same topic. The historical, present, and future positioning of speakers and those of their interlocutors are expressed in the words that constitute an utterance—words that are not neutral but express particular predispositions and value systems. In this view, rather than seeing SLA as a gradual, individual process of internalizing a neutral set of rules, structures, and vocabulary of a standard language, Bakhtin's work encourages us to think about the learning of language within particular discourses and with particular interlocutors. Speakers need to struggle to appropriate the voices of others, and to use those voices for their own purposes. What others say, the customary discourse of any particular community, may privilege or debase certain speakers. Finding answering words for others, joining the chain of speech communication, is as much a social as a linguistic struggle.

Pierre Bourdieu (1977, 1984), a French sociologist, focused on the often unequal relationships between interlocutors and the importance of power in structuring speech. In arguing that "speech always owes a major part of its value to the value of the person who utters it" (1977, p. 652), Bourdieu suggested that the value ascribed to speech cannot be understood apart from the person who speaks, and that the person who speaks cannot be understood apart from larger networks of social relationships. He argued that, when a person speaks, the speaker wishes not only to be understood, but to be "believed, obeyed, respected, distinguished" (p. 648). However, speakers' abilities to command respect are unequally distributed because of the symbolic power relations between interlocutors. To redress the inequities between what Bourdieu called "legitimate" and "illegitimate" speakers, he argued that an expanded definition of competence should include the "right to speech" or "the power to impose reception" (p. 648). Like Bakhtin then, Bourdieu reminds the SLA theorist that language cannot be idealized and that we cannot take for granted that good faith will prevail between participants in oral or literate activities. Bourdieu's foregrounding of power relations in language use has important implications for how language learners are positioned by others, for the opportunities they get to speak, and for the varieties of language that we teach and that they use.

Poststructuralist Theories of Subjectivity

The work of feminist poststructuralist Christine Weedon (1987/1997), like that of Bakhtin and Bourdieu, is centrally concerned with the conditions under which people speak, within both institutional and community contexts. Like other poststructuralist theorists who inform her work, Weedon has foregrounded the central role of language in her analysis of the relationship between the individual and the social, arguing that language not only defines institutional practices, but serves to construct our sense of ourselves—our *subjectivity*: "Language is the place where actual and possible forms of social organization and their likely social and political consequences are defined and contested. Yet it is also the place where our sense of selves, our subjectivity, is constructed" (p. 21).

The use of the term "subjectivity", derived from the term *subject*, is compelling because it serves as a reminder that a person's identity must always be understood in relational terms: One is either subject *of* a set of relationships (i.e., in a position of power) or subject *to* a set of relationships (i.e., in a position of reduced power). Weedon noted that the terms "subject" and "subjectivity" signify a different conception of the individual than that associated with humanist conceptions of the individual dominant in Western philosophy. While humanist conceptions of the individual presuppose that every person has an essential, unique, fixed, and coherent core, poststructuralism depicts the individual (i.e., the subject) as diverse, contradictory, dynamic, and changing over historical time and social space. Drawing on the Foucauldian notions of discourse and historical specificity, subjectivity in poststructuralism is understood as discursively constructed and as always socially and historically embedded. As noted above, these theories of subjectivity have been central in the work of many identity theorists in SLA.

Poststructuralist approaches to theorizing identity have also been fruitfully put to work by cultural theorist Stuart Hall (1992a, 1992b) and postcolonial theorist Homi Bhabha (1994) to de-essentialize and deconstruct identity categories such as race and gender. In theorizing cultural identity, Hall focused on identity as in-process, and stressed the importance of representation following from the discursive construction of identity. In his notion of *new ethnicities*, Hall provided an alternative theorizing of race that recognizes experiences of race without homogenizing them. Hall emphasized a multifaceted rootedness that is not limited to ethnic minorities and that can be applied to other forms of difference. However, one of the difficulties in theorizing difference in this way is that people often wish to assert their identities as homogeneous and unitary, foregrounding a particular aspect of their experience such as gender, race, or religious affiliation. We see this in the current strength of nationalisms and religious fundamentalism in different parts of the globe. Such unitary assertions of identity are often referred to as "strategic essentialism" (cf. Spivak, in Fuss, 1989; Yon, 1999). The terms *identity politics* or the *politics of difference* reference this particular coalescence of identity and power relations, emphasizing the material effects of difference.

Sociocultural Theories of Learning

Rather than viewing SLA as a predominantly mental and individual process (Davis, 1995), the identity approach investigates SLA as a sociocultural practice. SLA is conceptualized as a relational activity that occurs between specific speakers situated in specific sociocultural contexts. A shift from seeing learners as individual language producers to seeing them as members of social and historical groups calls for an examination of the conditions for learning, or the appropriation of practices, in any particular community. This view is informed by anthropologists Jean Lave and Etienne Wenger (1991), who argued that "situated learning" is an integral and inseparable part of social practice. Through a process of *legitimate peripheral participation*, newcomers interact with old-timers in a given community setting, become increasingly experienced in the practices that characterize that community, and gradually move toward fuller participation in that community. Lave and Wenger recognized, however, that particular social arrangements in any community may constrain or facilitate movement toward fuller participation.

In developing these ideas, Wenger (1998) focused on the relationship of participation to the construction of a learner's identity. He argued that our relation to communities of practice involves both participation and non-participation, and that our identities are shaped by combinations of the two. Non-participation in some communities is inevitable because our experiences include coming into contact with communities to which we do not belong. This kind of non-participation differs from that which occurs when we are non-participatory in the practices of communities to which we do belong. In the latter case, Wenger's distinction between *peripherality* and *marginality* is a useful one. By peripherality, Wenger refers to the fact that some degree of non-participation can be an enabling factor of participation, while marginality is a form of non-participation that prevents full participation.

In conceptualizing learning in SLA, such theories are particularly apt in situations where L2 learners (newcomers) enter a classroom in which speakers of the target language (old-timers) constitute the more experienced members of the community. Toohey's (2000, 2001) research with ESL children in a public school who attended classes in which the majority of children were native English speakers showed a community that included many mentors who were experienced English speakers. In other classrooms, however, such as the adult immigrant language classes discussed by Norton (2001), all of the members of the classroom community, apart from the teacher, were newcomers; the only old-timer was the teacher. The question that arose then was what community practices did these adults seek to learn? What, indeed, constituted the community for them?

To address this question, Norton (2001) found Wenger's discussion on identity and modes of belonging particularly useful. Drawing on his research with insurance claims processors, Wenger (1998) noted that the claims processors' experience of both participation and non-participation reached beyond the walls of their office, and that they had to use their imagination to get a picture of these broader connections. In this view, imagination, as one mode of belonging, addresses the extent to which we create images of the world and see connections through time and space via the extrapolation of experience. As Wenger noted:

> My use of the concept of imagination refers to a process of expanding our self by transcending our time and space and creating new images of the world and ourselves. Imagination in this sense is looking at an apple seed and seeing a tree.
>
> (p. 176)

Wenger emphasized further that imagination should not be confused with misleading fantasy or withdrawal from reality. This mode of belonging, he argued, is a creative process of producing new images of possibility and new ways of understanding one's relation to the world that transcend more immediate acts of engagement.

Drawing on data from two adult immigrant language learners—Katarina and Felicia, both of whom chose not to participate in their classroom communities—Norton (2001) argued that the communities of practice that characterized Katarina and Felicia's learning trajectories were communities of the imagination. When Katarina and Felicia entered their language classrooms, they not only saw a classroom with four walls, but also envisioned an imagined community outside the classroom that transcended time and space. However, while highly motivated students, they were not invested in the language practices of their respective classrooms, and both chose to withdraw from class.

The connection between non-participation and imagined communities is well illustrated in the example of Katarina, who withdrew from her language course after four months in response to her teacher's evaluative comment that Katarina's English was not "good enough" to take a computer course. In her native country, Katarina had been a teacher for 17 years and was a highly respected professional in this position; she eagerly sought recognition from people who were fellow professionals, and wished to have a profession in Canada in which she could meet people who shared her views and aspirations. As she said, "I choose computer course, not because I have to speak, but because I have to think." Katarina's imagined community was thus a community of professionals, and was as much a reconstruction of her professional past in Poland as it was an imaginative construction of her future in Canada. Katarina's language teacher was an old-timer in this imagined community, a community in which Katarina believed she had already achieved old-timer status. When Katarina felt that her teacher failed to acknowledge her professional identity, thereby positioning her as a newcomer, she was greatly distressed. When, indeed, the teacher appeared to discourage Katarina from taking a computer course that would give her greater access to her imagined community, Katarina refused to continue participating in the language class. Norton concluded that Katarina's act of non-participation helped her to preserve the integrity of her imagined community.

The theoretical assumptions of an identity approach to SLA, reviewed above, suggest that language learning is not a gradual individual process of internalizing a neutral set of rules, structures, and vocabulary of a standard language. Rather, such theoretical principles suggest that language learners need to struggle to appropriate the voices of others; they need to learn to command the attention of their listeners; and they need to negotiate language as a system and as a social practice. Further, learners' investments in the practices of their communities, whether real or imagined, are also important for SLA. An imagined community assumes an imagined identity, and investment in target language practices can be understood within this context.

Research Methods

Given the focus of an identity approach to SLA, the key methodological question to be answered is what kind of research enables scholars to investigate the relationship between language learners as social beings and the frequently inequitable worlds in which learning takes place? Since an identity approach to SLA characterizes learner identity as multiple and changing, a quantitative research paradigm relying on static and measurable variables will generally not be appropriate. The focus on issues of power also necessitates that qualitative research designs are framed by critical research. For these reasons, methods that scholars use in identity approaches to SLA tend to be qualitative rather than quantitative, and often draw on critical ethnography, feminist poststructuralist theory, sociolinguistics, and linguistic anthropology. There are a number of common assumptions that such scholars bring to their qualitative research projects, three of which are as follows:

First, much identity research rejects the view that any research can claim to be objective or unbiased. In this view, researchers have to understand their own experience and knowledge as well as those of the participants in their studies (Norton & Early, in press). This does not suggest that qualitative research is lacking in rigor; on the contrary, all research studies are understood to be situated, and the researcher integral to the progress of a research project. In her research in India, Ramanathan (2005) noted, for example, "Questions and issues of what are 'present' and 'absent' clearly underlie what are 'visible' and 'invisible' in literacy events and practices and are determined, to a large extent, by the researcher's lens" (p. 15).

Second, identity researchers aim to investigate the complex relationship between social structure on the one hand, and human agency on the other, without resorting to deterministic or reductionist analyses. While taking race, class, gender, and other structural issues into account in their analysis, they need to ensure that they leave conceptual room for the actions and investments of human agents. Menard-Warwick (2005) has made the case that Bakhtin's theories of language have the potential to resolve some of the contradictions between continuity and change that characterize debates on identity in the fields of SLA and literacy.

Third, identity researchers seek to better understand how power operates within society, constraining or enabling human action (Cummins, 2000; Fairclough, 1989; Janks, 2010; Pennycook, 2007). They often draw on Foucault (1980) to understand not only the relationship between knowledge and power, but the subtle ways in which power operates in society. Foucault noted, for example, that power is often invisible in that it frequently naturalizes events and practices in ways that come to be seen as "normal" to members of a community. As Pennycook pointed out:

> Foucault brings a constant skepticism toward cherished concepts and modes of thought. Taken-for-granted categories such as man, woman, class, race, ethnicity, nation, identity, awareness, emancipation, language or power must be understood as contingent, shifting and produced in the particular, rather than having some prior ontological status.
>
> (2007, p. 39)

In an identity approach to SLA, there has thus been a strong methodological focus on narratives, whether collected through fieldwork (Barkhuizen, 2008;

Block, 2006; Botha, 2009; Goldstein, 1996; McKay & Wong, 1996; Miller, 2003; Norton, 2000) or from existing autobiographical and biographical accounts (Norton & Early, in press; Pavlenko, 2001a, 2001b, 2004). This methodological focus has many potential synergies with a critical research paradigm in that it foregrounds an individual's sense-making of their experience as well as the complexity of individual/social relationships. As Block (2007a) has pointed out, the focus on narrative in SLA research follows its recent popularity in social science research, and is part of a wider "social turn" (Block, 2003) in SLA research. Pavlenko has made a strong case for the particular contribution that narrative can make:

> L2 learning stories . . . are unique and rich sources of information about the relationship between language and identity in second language learning and socialization. It is possible that only personal narratives provide a glimpse into areas so private, personal and intimate that they are rarely—if ever— breached in the study of SLA, and at the same time are at the heart and soul of the second language socialization process.
>
> (2001b, p. 167)

Turning our attention to fieldwork-based research on identity and language learning, we find that researchers often combine a range of methods of data collection such as ethnographic observation, interviews (including life history interviews), diary studies, and written responses (narrative or other) to researcher questions. Extended time frames provide particular depth. For example, Toohey's (2000, 2001) longitudinal study of six young learners from minority language backgrounds in a Canadian school tracked their development over a three-year period. Toohey combined several ethnographic data collection methods: regular classroom observations were captured in fieldnotes and audio recordings and supported by monthly video recordings; interviews and ongoing informal discussions were held with the children's teachers; and home visits where parents were interviewed were common. It was the combination of such methods that provided the rich data necessary to understand the learners and their classroom language learning as socially, historically, and politically constructed, and the classroom as a site of identity negotiation.

Qualitative research on language and identity is not without its challenges, however, and the following two studies are illustrative of some of its difficulties. Drawing on their research on task-based language learning in urban settings in the United Kingdom, Leung, Harris, and Rampton (2004) examined the inelegance of qualitative research, arguing that the "epistemic turbulence" in qualitative research in second language acquisition centers on the question of what constitutes or represents reality. The methodology adopted in their study was to collect naturally occurring data with the use of video and audio recordings, which were supplemented by field notes. They described the data as "messy" in that it was difficult to represent and account for data that did not fit neatly into the theoretical construct of task-based language use. Leung et al. made the case that researchers need a conceptual framework that acknowledges rather than obscures the messiness of data.

In a very different context, Toohey and Waterstone (2004) described a research collaboration between teachers and researchers in Vancouver, Canada, with the mutual goal of investigating what practices in classrooms would make a difference to the learning opportunities of minority-language children. While teachers were comfortable discussing and critiquing their educational practices, they expressed ambivalence about translating their practice into publishable academic papers, noting that they felt little ownership over the academic language characteristic of many published journals. To address precisely this type of challenge, Sharkey and Johnson (2003) initiated a productive and engaging dialogue between researchers and teachers, with the expressed aim of demystifying research and theory that addresses themes of identity, power, and educational change.

Supporting Findings

Apart from Norton's own work, numerous researchers, as discussed above, have investigated the relationship between identity and SLA. While some have focused particularly on the notion of investment in explaining language learning processes (e.g., Cummins, 2006; Haneda, 2005; McKay & Wong, 1996; Pittaway, 2004; Potowski, 2007; Skilton-Sylvester, 2002), others have taken up the idea of imagined communities (Carroll, Motha, & Price, 2008; Dagenais, 2003; Kanno, 2008; Kanno & Norton, 2003; Kendrick & Jones, 2008; Pavlenko & Norton, 2007). Here we present evidence of the usefulness of both of these concepts in understanding SLA.

All five of the immigrant women in Norton's original study (Norton Peirce, 1995; Norton, 2000) were highly motivated learners of English, yet there were particular social conditions under which the women in this study were most uncomfortable and unlikely to speak. The data suggest that a language learner's motivation is mediated by investments that may conflict with the desire to speak, or, paradoxically, may make it possible for the language learner to claim the right to speak. The case study of Martina, a Czech immigrant and mother of three children, is a powerful case in point. Despite never feeling comfortable speaking in English and despite what could be described as a high affective filter, Martina refused to be silenced. In her workplace, for example, where she worked alongside young native English speakers in a fast food restaurant, she saw herself positioned as a "broom," a position that dehumanized her and denied her the right to speak. Martina therefore reframed the relationship between herself and her co-workers as a domestic one, in which her co-workers were positioned as "children" rather than powerful native speakers. In claiming the right to speak as mother/parent/adult and resisting the identity of the immigrant, Martina positioned herself as a legitimate speaker in this encounter. In essence, while Martina was a highly motivated language learner, she was not invested in the language practices of her workplace. However, she could transform these language practices by drawing on an alternative and more powerful identity position from which to speak, with significant implications for SLA.

In a study of Chinese adolescent immigrant students in the United States, McKay and Wong (1996) extended the notion of investment. Like other identity theorists, they demonstrated how the specific needs, desires and negotiations of learners are not distractions from the task of language learning, but "must be regarded as constituting the very fabric of students' lives and as determining their investment in learning the target language" (p. 603). While Norton focused on opportunities to speak, McKay and Wong's research investigated students' investments in the four skills of listening, speaking, reading and writing. They argued that investment in each of these skills can be highly selective and that different skills can have different values in relation to learner identities. For example, in the case of one of the students, Michael Lee, his spoken discourse in English developed rapidly while his written language skills did not improve. Unlike the other students in the study, Michael's sporting ability enabled him to make friends and to socialize primarily with non-Chinese immigrant students. McKay and Wong provided fascinating evidence of Michael's ability to resist and counteract his powerless positioning by school staff as "ESL student" (see also Talmy, 2008). Their study provides further powerful evidence of the impact of social positioning by teachers and peers on an individual's language learning. It is no coincidence that the student from the lowest socio-economic background, Brad Wang, was consistently positioned unfavorably and as a low achiever, despite his excellent writing skills relative to the other students in the first writing assessment completed by the students.

Skilton-Sylvester (2002), drawing on her research with four Cambodian women in adult ESL classes in the United States, has argued that traditional views of adult motivation and participation do not adequately address the complex lives of adult learners, and that an understanding of a woman's domestic and professional identities is necessary to explain her investment and thus participation in particular adult ESL programs. Haneda (2005) has drawn on the construct of investment to understand the engagement of two university students in an advanced Japanese literacy course, concluding that their multiple membership in differing communities may have shaped the way they invested differently in writing in Japanese. Potowski (2007) has used the construct of investment to explain students' use of Spanish in a dual Spanish/English immersion program in the United States, noting that, even if a language program is well run, a learner's investment in the target language must be consistent with the goals of the program if language learning is to meet expectations. Cummins (2006) has drawn on the construct of investment to develop the notion of the identity text, arguing that the construct has emerged as a "significant explanatory construct" (p. 59) in the L2 learning literature.

As noted in the discussion of "Theoretical Principles" above, Norton (2001) adapted the construct of imagined communities to explain the non-participation of two adult immigrant learners in their language classes. In 2003, a special issue of the *Journal of Language, Identity, and Education*, entitled "Imagined Communities and Educational Possibilities" (Kanno & Norton, 2003), helped to place this construct on the SLA agenda, and interest in the topic has continued to grow (cf. Carroll et al., 2008; Dagenais, Moore, Sabatier, Lamarre, & Armand, 2008; Kanno, 2008; Kendrick & Jones, 2008; Pavlenko & Norton, 2007). In the Japanese context, for example, Kanno (2008) examined the relationship between school education and inequality of access to bilingualism in five different Japanese schools promoting bilingual education. She found that, while additive bilingualism was promoted for upper middle-class students, subtractive bilingualism was far more common in schools serving immigrant and refugee children. Kanno argued that, in the schools she researched, different visions of children's imagined communities called for different forms of bilingual education, exacerbating existing inequities between students with unequal access to resources.

In Canada, Dagenais et al. (2008) investigated the linguistic landscape in the vicinity of two elementary schools in Vancouver and Montreal, illustrating the ways in which the children imagined the language of their neighborhoods, and con-structed their identities in relation to them. Dagenais et al. described the innovative ways in which researchers and students drew on multimodal resources such as digital photography to document the linguistic landscape of these neighborhoods, and the way children in both cities were encouraged to exchange letters, posters, photographs, and videos. Dagenais et al. argued that documenting the imagined communities of neighborhoods, as depicted and understood by children, can provide much information on the children's understanding of their community, an important consideration for language educators. In another region of the world, Kendrick and Jones (2008) drew on the notion of imagined communities to analyze the drawings and photographs produced by primary and secondary schoolgirls in the Ugandan context. Their research, using multimodal methodologies, sought to investigate the girls' perceptions of participation in local literacy practices, and to promote dialogue on literacy, gender, and development. What the authors found was that the girls' visual images provided insight into their imagined communities, which were associated with command of English and access to education.

Differences vis-à-vis Other Approaches

In common with most of the other alternative approaches to SLA represented in this volume, a focus on identity developed as a response to the largely asocial character of SLA theory, with its exclusive attention on individual language learners and individual cognition, acknowledged by many SLA scholars (Atkinson, 2002; Larsen-Freeman, 2007; Ricento, 2005; Swain & Deters, 2007; Zuengler & Miller, 2006). An identity approach thus has many synergies with other approaches that foreground the profoundly social nature of language learning. In line with this, the identity approach does not in any way claim to be able to answer all the questions pertaining to SLA, nor does it claim to invalidate other approaches such as sociocultural theory, conversation analysis, sociocognitive approaches, and so on. What we do argue is that failing to consider the centrality of learners' identities, as well as issues of power and inequality in the language learning process, will produce an inadequate understanding of SLA.

What is distinctive about the identity approach in relation to mainstream, cognitivist approaches to SLA, as well as the alternatives presented in this volume, is the focus on issues of power and inequality as central to our understanding of language learning. Opportunities to speak and exposure to target language speakers, essential to language learning, are fundamentally socially structured. As Norton (1997, p. 410) argued, "speech, speakers and social relationships are inseparable." The difference between an identity approach and the others in this volume is thus largely a matter of emphasis: Social identities and power are foregrounded in understanding SLA, whether in naturalistic settings or classroom language learning settings. In this sense, the focus on identity does not attempt to bridge the gap between social and cognitive approaches, as does the sociocognitive approach (Atkinson, 2002) or chaos/complexity theory (Larsen-Freeman, 2007), but is better characterized as an unequivocally social approach to SLA.

In common with a sociocultural theory (SCT) approach (Lantolf, 2000), an identity approach views learners as historically and socially situated agents, and learning as not just the acquisition of linguistic forms but as growing participation in a community of practice. Learning in both approaches is thus seen as part of the ongoing process of identity construction. However, the SCT approach to understanding SLA is centrally concerned with individual cognitive processes, for example the learner's zone of proximal development or use of private and inner speech, rather than with social processes. The theorizing of language further differs in that an identity approach sees language as always socially situated; language can never be fully internalized because the sign is seen as always unstable and the word as always populated with the intentions and meanings of others (Bakhtin, 1981).

The identity approach shares a social view of learning as participation in communities of practice with conversation analysis (CA) (e.g., Wagner, 2004). Two main differences with a CA approach, however, are the focus on different kinds of data and the value attached to such data. An identity approach aims to include an emic understanding, which aims to access participants' own understandings of their experiences; in line with this, self-reported and reflective data are highly valued. CA focuses exclusively on naturally occurring conversation and is not necessarily concerned with issues of power. Finally, an identity approach has most in common with the language socialization approach to SLA. Much of the research discussed in this chapter could be included in reviews of a language socialization approach (e.g., Duff, 2002). However, power may not always be foregrounded in a language socialization approach (e.g. Swain & Deters, 2007; Watson-Gegeo, 2004), and Duff has pointed out that "language socialisation models tend to imply that the appropriation of target culture norms and practices is *always* desirable, virtuous, inevitable and complete" (p. 291). Duff's own research, carried out within a language socialization framework, does however foreground issues of power and shows how appropriation of target culture norms is an uneven process that may well be strategically resisted.

Future Directions

With regard to future directions in research focused on identity and power in SLA, there is scope for expanding the methodological tools used. First, Wagner (2004) and Block (2007a) have recently commented on the potential of the analysis of naturally occurring interaction to enrich research in the area of identity in SLA, particularly in exploring the negotiation of participation. As Wagner argued, "the understanding of learning as empowerment of social participation can recruit strong empirical support in a CA-based analysis of second language talk" (p. 614). While there are several identity-focused analyses of L2 classroom talk (e.g. Duff, 2002; Makoe & McKinney, 2009; Pomerantz, 2008; Talmy, 2008; Toohey, 2000), analyses of talk outside of the classroom are less common.

Second, much emerging research on identity and L2 learning addresses technology as a site of language learning, and this trend will likely continue in the future. Lam (2000), for example, who studied the internet correspondence of a Chinese immigrant teenager in the United States who entered into transnational communication with a group of peers, demonstrated how this experience in what she called "textual identity" related to the student's developing identity in the use of English. In another context, White (2007) investigated innovation in distance language teaching in the Australian context, arguing that attention to issues of identity can enhance our understanding of educational innovation. The research of Kramsch and Thorne (2002) has indicated, however, that not all transnational internet communication leads to positive identity outcomes. In their study of the synchronous and asynchronous communication between American learners of French in the United States and French learners of English in France, they found that students had little understanding of the larger cultural framework within which each party was operating, leading to problematic digital exchanges. Further, as scholars such as Andema (2009), Snyder and Prinsloo (2007), and Warschauer (2003) have noted, much of the digital research on language learning has focused on research in wealthier regions of the world, and there is a great need for research in poorly resourced communities to impact global debates on new technologies, identity, and language learning.

Third, we would argue that an understanding of SLA processes focused on identity would be greatly enriched by research conducted in postcolonial sites where multilingualism is the norm and language acquisition processes can be quite different from immigrant language learning experiences in the north or study abroad contexts. In an article that challenges monolingualist assumptions underlying much of SLA theory, Canagarajah (2007, p. 935) argued that "insights from non-Western communities should inform the current efforts for alternate theory building in our field." In such multilingual contexts it is unlikely that the term SLA itself is appropriate. As Block (2003, p. 5) has noted, the term "second" doesn't capture the "experiences of multilinguals who have had contact with three or more languages in their lifetimes." Recently scholars have called for the field of language education to decolonize English language teaching in particular, and to restore agency and professionalism in periphery communities (Canagarajah, 2002, 2005, 2007; Higgins, 2009; Kumaravadivelu, 2003; Morgan & Ramanathan, 2005; Tembe & Norton, 2008).

To take but one area of focus, postcolonial multilingual contexts have much to contribute to our thinking on processes of identity and language learning (e.g. Makubalo, 2007; McKinney, 2007; Nongogo, 2007). McKinney's study of the language practices of black South African students attending previously white high schools showed the complex self- and other-positioning of black youth in relation to different "brands" of English as well as to the use of local African languages. In a country with 11 official languages, but where English is the language of power, one learner referred to the prestige variety of English as "Louis Vuitton English," illustrating the idea of English as a commodity (p. 14). Despite the accusations aimed at these black students who are acquiring a prestige variety of English that they are becoming white, or the use of derogatory labels such as "coconuts," such students resist these identities and show their awareness of the different kinds of cultural capital carried by varieties of English and local languages. They are clearly appropriating English for their own uses rather than identifying with white L1 speakers of English in their language acquisition processes.

Fourth, the relationship between language, identity, and resistance will become increasingly important in SLA research. In exploring what he called the subversive identities of language learners, Canagarajah (2004) addressed the intriguing question of how language learners can maintain membership in their vernacular communities and cultures while still learning a second language or dialect. He drew on his research with two very different groups, one in the United States and the other in Sri Lanka, to argue that language learners are sometimes ambivalent about the learning of a second language or dialect, and that they may resort to clandestine literacy practices to create "pedagogical safe houses" in the language classroom. In both contexts, the clandestine literacy activities of the students are seen to be forms of resistance to unfavorable identities imposed on the learners. At the same time, however, these safe houses serve as sites of identity construction, allowing students to negotiate the often contradictory tensions they encounter as members of diverse communities.

In sum, we have drawn on a burgeoning body of research to argue that identity is always in process, and that learners often have differential investments in the language practices of their classrooms and communities. Further, we have made the case that the imagined identities and imagined communities of learners are central in the struggle for legitimacy. As language learners in every region of the world claim the right to speak, their identities and investments are now firmly on the SLA agenda.

References

Andema, S. (2009). *Digital literacy and teacher education in East Africa: The case of Bondo Primary Teachers' College, Uganda.* Unpublished master's thesis, University of British Columbia.

Anderson, B. (1991). *Imagined communities: Reflections on the origin and spread of nationalism* (Rev. ed.). New York: Verso.

Atkinson, D. (2002). Toward a sociocognitive approach to second language acquisition. *Modern Language Journal, 86*(4), 525–545.

Bakhtin, M. (1981). *The dialogic imagination: Four essays by M.M. Bakhtin.* Austin, TX: University of Texas Press.

Bakhtin, M. (1984). *Problems of Dostoevsky's poetics* (C. Emerson, Trans.). Minneapolis, MN: University of Minnesota Press.

Barkhuizen, G. (2008). A narrative approach to exploring context in language teaching. *English Language Teaching Journal, 62*(3), 231–239.

Bhabha, H. K. (1994). *The location of culture.* London & New York: Routledge.

Blackledge, A., & Creese, A. (2010). *Multilingualism: A critical perspective.* London & New York: Continuum.

Block, D. (2003). *The social turn in second language acquisition.* Edinburgh: Edinburgh University Press.

Block, D. (2006). *Multilingual identities in a global city: London stories.* London: Palgrave.

Block, D. (2007a). The rise of identity in SLA research, post Firth and Wagner (1997). *Modern Language Journal, 91*(5), 863–876.

Block, D. (2007b). *Second language identities.* London & New York: Continuum.

Botha, E. K. (2009). 'Them and us': Constructions of identity in the life history of a trilingual white South African. *African Identities, 7*(4), 463–476.

Bourdieu, P (1977). The economics of linguistic exchanges. *Social Science Information, 16*(6), 645–668.

Bourdieu, P. (1984). *Distinction: A social critique of the judgment of taste* (R. Nice, Trans.). London: Routledge & Kegan Paul.

Bourdieu, P., & Passeron, J. (1977). *Reproduction in education, society, and culture.* London & Beverly Hills, CA: Sage Publications.

Canagarajah, A. S. (2002). Globalisation, methods, and practice in periphery classrooms. In D. Block & D. Cameron (Eds.), *Globalisation and language teaching* (pp. 134–150). London & New York: Routledge.

Canagarajah, A. S. (2004). Subversive identities, pedagogical safe houses, and critical learning. In B. Norton & K. Toohey (Eds.), *Critical pedagogies and language learning* (pp. 116–137). New York: Cambridge University Press.

Canagarajah, A. S. (2005). Reconstructing local knowledge, reconfiguring language studies. In A. S. Canagarajah (Ed.), *Reclaiming the local in language policy and practice* (pp. 3–22). Mahwah, NJ: Erlbaum.

Canagarajah, A. S. (2007). Lingua franca English, multilingual communities, and language acquisition. *Modern Language Journal, 91*(focus issue), 923–939.

Carroll, S., Motha, S., & Price, J. (2008). Accessing imagined communities and reinscribing regimes of truth. *Critical Inquiry in Language Studies, 5*(3), 165–191.

Clarke, M. (2008). *Language teacher identities: Co-constructing discourse and community.* Clevedon: Multilingual Matters.

Crookes, G., & Schmidt, R. (1991). Motivation: Reopening the research agenda. *Language Learning, 41*(4), 469–512.

Cummins, J. (2000). *Language, power and pedagogy: Bilingual children in the crossfire.* Clevedon: Multilingual Matters.

Cummins, J. (2006). Identity texts: The imaginative construction of self through multiliteracies pedagogy. In O. Garcia, T. Skutnabb-Kangas, & M. Torres-Guzman (Eds.), *Imagining multilingual schools: Language in education and glocalization* (pp. 51–68). Clevedon: Multilingual Matters.

Dagenais, D. (2003). Accessing imagined communities through multilingualism and immersion education. *Journal of Language, Identity, and Education, 2*(4), 269–283.

Dagenais, D., Moore, D., Lamarre, S., Sabatier, C., & Armand, F. (2008). Linguistic landscape and language awareness. In E. Shohamy & D. Gorter (Eds.), *Linguistic landscape: Expanding the scenery* (pp. 253–269). New York & London: Routledge.

Davis, K. (1995). Qualitative theory and methods in applied linguistic research. *TESOL Quarterly, 29*(3), 427–454.

Davis, K., & Skilton-Sylvester, E. (Eds.). (2004). Gender in TESOL [Special issue]. *TESOL Quarterly, 38*(3).

Day, E. M. (2002). *Identity and the young English language learner.* Clevedon: Multilingual Matters.

Derrida, J. (1980). *Writing and difference.* Chicago, IL: University of Chicago Press.

Dörnyei, Z. (1994). Motivation and motivating in the foreign language classroom. *Modern Language Journal, 78*(3), 273–284.

Dörnyei, Z. (1997). Psychological processes in cooperative language learning: Group dynamics and motivation. *Modern Language Journal, 81*(4), 482–493.

Duff, P. A. (2002). The discursive co-construction of knowledge, identity, and difference: An ethnography of communication in the high school mainstream. *Applied Linguistics, 23*(3), 289–322.

Fairclough, N. (1989). *Language and power.* London: Longman.

Foucault, M. (1980). *Power/Knowledge: Selected interviews and other writings 1972–1977* (C. Gordon, Trans.). New York: Pantheon Books.

Fuss, D. (1989). *Essentially speaking: Feminism, nature and difference.* New York & London: Routledge.

Gardner, R. C., & Lambert, W. E. (1972). *Attitudes and motivation in second language learning.* Rowley, MA: Newbury House.

Goldstein, T. (1996). *Two languages at work: Bilingual life on the production floor.* Berlin & New York: Mouton de Gruyter.

Hall, S. (1992a). The question of cultural identity. In S. Hall, D. Held, & T. McGrew (Eds.), *Modernity and its futures* (pp. 274–325). Cambridge: Polity Press in association with Blackwell Publishers and The Open University.

Hall, S. (1992b). New ethnicities. In J. Donald & A. Rattansi (Eds.), *'Race', culture and difference* (pp. 252–259). London: Sage.

Haneda, M. (2005). Investing in foreign language writing: A study of two multicultural learners. *Journal of Language, Identity & Education, 4*(4), 269–290.

Heller, M. (2007). *Linguistic minorities and modernity: A sociolinguistic ethnography* (2nd ed.). London: Continuum.

Higgins, C. (2009). *English as a local language: Post-colonial identities and multilingual practices.* Bristol: Multilingual Matters.

Ibrahim, A. E. K. M. (1999). Becoming Black: Rap and hip-hop, race, gender, identity, and the politics of ESL learning. *TESOL Quarterly, 33*(3), 349–369.

Janks, H. (2010). *Literacy and power.* New York & London: Routledge.

Kanno, Y. (2003). *Negotiating bilingual and bicultural identities: Japanese returnees betwixt two worlds.* Mahwah, NJ: Erlbaum.

Kanno, Y. (2008). *Language and education in Japan: Unequal access to bilingualism.* Basingstoke: Palgrave Macmillan.

Kanno, Y., & Norton, B. (Eds.) (2003). Imagined communities and educational possibilities [Special issue]. *Journal of Language, Identity and Education, 2*(4).

Kendrick, M., & Jones, S. (2008). Girls' visual representations of literacy in a rural Ugandan community. *Canadian Journal of Education, 31*(3), 372–404.

King, B. (2008). "Being gay guy, that is the advantage": Queer Korean language learning and identity construction. *Journal of Language, Identity, & Education, 7*(3–4), 230–252.

Kramsch, C. (2010). *The multilingual subject*. Oxford: Oxford University Press.

Kramsch, C., & Thorne, S. (2002). Foreign language learning as global communicative practice. In D. Block & D. Cameron (Eds.), *Globalization and language teaching* (pp. 83–100). London: Routledge.

Kress, G. (1989). *Linguistic processes in sociocultural practice*. Oxford: Oxford University Press.

Kubota, R., & Lin, A. (2006). Race and TESOL: Introduction to concepts and theories [Special issue]. *TESOL Quarterly, 40*(3).

Kubota, R., & Lin, A. (2009) *Race, culture, and identities in second language education: Exploring critically engaged practice*. London & New York: Routledge.

Kumaravadivelu, B. (2003). *Beyond methods: Macrostrategies for language learning*. New Haven, CT: Yale University Press.

Lam, W. S. E. (2000). L2 literacy and the design of the self: A case study of a teenager writing on the internet. *TESOL Quarterly, 34*(3), 457–482.

Lantolf, J. P. (Ed.). (2000). *Sociocultural theory and second language learning*. Oxford: Oxford University Press.

Larsen-Freeman, D. (2007). Reflecting on the cognitive-social debate in second language acquisition [Focus issue]. *Modern Language Journal, 91*, 773–787.

Lave, J., & Wenger, E. (1991). *Situated learning: Legitimate peripheral participation*. Cambridge: Cambridge University Press.

Leung, C., Harris, R., & Rampton, B. (2004). Living with inelegance in qualitative research on task-based learning. In B. Norton & K. Toohey (Eds.), *Critical pedagogies and language learning* (pp. 242–267). New York: Cambridge University Press.

Lin, A. (Ed). (2007) *Problematizing identity: Everyday struggles in language, culture, and education*. Mahwah, NJ: Erlbaum.

Luke, A. (2004). Two takes on the critical. In B. Norton & K. Toohey (Eds.), *Critical pedagogies and language learning* (pp. 21–29). Cambridge: Cambridge University Press.

Makoe, P., & McKinney, C. (2009). Hybrid discursive practices in a South African multilingual primary classroom: A case study. *English Teaching: Practice and Critique, 8*(2), 80–95. Retrieved June 6, 2010, from http://education.waikato.ac.nz/research/journal/index.php?id=1.

Makubalo, G. (2007). "I don't know . . . it contradicts": Identity construction and the use of English by learners in a desegregated school space. *English Academy Review, 24*(2), 25–41.

McKay, S., & Wong, S. C. (1996). Multiple discourses, multiple identities: Investment and agency in second language learning among Chinese adolescent immigrant students. *Harvard Educational Review, 66*(3), 577–608.

McKinney, C. (2007). "If I speak English does it make me less black anyway?" "Race" and English in South African desegregated schools. *English Academy Review, 24*(2), 6–24.

McKinney, C., & Norton, B. (2008). Identity in language and literacy education. In B. Spolsky & F. Hult (Eds.), *The handbook of educational linguistics* (pp. 192–205). Malden, MA: Blackwell.

Menard-Warwick, J. (2005). Both a fiction and an existential fact: Theorizing identity in second language acquisition and literacy studies. *Linguistics & Education, 16* (3), 253–274.

Miller, J. (2003). *Audible difference: ESL and social identity in schools*. Clevedon: Multilingual Matters.

Morgan, B., & Ramanathan, V. (2005). Critical literacies and language education: Global and local perspectives. *Annual Review of Applied Linguistics, 25*, 151–169.

Nelson, C. (2009). *Sexual identities in English language education: Classroom conversations*. New York: Routledge.

Nongogo, N. (2007) *"Mina 'ngumZulu phaqa"* Language and identity among multilingual Grade 9 learners at a private desegregated high school in South Africa. *English Academy Review, 24*(2), 42–54.

Norton, B. (1997). Language, identity and the ownership of English. *TESOL Quarterly, 31*(3), 409–429.

Norton, B. (2000). *Identity and language learning: Gender, ethnicity and educational change.* Harlow: Pearson Education.

Norton, B. (2001). Non-participation, imagined communities and the language classroom. In M. Breen (Ed.), *Learner contributions to language learning: New directions in research* (pp. 159–171). Harlow: Pearson Education.

Norton, B., & Early, M. (in press). Researcher identity, narrative inquiry, and language teacher education. *TESOL Quarterly, 45.*

Norton, B., & Gao, Y. (2008). Identity, investment, and Chinese learners of English. *Journal of Asian Pacific Communication, 18*(1), 109–120.

Norton, B., & Pavlenko, A. (2004). *Gender and English language learners.* Alexandria, VA: Teachers of English to Speakers of Other Languages.

Norton, B., & Toohey, K. (2001). Changing perspectives on good language learners. *TESOL Quarterly, 35*(2), 307–322.

Norton, B., & Toohey, K. (Eds.). (2004). *Critical pedagogies and language learning.* New York: Cambridge University Press.

Norton Peirce, B. (1995). Social identity, investment, and language learning. *TESOL Quarterly, 29*(1), 9–31.

Oxford, R., & Shearin, J. (1994). Language learning motivation: Expanding the theoretical framework. *Modern Language Journal, 78*(1), 12–28.

Pavlenko, A. (2001a). Language learning memoirs as gendered genre. *Applied Linguistics, 22* (2), 213–240.

Pavlenko, A. (2001b). "How am I to become a woman in an American vein?": Transformations of gender performance in second language learning. In A. Pavlenko, A. Blackledge, I. Piller, & M.Teutsch-Dwyer (Eds.), *Multilingualism, second language learning, and gender* (pp. 133–174). New York: Mouton de Gruyter.

Pavlenko, A. (2004) "The Making of an American": Negotiation of identities at the turn of the twentieth century. In A. Pavlenko & A. Blackledge (Eds.), *Negotiation of identities in multilingual contexts* (pp. 34–67). Clevedon: Multilingual Matters.

Pavlenko, A., & Blackledge, A. (Eds.) (2004). *Negotiation of identities in multilingual contexts.* Clevedon: Multilingual Matters

Pavlenko, A., & Norton, B. (2007). Imagined communities, identity, and English language teaching. In J. Cummins & C. Davison (Eds.), *International handbook of English language teaching* (pp. 669–680). New York: Springer.

Pennycook, A. (2007). *Global Englishes and transcultural flows.* London & New York: Routledge.

Pittaway, D. (2004). Investment and second language acquisition. *Critical Inquiry in Language Studies, 4*(1), 203–218.

Pomerantz, A (2008). "*Tú necisitas preguntar en Español*": Negotiating good language learner identity in a Spanish classroom. *Journal of Language, Identity, & Education, 7*(3/4), 253–271.

Potowski, K. (2007). *Language and identity in a dual immersion school.* Clevedon: Multilingual Matters.

Ramanathan, V. (2005). *The English–vernacular divide: Postcolonial language politics and practice.* Clevedon: Multilingual Matters.

Ricento, T. (2005). Considerations of identity in L2 learning. In E. Hinkel (Ed.), *Handbook of research on second language teaching and learning* (pp. 895–911). Mahwah, NJ: Erlbaum.

Saussure, F. de (1966). *Course in general linguistics.* New York: McGraw-Hill.

Sharkey, J., & Johnson, K. (Eds). (2003). *The TESOL Quarterly dialogues: Rethinking issues of language, culture, and power.* Alexandria, VA: Teachers of English to Speakers of Other Languages.

Skilton-Sylvester, E. (2002). Should I stay or should I go? Investigating Cambodian women's participation and investment in adult ESL programs. *Adult Education Quarterly, 53*(1), 9–26.

Snyder, I., & Prinsloo, M. (Eds.) (2007). The digital literacy practices of young people in marginal contexts [Special issue]. *Language & Education: An International Journal, 21*(3).

Spolsky, B. (1989). *Conditions for second language learning.* Oxford: Oxford University Press.

Swain, M., & Deters, P. (2007). "New" mainstream SLA theory: Expanded and enriched [Focus issue]. *Modern Language Journal, 91*, 820–836.

Talmy, S. (2008). The cultural productions of the ESL student at Tradewinds High: Contingency, multidirectionality, and identity in L2 socialization. *Applied Linguistics, 29*(4), 619–644.

Tembe, J., & Norton, B. (2008). Promoting local languages in Ugandan primary schools: The community as stakeholder. *Canadian Modern Language Review, 65*(1), 33–60.

Toohey, K. (2000). *Learning English at school: Identity, social relations and classroom practice.* Clevedon: Multilingual Matters.

Toohey, K. (2001). Disputes in child L2 learning. *TESOL Quarterly, 35*(2), 257–278.

Toohey, K., & Waterstone, B. (2004). Negotiating expertise in an action research community. In B. Norton & K. Toohey (Eds.), *Critical pedagogies and language learning* (pp. 291–310). Cambridge: Cambridge University Press.

Tsui, A., & Tollefson, J. (Eds). (2007). *Language policy, culture, and identity in Asian contexts.* Mahwah, NJ: Erlbaum.

Wagner, J. (2004). The classroom and beyond. *Modern Language Journal, 88*(4), 612–616.

Warschauer, M. (2003). *Technology and social inclusion: Rethinking the digital divide.* Boston, MA: MIT Press.

Watson-Gegeo, K. A. (2004). Mind, language, and epistemology: Toward a language socialization paradigm for SLA. *Modern Language Journal, 88*(3), 331–350.

Weedon, C. (1987/1997). *Feminist practice and poststructuralist theory* (2nd ed.). London: Blackwell.

Wenger, E. (1998). *Communities of practice: Learning, meaning, and identity.* Cambridge: Cambridge University Press.

White, C. (2007). Innovation and identity in distance language learning and teaching. *Innovation in Language Learning and Teaching, 1*(1), 97–110.

Yon, D. A. (1999). Interview with Stuart Hall, London, August 1998, *Journal of Curriculum Theorising, 15*(4), 89–99.

Zuengler, J., & Miller, E. R. (2006). Cognitive and sociocultural perspectives: Two parallel SLA worlds? *TESOL Quarterly, 40*(1), 35–58.

4

LANGUAGE SOCIALIZATION APPROACHES TO SECOND LANGUAGE ACQUISITION

Social, cultural, and linguistic development in additional languages

Patricia A. Duff and Steven Talmy

Overview

Language socialization represents a broad framework for understanding the development of linguistic, cultural, and communicative competence through interaction with others who are more knowledgeable or proficient. As a branch of linguistic anthropology, it is often described as a theoretical and methodological approach, or "paradigm" (e.g., Ochs & Schieffelin, 2008; Watson-Gegeo, 2004). Based on early theorizing by Hymes (1972), Halliday (1980/2003), Vygotsky (1978), Heath (1983), Schieffelin and Ochs (1986a), and others, language socialization examines macro- and micro-contexts in which language is learned and used, and employs longitudinal research designs that feature ethnography and linguistic/discourse analytic methods.[1]

A primary aim of much cognitivist second language acquisition (SLA) research is to provide descriptions of and explanations for linguistic development, for example the acquisition of L2 morphosyntax, phonology, lexis, and pragmatic phenomena such as speech acts. There is naturally an attendant concern with cognition, particularly in terms of the internalization, integration, storage, retrieval, and use of linguistic knowledge. In contrast, language socialization research seeks to account for and explain learning in much broader terms, examining not only linguistic development, but also *the other forms of knowledge* that are learned in and through language. These other forms of knowledge include *culture*, for example stances of morality or respect that are learned along with the linguistic forms that mark them. They include *social knowledge* as well, such as how certain types of language practices produce and reflect social stratification, hierarchy, and status marking. Language socialization research also examines *ideologies* (e.g., of the world, of nationality, of language itself); *epistemologies* (reflecting sources of knowledge, degrees of certainty, evidentiality); gendered and other *identities and subjectivities* (e.g., "nonnative speakers"); and *affect* (e.g., the expression of positive or negative emotions such as pleasure or shame), to name a few commonly studied dimensions. Furthermore, because of language socialization's origins in the study of children's social, cultural, and first language (L1) development through interaction, much language socialization research looks not at discrete linguistic items at the level of lexis and morphology, but at interactional or sociolinguistic *routines* that become part of language learners' and users' communicative repertoires. In other words, the learning object, or "language," is fundamentally redefined from a language socialization perspective: In contrast to a restricted and decontextualized view of language as a neutral transmitter of information made up of morphemes, syntactic structures, lexis, and pragmatic norms, language socialization conceives of language as one of a multitude of in-flux, contested, and ever-changing *social practices* that in part constitute particular dynamic communities of practice. Language socialization also differs from cognitivist SLA in its focus on the local social, political, and cultural contexts in which language is learned and used, on historical aspects of language and culture learning, on contestation and change across timescales, and on the cultural content of linguistic structures and practices.

Like other alternative approaches to SLA, L2 socialization, as it has entered its "second wave" (Bronson & Watson-Gegeo, 2008) of scholarship, is now garnering greater attention, acceptance, and visibility than ever before. Evidence of this development can be found in recent comprehensive volumes on SLA in which L2 socialization is discussed (e.g., Ellis, 2009; Mitchell & Myles, 2004; Ortega, 2009); in the addition of a new volume on language socialization to the *Encyclopedia of Language and Education* (Duff & Hornberger, 2008); in the multitude of handbooks and related reference works on language acquisition that have appeared in recent years (e.g., Watson-Gegeo & Nielsen, 2003); in articles in mainstream journals directly relevant to language learning and education (e.g., *Applied Linguistics; Journal of Pragmatics; Linguistics and Education; TESOL Quarterly*); and in a recent volume on sociocognitive approaches to second language learning and use (Batstone, 2010).

With some important differences (see below), L2 socialization shares many underlying principles with other socially oriented theories, models, or accounts of SLA, including several discussed in this volume. Commonalities include a commitment to a deeply ecological perspective of learning-in-context (Kramsch & Steffensen, 2008), and a concomitant analysis of learning through praxis—that is, through observation, participation, and performance—in the everyday activities of communities of language users (Bourdieu, 1991). L2 socialization also shares important theoretical linkages with other alternative approaches to SLA, including neo-Vygotskian sociocultural theory (Duff, 2007; Ochs, 1996), ethnomethodology (Garrett & Baquedano-López, 2002; Schieffelin & Ochs, 1986a), and systemic functional linguistics (see, e.g., Bernstein, 1972; Williams, 2008). Additionally, there is acknowledgment that L2 learning is mediated not only by social agents but also by other affordances of the learning setting, such as modality (oral, written, visual, electronic) and additional semiotic resources, including physical artifacts, other people, and language itself. As well, L2 socialization views language learners/users as sociohistorically, socioculturally, and sociopolitically situated individuals with multiple subjectivities and identities (e.g., not only as *language learners*), which are inculcated, enacted, and co-constructed through social experience in everyday life.

Theoretical Principles

Language socialization has its theoretical roots in a variety of disciplines that are drawn on to different degrees by scholars doing L2 or multilingual socialization research: linguistic anthropology (Duranti, Ochs, & Schieffelin, in press; Hymes, 1972; Schieffelin & Ochs, 1986a), sociology (e.g., Bernstein, 1972; Bourdieu, 1977; Giddens, 1979, 1984), cultural psychology (Lave & Wenger, 1991; Rogoff, 1995, 2003), cultural-historical psychology/sociocultural theory and activity theory (Engestrom, 1999; Leontiev, 1981;Vygotsky, 1978), systemic functional linguistics (e.g., Halliday, 1980/2003), semiotics (e.g., Hanks, 1992), literary theory (e.g., Bahktin, 1981) and, more recently, discursive psychology (e.g., positioning theory; Bamberg, 2000; Korobov & Bamberg, 2004).[2] Recent work drawing on poststructuralist theories focuses especially on subjectivity in language learning and use, and the emergence of a sense of self through socialization (e.g., Garrett, 2007).

In contrast to L1 socialization, L2 socialization addresses the manifold complexities of children or adults with already developed repertoires of linguistic, discursive, and cultural practices as they encounter new ones. Thus, the interactions between prior and current learning go well beyond those described traditionally in SLA as "cross-linguistic influence" or "transfer" (Duff, in press-a). Learners in L2 socialization, like those undergoing L1 socialization, may be in home, school, peer group, university, or workplace contexts.

Language socialization researchers have typically acknowledged some degree of agency, contingency, unpredictability, and multidirectionality in terms of learners and their language learning trajectories—that is, learners are *agents* who may contest or transform as well as accommodate practices others attempt to induct them into (e.g., Duff, 2002; Kulick & Schieffelin, 2004; Talmy, 2008). Furthermore, learners socialize caregivers, teachers, and other "experts" into *their* identities and practices. A great deal of L1 socialization research has nonetheless focused on socialization as a powerful process whereby newcomers or novices accommodate, apprentice to, and resist linguistic and cultural norms they are exposed to. Yet, for a variety of reasons, some L2 learners do not experience the same degrees of access or acceptance within their new discourse communities as their L1 counterparts do. Despite their desire in many cases to be apprenticed into the practices of new L2 communities, they may face opposition from others (see Norton, 2000; Norton & McKinney, this volume). Or they may be embraced by new communities but themselves not be fully invested in learning particular community ways because their future goals may not require it, or because they remain actively committed to competing social networks. They may want to retain an identity that is distinct from a particular (e.g., target language) community (e.g., Bronson & Watson-Gegeo, 2008), or for practical reasons they may be unwilling to straddle both (and perhaps other) community expectations and learning/performance demands simultaneously. Furthermore, they may feel conflicted about becoming fuller members in certain new L2-mediated social worlds.

To summarize, from a (second) language socialization perspective, social interaction with more proficient members of a particular community centrally mediates the development of both communicative competence *and* knowledge of the values, practices, identities, ideologies and stances of that community. However, these more proficient interlocutors are also socialized by novices/newcomers into their expert/old-timer roles, identities, and subjectivities, they learn from novices/newcomers their specific and perhaps unique communicative needs, and they also learn from these learners' own perspectives and prior experiences. Thus, socialization is bidirectional (or multidirectional) and can lead to the internalization and reproduction of existing L2 cultural and communicative practices. However, because socialization involves myriad complexities concerning relations of power, access, identity, and sociopolitical and sociohistorical constraints, it is a necessarily contingent process, and can thus lead to unanticipated outcomes, such as the development of hybrid practices, identities, and values, the incomplete or partial appropriation of the L2, or a lower-than-desired status within the L2 community. Finally, because language learning and socialization are lifelong processes in which new ways of acting, communicating, and thinking require new discursive practices, longitudinal perspectives are important for better understanding learner trajectories.

Research Methods

In language socialization, studies are typically ethnographic, providing a broad description of the cultures, communities, classrooms, and other dynamic social settings in which language is learned and used, based on persistent engagement in and extensive observation of the context (Bronson & Watson-Gegeo, 2008; Duff, 1995, 2002; Garrett, 2008; Kulick & Schieffelin, 2004; Schieffelin & Ochs, 1996). Ethnographic research involves understanding the cultural patterns and values of groups in their local contexts. For example, Duff (1995, 1996) video-recorded dual-language English/Hungarian classrooms over two years in three schools in different parts of post-1989 Hungary. She examined the changing dynamics of oral classroom discourse as it connected with the introduction of English as a medium of instruction and emerging notions of democratization. Specifically, she demonstrated how the quest for democratization outside of schools was paralleled in classrooms, for example in the abandonment of a cornerstone of Hungarian education and assessment—daily classroom recitations called *felelés*—which were being replaced by new forms of discourse, interaction, and assessment. The study exemplifies the effort that is common in language socialization research to bring together both macro- and microanalysis, that is, how processes that are evident in a wider sociocultural context (e.g., democratization in post-1989 Hungary) are realized in particular local circumstances (e.g., a shift to new forms of assessment). The study also looked at language acquisition: how teachers and students corrected one another as part of the negotiation and internalization of correct English forms and as a way of showcasing their (emerging) identities as proficient English speakers or bilingual Hungarians.

True to its ethnographic orientation, data sources in language socialization research, as illustrated by Duff's (1995, 1996) study, typically include some combination of the following:

- fieldnotes generated from some form of participant observation;
- site artifacts such as relevant policy documents, books, magazines, and other print-text materials; multimodal texts including photographs, pictures, and artwork; and participant-generated texts such as classwork, writing assignments, drawings, among much else;
- interviews, ranging from one-on-one semi-structured or unstructured formats, to focus groups, to retrospective "stimulated recall" sessions, to email and other forms of computer-mediated communication;
- audio- and/or video-recordings of socializing interactions from the particular speech event, activity, interaction type, or other language/social practice under investigation.

Typically, data are subjected to intensive, iterative analysis of the linguistic and other social and cultural practices being investigated, with a focus on the contextual dimensions within which these practices occur, as well as close analysis of the changes in and development (if any) of participants' competencies over time.

Ordinarily, a longitudinal presence on site or engagement with the community ensures that the research will involve regular observations by researchers over an extended period. One reason for this sort of prolonged engagement with the community is to understand recurring cultural and linguistic patterns of interaction that constitute processes of socialization. For example, Talmy's (2008, 2009) 2.5-year critical ethnography in a Hawai'i high school described several social practices that constituted an old-timer "Local ESL" community of practice in the school's ESL program. He showed how student participation in these practices worked on the one hand to socialize newcomer ESL students into negative language ideologies constituting the "stigma" associated with ESL, and, on the other, to apprentice three novice ESL teachers into an infantilizing ESL pedagogical practice.

A focal social practice, speech event, or activity may be selected so comparisons can be made over time. Within this activity, particular interactional routines (e.g., greetings), linguistic elements (e.g., sentence-final particles in Japanese), or turn-taking behaviors may be examined. Morita (2000), for example, studied the socialization of international and domestic graduate students into an academic community, specifically as they participated in the speech event of the oral academic presentation in their classes. Vickers (2007), too, examined a single speech event—the "team meeting"—in her study of nonnative English-speaking students' socialization into the practices of a group of student engineers. These researchers then engaged in discourse analyses of data concerning the speech event under consideration. Common approaches for such discourse analyses in language socialization include systemic-functional grammar, conversation analysis, interactional sociolinguistics, or positioning analysis. Coding, counting, or content analysis may be undertaken, or the analysis may be completely qualitative.

Language socialization research often pays more attention to the interactional and linguistic *processes* of socialization in real interactional time than to the systematic study of *outcomes*. Indeed, since language socialization is a complex, lifelong process, no single study can be sufficiently longitudinal to capture the ebb and flow of socialization and its many milestones over a lifetime. In shorter-term studies, the process of language education and enculturation often supersedes detailed analyses and evidence of linguistic, affective, and other (e.g., cognitive) outcomes of language socialization. That is because language socialization underscores the values being inculcated, the challenges facing learners and agents of socialization, and (although less so) the degree of success in learning such practices. This characteristic of L2 socialization may be a by-product of L1 socialization studies in which the eventual attainment of target practices was often taken for granted.

However, some L2 socialization studies focus less on the particular activity settings and more on the sociolinguistic dispositions and forms to be mastered, such as those entailed in showing respect to one's elders (Howard, 2008) or politeness and empathy (Cook, 2008a, 2008b). As in much other ethnographic research, participants' own (or *emic*) perspectives on socialization processes are often generated with researchers through interviews, if interviewees have the ability to engage in metalinguistic reflections. Exceptions to typical instances of socialization toward desired goals are also important to note.

Although these methodological principles are commonly acknowledged as being hallmarks of language socialization, some concerns have been raised about the orientation of earlier (L1) studies in this tradition. Articulated most clearly by scholars of L2 socialization (e.g., Bayley & Schecter, 2003a; Duff, 2003; He, 2003a, 2003b; Schecter & Bayley, 2004), the concerns include a prevailing focus on socializing processes that take place in comparatively homogeneous, monolingual contexts; on the socialization of young children by parents and caregivers; on successful cases of language socialization; and on socialization through face-to-face interaction. Such empirical foci have resulted, Schecter and Bayley argued, in a "more restricted . . . [and] deterministic" (p. 620) conception of language socialization, one that is "static, bounded and relatively unidirectional" (p. 605). Because of the emphasis on how experts socialize novices, He (2003b) has maintained that "the process of socialization [is] often characterized as smooth and seamless, [with] novices . . . presumed to be passive, ready, and uniform recipients of socialization" (p. 128). Consequently, the categories of "novice" and "expert" have been reified and power relations obscured, it has been argued, as have the fundamentally contested and contingent character of socializing processes, the agency of novices, and how experts themselves are socialized through participation in socializing interactions. Additional concerns include the comparative neglect of the socialization of older youth and adults, socialization in more heterogeneous, multilingual, and transnational contexts, and the multiple modalities through which language socialization can occur, including computer-mediated communication, academic discourses, and popular media. Such problematics have resulted in a call for a "dynamic model" of language socialization (Bayley & Schecter, 2003a), one which works to complicate and go beyond "the limitations of more static models of language socialization" (Schecter & Bayley, 2004, p. 611) by focusing on power, contingency, and multidirectionality in socializing processes, socialization across the lifespan, and "the complexities of language socialization in bilingual and multilingual settings" (p. 606).

The implications of these critiques are significant. First, they entail an expansion in the scope of study for language socialization research in terms of populations (from children to include youth and adults), settings (from monolingual to bi- and multilingual settings; from naturalistic home and community settings to school and workplace contexts), empirical focus (from successful socialization to cases of unsuccessful or unexpected socialization), and modality (from face-to-face interaction to multiple modalities). Second, methodologically, such critiques imply a need to broaden the range of options for conducting language socialization research, from long-term ethnographically based accounts of a community's language and other social practices, derived from analysis of observational fieldnotes, site artifacts, and audio- and/or video-recordings, to potentially shorter-term research engagements, smaller data sets, data generated primarily or even exclusively from interviews (i.e., participant reports of socialization experiences), and, thus, little or perhaps even no direct firsthand ethnographic fieldwork in the community whose practices are under investigation.

It should come as no surprise that the critiques enumerated above, and their implications for language socialization research, have themselves engendered critical response. One form of response has been to reject the underlying premises of these critiques. Garrett (2004), for example, disputed the contention that language socialization has neglected power, learner agency, bi-directionality, and socialization across the lifespan. Talmy (2008, pp. 620–621) argued that the call for a "dynamic model" of language socialization, while superficially "compelling," was in fact "unwarranted" because language socialization's analytic framework not only "allows . . . analyses to be grounded in ways unavailable to other [sociological and anthropological] models of socialization" but also provides "the means to demonstrate the fundamental contingency and multidirectionality of socialization as it is—or is not—collaboratively achieved" (p. 620).

A second form of response to the above-mentioned critiques is an apparent effort to secure the boundaries of what constitutes "genuine" language socialization research. Such an effort is evident in Baquedano-López and Kattan (2008), who distinguished two different approaches to language socialization research: (1) as a "theoretical and methodological paradigm," which holds true to principles enumerated by, for example, Schieffelin and Ochs (1986a) and Kulick and Schieffelin (2004); and (2) as a "theme of study," which includes studies in which the above critiques were raised. Bronson and Watson-Gegeo (2008), too, suggested an informal four-part taxonomy to describe the differing degrees to which language socialization research conforms to the paradigmatic principles put forth by its originators. Similar to Baquedano-López and Kattan's "theme of study," they asserted that *language socialization as topic* "is often based on relatively thin data sets, perhaps interviews and a few examples without intensive analysis of primary discourse data in a longitudinal frame" (Bronson & Watson-Gegeo, p. 48). In contrast, their *language socialization as method* is research that:

> adhere[s] to the highest standards, including full-blown longitudinal ethnographic research and discourse analyses of relevant data. Well-designed language socialization research must embody design and methods that are congruent with the theoretical and philosophical underpinnings of the tradition in order to count as genuine contributions. A high degree of transparency about the nature of the context, participants, setting, data, and analysis is essential. Methods may be eclectic . . . [However, t]o achieve what we might call a "gold standard" for design and methodological rigor . . . certain characteristics and strategies are essential.
>
> (p. 48)

On the one hand, these sorts of "intra-paradigmatic" debates attest to the theoretical and methodological development and expansion of language socialization since its original articulation by Schieffelin and Ochs (e.g., 1986a), and point to its viability as an approach to investigating the complex set of phenomena that has been glossed as "L2 learning." On the other hand, attempts to define "genuine" language socialization, calls for "gold standards," mention of a language socialization "canon" (Bronson & Watson-Gegeo, 2008, p. 48), and methodological prescriptions for conducting research may perhaps be premature and overly restrictive. Certainly, to qualify as "language socialization," research ought (ideally) to be ethnographic, document changes in language and other social practices, explain development in terms of socialization, and involve close analysis of a rich primary data record derived from participant observation, documents, and audio- and/or video-recordings, among other methods. Further, research that relies on data generated in interviews in language socialization (or any other approach to investigating SLA, either alternative or cognitivist), should have an adequately conceptualized theory of interview, that is, as a speech event into and through which interlocutors are socialized and positioned, and through which "content" is co-constructed. However, our concern with the unequivocal demarcation of paradigmatic boundaries, at least at this point in the "second wave" of language socialization's development, is that it could foreclose potentially important avenues and methods of inquiry in the future, thus delimiting investigation into the diverse, variable, and ever-changing means and social practices that novices/newcomers and experts/old-timers may be socialized through and into. Thus, in certain respects (and somewhat ironically), the debates about the need to secure language socialization's paradigmatic boundaries resemble the dispute that arose in the mid-1990s among proponents of cognitivist SLA with those of alternative approaches (see, e.g., Block, 1996; Firth & Wagner, 1997; Kasper, 1997; Long, 1997), when the former decried the proliferation of sociocultural approaches to L2 learning (including language socialization). One implication of these critiques in L2 socialization research, as a particular orientation to SLA research, is that cognitivist SLA, too, would do well to include more critical reflection on its paradigmatic assumptions, epistemology, favored approaches to research, methods of data analysis, and the claims about SLA that are generated on the basis of these.

Supporting Findings

We emphasize that the goals of cognitivist SLA and L2 socialization research overlap in important ways, but are by no means the same. Therefore, the findings that support L2 socialization research might not be considered adequate as evidence of SLA, particularly if the focus of SLA is primarily on linguistic forms. Although both L2 socialization and cognitivist SLA deal with language learning and language learners, and both ideally are concerned with learners' development and increasing participation in social life, in L2 socialization, what is learned is much more than aspects of a linguistic code (e.g., grammar). Furthermore, much SLA research looks at "learning" in the short term—over the negotiations for meaning in a single task-based interaction session, for example, or over a two-week period; there are relatively few studies of the lasting effects of instructional or interactional interventions on particular linguistic forms or functions (Lightbown & Spada, 2006). In addition, unlike cognitivist SLA research, the focus in language socialization tends to be the *group* or *community* and a set of communal practices more than the individual, though focal case study participants are frequently very helpful at illustrating language acquisition and socialization processes (Duff, 2008).

One of the criticisms of L2 socialization research from cognitivist SLA researchers—and one that is justified to some extent—is that it tends to focus more on the macro/sociological than micro/linguistic aspects of language development, even when there is fine-grained analysis of discourse. A macro perspective permits an examination of the linguistic affordances of speech events or situations and not only what is said or done at the micro level. Alternatively, the critique focuses on the privileging of personal experience—the emic perspective—over etic analysis (by the researcher) of attested language capabilities. Ellis (2009), for example, while observing that some of the most robust findings in L2 socialization research to date have been in the area of L2 pragmatics, suggested that a "narrower, more linguistic focus . . . will make language socialization theory relevant to [cognitivist] SLA" (p. 335), and that "ideally, language socialization theory needs to marry a broad scope of explanation with a narrow, linguistic focus" (p. 335). Although perhaps in the minority, detailed analyses of this sort do exist. One such example is Cook's

(2008b) longitudinal analysis of the acquisition of -*masu*/-*desu* versus unmarked verb endings by learners of L2 Japanese in Japan, which Cook contextualized within a wider cultural and sociolinguistic framework.

While Ellis's (2009) observation may have merit, the influence of broader macro-social and cultural processes should not be underestimated in either cognitivist SLA or language socialization. After all, current mainstream SLA theory holds that opportunities for appropriate input/intake, interaction, and output, plus feedback of particular types, are indispensable for SLA. Therefore, if students' access to meaningful input is blocked or if they are provided insufficient or inhospitable opportunities to interact in significant ways, their language production will also be curtailed and their learning goals (plus their sense of themselves as people whose learning is valued and supported) will likely be negatively influenced. A common consequence, studied too seldom in SLA, is attrition in language learning programs and the reasons underlying the termination of students' L2 study.

Indeed, the advantage of a longitudinal approach that permits tracking students' learning trajectories is clear. If students learn prescribed linguistic forms in the first month of their coursework but end up dropping out of their classes because they feel neglected or discriminated against (to use extreme cases), their short-term successes will have little meaning. A similar point was made by Atkinson (2003) when he described Indian students' "socialization and dys-socialization" in a South Indian college context where English was the medium of instruction. By dys-socialization, he meant that "some students appear[ed] to be developing and having reinforced social identities that militate[d] *against* the acquisition of English" (p. 148). The disadvantaged students in that context were lower caste, lower socio-economic background, first-generation male college students who did not come from English-speaking backgrounds and who had had little prior instruction in English, in contrast to their wealthier, more cosmopolitan, and more English-proficient classmates. However, the practices of the disadvantaged students—not bringing or having their English textbooks, sleeping or chatting in class, their seating position (at the back), and other forms of "resistance"—were in no way helping them acquire the valued standard English proficiency and academic skills necessary for their longer-term academic success and upward social mobility.

Talmy (2008, 2009) observed a similar phenomenon in secondary ESL classrooms in Hawai'i, with students who had been in the state for several years already but continued to be positioned as recently arrived immigrants with little competence in English. Norton (2000), too, observed that motivation and good will on the part of her immigrant language learners were not enough to ensure that they would be able to engage with English speakers in society in a manner that would facilitate further learning.

Ortega's (2009) brief overview of language socialization in her SLA textbook identified the constructs of *access* and *participation* as being at the core of language socialization studies as well as other alternative approaches (e.g., Norton, 2000; Norton & McKinney, this volume; Wenger, 1998). Ortega cited Morita's (2004) study of Japanese women studying at a Canadian university to support the notion that, if learners are positioned in disadvantageous ways and thereby silenced by their interlocutors (e.g., instructors, peers), either knowingly or unknowingly, the students' opportunities for learning, participating in classroom discourse, and feeling like they are legitimate speakers may also be stifled. Abdi (2009) reported on this phenomenon in her Canadian high school study of learners of L2 Spanish from various ethnolinguistic backgrounds, including Spanish-speaking backgrounds in Latin America. The Anglophone Spanish teacher assumed that certain students were not from Spanish-speaking homes, when in fact they were, thereby denying them—but giving others—opportunities to display their Spanish skills prominently in class and to be conferred the status of proficient Spanish speakers. Some students' opportunities for SLA were inadvertently impacted in other ways as well, based on something as seemingly mundane as the seating plan (cf. Toohey, 1998). For example, when one (heritage-language) Grade 9 student who had previously been an enthusiastic classroom participant was assigned to sit with several Grade 12 students, she was effectively silenced because her new group members positioned her as immature and not a valued peer. Her opportunities for learning and using Spanish, or for socializing others into Spanish language practices, were therefore reduced. Thus, studies of the social conditions of learning and local classroom cultures can have a great bearing on students' global possibilities for SLA, as well as their academic advancement and affective states, even if the details of, say, their L2 morphological development, question formation, or word order are not systematically tracked. If students are made to feel like outsiders and illegitimate users of a language, their prospects for longer-term language learning success are compromised (Duff, in press-b; Toohey, 1998).

Access and participation are, to be sure, key components of language socialization and optimal SLA, particularly within a community of practice perspective (Lave & Wenger, 1991). However, language socialization entails much more: It is not only concerned with the affordances of particular language learning contexts or participation frameworks, but also with the social, cultural, pragmatic, and other meanings that come bundled with language and various interactional routines and activities. Thus, the meanings conveyed by the linguistic and nonlinguistic forms that students encounter in SLA, the textbooks used, the prevailing ideologies of learning and using language, plus the identities made available to learners and whether they are taken up or contested are all important aspects of L2 socialization, and clearly extend far beyond the acquisition of linguistic forms and their meanings. The systematic "error" correction reported by Friedman (2010) in the national language classrooms she studied in Ukraine, for example, did not represent random phonological or lexical deviations from the "pure" Ukrainian sought by—and actively socialized by—the teacher; rather, the forms that got corrected were phonologically or lexically Russian in origin, though often quite similar to the corresponding Ukrainian words. However, the Russian forms betrayed colonial (Russian-dominant) ideologies of nation, based on the Russian language that teachers were trying to eradicate in the post-Soviet era. Error correction itself was therefore a significant form of language socialization, revitalization, and nation rebuilding.

A number of publications on L2 Japanese pragmatic and grammatical development (e.g., Ohta, 1994, 2001) have looked more systematically at L2 development in relation to socialization. In general, the studies demonstrate how learners of Japanese are socialized to be *empathetic* listeners and members of society, able to use linguistic resources (e.g., sentence-final particles) that display their affective engagements appropriately. Relevant studies include those in the 1999 special issue of the *Journal of Pragmatics* (Kanagy, 1999), with a set of articles on L1 and L2 socialization in Japanese, plus Cook's (2008a) review of this and related research, including her own on L2 socialization in Japanese, as well as earlier work by Siegal (1994, 1996) on Western women learning Japanese. These studies offer insights into how Japanese experts mentor novices into the language and culture, as seen in the novices' growing proficiency with various kinds of sentence particles (e.g., *ne*, *no*), tag questions (*deshoo*), and other constructions. Ohta's (1999) year-long study of multiple lessons taught by the same four teachers examined socialization into Japanese-specific "interactional style." She described how the process of acquisition (through socialization) requires that novices become more aware of the function of the target routines they are learning, then understand what resources are available to enact the routines and the social roles involved, and, finally, extend them to an ever wider range of contexts. In particular, Ohta examined the discursive and affective alignments between listeners and speakers through verbal assessments, equivalent to expressions of concern or empathy, such as *Wow, that's too bad*, especially those using the Japanese utterance-final particle *ne*. Using data from one of her participants at four points in time, Ohta illustrated how the participant, with support from the modeling of assessments by the teacher, became increasingly adept at such expressions of alignment/assessment herself. In the same special issue, Yoshimi (1999) studied *ne* and its role in creating harmony, cooperation, and rapport between speaker and listener. As a set, studies of this sort demonstrate that studying morphology without also capturing its social role in interactional contexts to index affective stances and relationships is inadequate in SLA. Furthermore, by examining interactional routines, L2 socialization goes beyond the morpheme/particle, word, phrase, or clause level and deals with pragmatics within a larger interpersonal discourse context.

In a number of studies, He (2000, 2003a, 2003b, 2004, 2008) has examined Chinese-American children's socialization into Chinese as a heritage language in the United States. Her focus has included different forms and functions of teachers' directives to students, their use of modal auxiliaries, the use of pronouns such as *women* (we/us) and *tamen* (they/them) to index in-group ("we/Chinese") versus out-group ("they/Americans") membership and identities, and the kinds of interactional roles or participation statuses that are attributed to the students by the teacher. Although He didn't track students' use of these same constructions over time, she did analyze the cultural foundations for the teachers' behaviors and sometimes the students' subversive responses. She also inferred from the classroom observations and discourse analysis that students would eventually internalize teachers' messages.

In L2 English contexts, SLA-oriented language socialization research has examined learners' development over time as well. Li (2000) observed how the requesting behaviors of the adult immigrant women participating in her study became increasingly target-like on the basis of their growing confidence and exposure to appropriate L2 forms in class and at work. In a high school context, Huang (2004) observed changes in ESL students' use of definitions, nominalization, and generic nouns over time in their science class, and Duff (1995) noted how students learned to correct one another's L2 English mistakes—and eventually to correct their teachers' mistakes as well. Finally, Kobayashi's research (e.g., 2003, 2004; Duff & Kobayashi, 2010) revealed how, in one program context, Japanese exchange students in Canada learned to socialize one another, with the assistance of modeling and preparation by their teacher, in their joint planning of oral group presentations. Kobayashi tracked students' use of their L1 (Japanese) to mediate their cognitive and linguistic planning, focusing on how they prepared their oral presentations, including helping each other to correct mistakes. He also examined some of the interactional routines and strategies used by the students, such as displaying mock gratitude to their teacher during a presentation (e.g., to make the veiled complaint: "We really appreciate [the teacher] giving us such a good opportunity [forcing us to work together]"). By following up on their performance, Kobayashi could determine whether the students repeated utterances they had carefully co-constructed days earlier and refined grammatically. These forms had not been taught by the teacher but were elicited and negotiated by the students in their group meetings. However, studies such as this one and many others on L2 socialization, apart from the Japanese studies and Li's aforementioned research, have not typically focused on the development of just one type of grammatical or pragmatic construction (e.g., a particular adjective, relative clause, morpheme, or type of request). Rather, they have looked at the development of growing grammatical and pragmatic sensitivity and performance through social interaction, negotiation, and in some cases explicit instruction and correction across a range of linguistic areas.

Differences vis-à-vis Other Alternative Approaches to SLA

The similarities that a language socialization approach to SLA shares with the other approaches presented in this volume are perhaps as important as the differences. In this section we briefly consider both similarities and differences between language socialization and conversation analysis (CA), identity and power, complexity theory, neo-Vygotskyan sociocultural theory, and sociocognitive and ecological theories of learning.

CA-SLA

CA (see Kasper & Wagner, this volume) has had substantive influences on theory and methodology in language socialization (e.g., Schieffelin & Ochs, 1986a, 1996).

Language socialization in part traces its "roots" (Garrett & Baquedano-López, 2002, p. 343) to CA's intellectual forebear, ethnomethodology, specifically the ethnomethodological interest in people's sense-making practices in everyday social life. Methodologically, CA has contributed to language socialization's powerful analytic framework, providing access to socializing processes in situ, and "to the ways in which social relations (including caregiver–child and novice–expert relations) are maintained, contested, and transformed across a variety of socializing interactions" (p. 342). That said, language socialization researchers employ CA to varying extents, and some not at all, preferring discourse analysis or the ethnography of communication instead (Duff, 2007).

Language socialization differs most substantively from CA in terms of its in-built *theory of learning*: The former has been developed specifically to document and explain (a lack of) change in and the (non)development of linguistic, cultural, and communicative competence over time. In contrast, as Kasper (2009) noted, CA's "object of study, in the broadest sense, is the interactional competencies of social members, specifically their sense-making practices and their methods to establish and maintain social order in their activities" (p. 11). It is because CA does not have its own (endogenous) theory of learning that scholars in CA-SLA have, in the past, turned to sociocultural theory (e.g., Mondada & Pekarek-Doehler, 2004), situated learning (e.g., Hellermann, 2008), and language socialization (e.g., He, 2003a, 2004) for (exogenous) theories of learning for their studies, although calls are increasing (e.g., Kasper, 2009; Markee & Seo, 2009) for a move to discursive psychology (Edwards & Potter, 1992, 2005) as a more compatible theoretical alternative for conversation-analytic studies of SLA.

Identity and Power

As described above, social identity has long been a central consideration in language socialization. The same has become true more recently in SLA based on other social approaches (see Norton & McKinney, this volume). Whereas identity studies in SLA have strong roots in poststructuralist feminist theory, the centrality of identity in language socialization can be traced more to its practice-oriented theoretical framework (e.g., Bourdieu, 1977; Giddens, 1979), its four-dimensional conceptualization of "social context" (as consisting of social identities, social acts, social activities, and affective and epistemic stances), and what Ochs (1996) called the Indexicality Principle, whereby "*indexical meanings* (e.g., temporal, spatial, social identity, social act, social activity, affective or epistemic meanings)" are assigned "to particular [linguistic] forms (e.g., interrogative forms, diminutive affixes, raised pitch, and the like)" (p. 410, italics in original). Simply put, participation in socializing interactions fundamentally implicates identity, as individuals accommodate, resist, subvert, and/or transform the acts, stances, and activities that constitute particular social identities/identity categories.

Power, too, is an inherent focus of language socialization, critiques such as those enumerated above (e.g., Bayley & Schecter, 2003a) notwithstanding. It is most clearly evident in the related concepts of *contingency*, that is, the basically unpredictable nature of socializing processes, and *multidirectionality*, or the consequences of socialization, not only on those being socialized, but on those doing the socializing (see Schieffelin & Ochs, 1986b, p. 165; see also Duff, 2002; Talmy, 2008). That is, power here is not a fixed or assured attribute of those who are older, more experienced, and so on, but can also be demonstrated by novices who contest practices or demonstrate expertise or understanding lacking in their mentors. However, power has not always been as prominently featured in language socialization research, especially in earlier "first generation" studies. As Kulick and Schieffelin argued:

> That the majority of language socialization studies have focused on [cultural and social] reproduction is a strength—they provide us with methodological and analytical tools for investigating and interpreting . . . continuity across generations. But the focus on expected and predictable outcomes is a weakness if there is not also an examination of cases in which socialization doesn't occur, or where it occurs in ways that are not expected or desired. To the extent that [language socialization] studies only document the acquisition of normatively sanctioned practices, they open themselves up to the charge that they are merely behaviorism in new clothes.
>
> (2004, p. 355)

Implicit in this comment is a recognition that power, agency, contestation, and resistance, and, by extension, the contingent and bi- or multidirectional character of socializing processes, need foregrounding in language socialization research, lest the image emerge that cultural and social reproduction is inevitable. Talmy (2008) has argued that the comparative lack of attention to these topics in especially "first generation" studies of language socialization:

> appears to come down to at least some combination of empirical focus . . . (e.g., highlighting processes involved when L1 socialization is achieved) and historical moment (i.e., establishing and elaborating the [language social-ization] paradigm) . . . rather than some problem endemic to [language socialization] itself.
>
> (pp. 622–623)

Although there is a great deal that language socialization research shares with studies that highlight identity and power in L2 learning, it also departs from them in significant ways. Once again, it is distinguished most clearly by its theory of learning. It also differs in terms of its clear methodological specifications, particularly those concerning longitudinality, an ethnographic orientation, and the detailed analysis of the language and other social practices that are the learning object in language socialization. Although these may be implied in accounts of identity in language learning, often the latter's empirical approach involves retrospection on the part of learners about their experiences in accounts generated in interviews, for example, or written in journals, with little direct, on-the-ground evidence of how identity is negotiated or the L2 learned in specific interactions, with particular interlocutors, in actual settings, as is typically the case in language socialization. Finally, most of the current work on language, identity, and power comes from sociology (with some significant earlier work coming out of the sociology of language and sociolinguistics), whereas language socialization originates from linguistic anthropology.

Complexity Theory

Complexity theory is still so new in empirical investigations of SLA that it remains unclear what its typical methodological approach or linguistic focus will be. To date, at least to us, the approach represents more a philosophical and metaphorical framework than a sustained and systematic empirical approach to tracking SLA, although the science it is based on has a firm empirical basis.

Sociocultural, Sociocognitive, and Ecological Approaches

As we pointed out earlier and elsewhere (e.g., Duff, 2007), language socialization has much in common with neo-Vygotskian sociocultural theory and related sociocognitive and ecological accounts of learning (e.g., Atkinson, this volume; Lantolf, this volume). These approaches all have a social, interactional, and cognitive orientation to language learning. They also share an appreciation for the importance of culturally organized activities (or tasks) and interactional routines as a locus for meaning-making and learning. Finally, they all acknowledge the key role played by more proficient interlocutors, peers, caregivers, or teachers in helping novices/ newcomers reach their potential by means of scaffolding or guided assistance. Learning, knowledge, and socialization—that is, the development of the human mind—are seen to be processes that are distributed across many co-participants or members in a community and that have historical antecedents.

However, language socialization differs from these approaches in important ways. These differences include the use in language socialization of anthropological methods, as well as its orientation to *enculturation*—i.e., not the accumulation of linguistic knowledge or communicative competence alone. Thus, whereas many recent social accounts of language acquisition conceive of it as the intersection of *social* and *cognitive* processes, often giving a privileged status to the linguistic forms that are acquired by learners in the context of social interaction, language socialization places a greater premium on the *social* and the *cultural* in psychological experience, including language learning. Also, much current language socialization research is distinctive in its focus on how learners can also be agents of socialization for those who are presumed to have greater expertise than they do, and that they can resist socialization or be highly selective in their own or others' socialization.

Additionally, language socialization research and theory has long been interested in both the language and literacy practices of novice or junior members of society and those of experts, as well as development across the lifespan as people encounter new forms of language and literacy use. It is only recently that SLA has become more interested in the relationship between literacy and oral language development (Tarone & Bigelow, 2009) and in the language learning of people with advanced levels of proficiency (Ortega & Byrnes, 2008). Furthermore, as mentioned earlier, L2 socialization research often looks simultaneously at the socialization of L1, L2, and multilingual learners in situations of language contact (e.g., Moore, 2008). The monolingual bias that is sometimes critiqued as part of SLA is often addressed in L2 socialization by attempts to capture the rich (often multilingual and multimodal) diversity of learners' semiotic repertoires, identities, and social engagements mediated through language.

Future Directions

If the past is any indication, the future of L2 socialization research holds tremendous promise. As the second wave of language socialization gives way to the third, we anticipate that its already impressive catalogue of research will yield even greater insights into the complex phenomenon that is typically referred to as L2 learning. In order to do so, we expect that future studies will move beyond past and current foci to include:

- more in-depth analysis of language capabilities and how they evolve over time;
- a wider range of target languages and language practices;
- greater attention to L1, L2, L3, etc. socialization in bilingual and multilingual settings;
- increased consideration of the essential unpredictability, contestedness, and fluidity of socialization, as it is or is not achieved, in ways anticipated or not;
- more investigation into the multiple and ever-changing modalities through which L2 socialization does (or does not) occur, including computer-mediated socialization through social networking sites, synchronous and asynchronous chat/texting, online gaming, and "simulated" environments such as *Second Life*;
- more sustained examination of language socialization in workplace and institutional settings in the current era of globalization, transmigration, and internationalization.

As the various alternative approaches to SLA, including language socialization, continue to evolve and perhaps cross-fertilize, SLA will be enriched by more deeply and broadly contextualized studies of contemporary linguistic and cultural development and use across time, space, and language communities. We have tried to indicate the distinctive contribution of second language socialization to this larger project here.

Notes

1 For historical overviews of language socialization, see, for example, Garrett and Baquedano-López (2002), Ochs and Schieffelin (2008), and Watson-Gegeo and Nielsen (2003).

2 See Garrett and Baquedano-López (2002) and chapters in Duff and Hornberger (2008) for more detailed discussion on theories informing language socialization.

References

Abdi, K. (2009). *Spanish heritage language learners in Canadian high school Spanish classes: Negotiating ethnolinguistic identities and ideologies.* Unpublished master's thesis, University of British Columbia.

Atkinson, D. (2003). Language socialization and dys-socialization in a South Indian college. In R. Bayley & S. Schecter (Eds.), *Language socialization in bilingual and multilingual societies* (pp. 147–162). Clevedon: Multilingual Matters.

Bakhtin, M. (1981). *The dialogic imagination: Four essays by M. M. Bakhtin* (M. E. Holquist, Ed.; C. Emerson & M. Holquist, Trans.). Austin, TX: University of Texas Press.

Bamberg, M. (2000). Critical personalism, language and development. *Theory & Psychology, 10*, 749–767.

Baquedano-López, P., & Kattan, S. (2008). Language socialization and schooling. In P. A. Duff & N. H. Hornberger (Eds.), *Encyclopedia of language and education, Vol. 8: Language socialization* (pp. 161–173). New York: Springer.

Batstone, R. (Ed.). (2010). *Sociocognitive perspectives on language use and language learning.* Oxford: Oxford University Press.

Bayley, R., & Schecter, S. R. (2003a). Introduction: Toward a dynamic model of language socialization. In R. Bayley & S. R. Schecter (Eds.), *Language socialization in bilingual and multilingual societies* (pp. 1–6). Clevedon: Multilingual Matters.

Bayley, R., & Schecter, S. R. (Eds.). (2003b). *Language socialization in bilingual and multilingual societies.* Clevedon: Multilingual Matters.

Bernstein, D. (1972). Social class, language and socialization. In P. P. Giglioli (Ed.), *Language and social context* (pp. 173–178). New York: Penguin Books.

Block, D. (1996). Not so fast: Some thoughts on theory culling, relativism, accepted findings and the heart and soul of SLA. *Applied Linguistics, 17*, 63–83.

Bourdieu, P. (1977). *Outline of a theory of practice.* Cambridge: Cambridge University Press.

Bourdieu, P. (1991). *Language and symbolic power* (G. Raymond & M. Adamson, Trans.). Cambridge, MA: Harvard University Press.

Bronson, M., & Watson-Gegeo, K. (2008). The critical moment: Language socialization and the (re)visioning of first and second language learning. In P. Duff & N. H. Hornberger (Eds.), *Encyclopedia of language and education, Vol. 8: Language socialization* (pp. 43–55). New York: Springer.

Cook, H. M. (2008a). Language socialization in Japanese. In P. A. Duff & N. H. Hornberger (Eds.), *Encyclopedia of language and education, Vol. 8: Language socialization* (pp. 313–326). New York: Springer.

Cook, H. M. (2008b). *Socializing identities through speech style: Learners of Japanese as a foreign language.* Bristol: Multilingual Matters.

Duff, P. A. (1995). An ethnography of communication in immersion classrooms in Hungary. *TESOL Quarterly, 29*, 505–537.

Duff, P. A. (1996). Different languages, different practices: Socialization of discourse competence in dual-language school classrooms in Hungary. In K. Bailey & D. Nunan

(Eds.), *Voices from the language classroom: Qualitative research in second language acquisition* (pp. 407–433). New York: Cambridge University Press.

Duff, P. A. (2002). The discursive co-construction of knowledge, identity, and difference: An ethnography of communication in the high school mainstream. *Applied Linguistics, 23*, 289–322.

Duff, P. A. (2003). New directions in second language socialization research. *Korean Journal of English Language and Linguistics, 3*, 309–339.

Duff, P. A. (2007). Second language socialization as sociocultural theory: Insights and issues. *Language Teaching, 40*, 309–319.

Duff, P. A. (2008). *Case study research in applied linguistics.* New York: Erlbaum/Taylor & Francis.

Duff, P. A. (in press-a). Second language socialization. In A. Duranti, E. Ochs, & B.B. Schieffelin (Eds.), *Handbook of language socialization.* New York: Blackwell.

Duff, P. A. (in press-b). Identity, agency, and SLA. In S. M. Gass & A. Mackey (Eds.), *Handbook of second language acquisition.* London: Routledge.

Duff, P. A., & Hornberger, N. H. (Eds.). (2008). *Encyclopedia of language and education, Vol. 8: Language socialization.* New York: Springer.

Duff, P. A., & Kobayashi, M. (2010). The intersection of social, cognitive, and cultural processes in language learning: A second language socialization approach. In R. Batstone (Ed.), *Sociocognitive perspectives on language use and language learning* (pp. 75–93). Oxford: Oxford University Press.

Duranti, A., Ochs, E., & Schieffelin, B. B. (in press). *Handbook of language socialization.* Malden, MA: Wiley Blackwell.

Edwards, D., & Potter, J. (1992). *Discursive psychology.* Thousand Oaks, CA: Sage.

Edwards, D., & Potter, J. (2005). Discursive psychology, mental states, and description. In H. te Molder & J. Potter (Eds.), *Conversation and cognition* (pp. 241–259). Cambridge: Cambridge University Press.

Ellis, R. (2009). *The study of second language acquisition* (2nd ed.). Oxford: Oxford University Press.

Engestrom, Y. (1999). Activity theory and individual and social transformation. In Y. Engestrom, R. Miettinen, & R. L. Punamaki (Eds.), *Perspectives on activity theory* (pp. 19–38). Cambridge: Cambridge University Press.

Firth, A., & Wagner, J. (1997). On discourse, communication, and (some) fundamental concepts in SLA research. *Modern Language Journal, 81*, 285–300.

Friedman, D. (2010). Speaking correctly: Error correction as a language socialization practice in a Ukrainian classroom. *Applied Linguistics, 30*, 346–367.

Garrett, P. B. (2004). Review of Bayley & Schecter, 2003. *Language in Society, 33*, 776–779.

Garrett, P. B. (2007). Language socialization and the (re)production of bilingual subjectivities. In M. Heller (Ed.), *Bilingualism: A social approach* (pp. 233–256). New York: Palgrave Macmillan.

Garrett, P. B. (2008). Researching language socialization. In K. A. King & N. H. Hornberger (Eds.), *Encyclopedia of language and education, Vol. 10: Research methods* (pp. 189–201). New York: Springer.

Garrett, P. B., & Baquedano-López, P. (2002). Language socialization: Reproduction and continuity, transformation and change. *Annual Review of Anthropology, 31*, 339–361.

Giddens, A. (1979). *Central problems in social theory.* Berkeley, CA: University of California Press.

Giddens, A. (1984). *The constitution of society.* Berkeley, CA: University of California Press.

Halliday, M. (1980/2003). Three aspects of children's language development: Learning language, learning through language, learning about language. Reprinted in J. Webster (Ed.), *The language of early childhood* (pp. 308–326). London: Continuum.

Hanks, W. (1992). The indexical ground of deictic reference. In A. Duranti & C. Goodwin (Eds.), *Rethinking context* (pp. 46–76). Cambridge: Cambridge University Press.

He, A. W. (2000). The grammatical and interactional organization of teachers' directives: Implications for socialization of Chinese American children. *Linguistics & Education, 11,* 119–40.

He, A. W. (2003a). Linguistic anthropology and language education: A comparative look at language socialization. In S. Wortham & B. Rymes (Eds.), *Linguistic anthropology of education* (pp. 93–120). Westport, CT: Praeger.

He, A. W. (2003b). Novices and their speech roles in Chinese heritage language classes. In R. Bayley & S. R. Schecter (Eds.), *Language socialization in bilingual and multilingual societies* (pp. 128–146). Clevedon: Multilingual Matters.

He, A. W. (2004). CA for SLA: Arguments from the Chinese language classroom. *Modern Language Journal, 88,* 568–582.

He, A. W. (2008). Heritage language learning and socialization. In P. A. Duff & N. H. Hornberger (Eds.), *Encyclopedia of language and education, Vol. 8: Language socialization* (pp. 201–213). New York: Springer.

Heath, S. B. (1983). *Ways with words: Language, life, and work in communities and classrooms.* Cambridge: Cambridge University Press.

Hellermann, J. (2008). *Social actions for classroom language learning.* Clevedon: Multilingual Matters.

Howard, K. M. (2008). Language socialization and language shift among school-aged children. In P. A. Duff & N. H. Hornberger (Eds.), *Encyclopedia of language and education, Vol. 8: Language socialization* (pp. 187–199). New York: Springer.

Huang, J. (2004). Socialising ESL students into the discourse of school science through academic writing. *Language & Education, 18,* 97–123.

Hymes, D. (1972). On communicative competence. In J. B. Pride & J. Holmes (Eds.), *Sociolinguistics: Selected readings* (pp. 269–293). Harmondsworth: Penguin.

Kanagy, R. (Ed.). (1999). Language socialization of affect in first and second language acquisition [Special issue]. *Journal of Pragmatics, 31*(11).

Kasper, G. (1997). "A" stands for acquisition: A response to Firth and Wagner. *Modern Language Journal, 81,* 307–312.

Kasper, G. (2009). Locating cognition in second language interaction and learning: Inside the skull or in public view? *International Review of Applied Linguistics in Language Teaching, 47,* 11–36.

Kobayashi, M. (2003). The role of peer support in ESL students' accomplishment of oral academic tasks. *Canadian Modern Language Review, 59,* 337–368.

Kobayashi, M. (2004). *A sociocultural study of second language tasks: Activity, agency, and language socialization.* Unpublished doctoral dissertation, University of British Columbia.

Korobov, N., & Bamberg, M. (2004). Positioning a "mature" self in interactive practices: How adolescent males negotiate "physical attraction" in group talk. *British Journal of Social Psychology, 22,* 471–492.

Kramsch, C., & Steffensen, S. V. (2008). Ecological perspectives on second language acquisition and socialization. In P. A. Duff & N. H. Hornberger (Eds.), *Encyclopedia of language and education, Vol 8: Language socialization* (pp. 17–28). New York: Springer.

Kulick, D., & Schieffelin, B. (2004). Language socialization. In A. Duranti (Ed.), *A companion to linguistic anthropology* (pp. 349–368). Malden, MA: Blackwell.

Lave, J., & Wenger, E. (1991). *Situated learning: Legitimate peripheral participation*. New York: Cambridge University Press.

Leontiev, A. (1981). *Psychology and the language learning process*. London: Pergamon.

Li, D. (2000). The pragmatics of making requests in the L2 workplace: A case study of language socialization. *Canadian Modern Language Review, 57*, 58–87.

Lightbown, P., & Spada, N. (2006). *How languages are learned* (3rd ed.). Oxford: Oxford University Press.

Long, M. (1997). Construct validity in SLA research: A response to Firth and Wagner. *Modern Language Journal, 81*, 318–323.

Markee, N. P., & Seo, M. S. (2009). Learning talk analysis. *International Review of Applied Linguistics in Language Teaching, 47*, 37–63.

Mitchell, R., & Myles, F. (2004). *Second language learning theories* (2nd ed.). London: Hodder Arnold.

Mondada, L., & Pekarek-Doehler, S. (2004). Second language acquisition as situated practice: Task accomplishment in the French second language classroom. *Modern Language Journal, 88*, 501–518.

Moore, L. C. (2008). Language socialization and second/foreign language and multilingual education in non-Western settings. In P. A. Duff & N. H. Hornberger (Eds.), *Encyclopedia of language and education, Vol. 8: Language socialization* (pp. 175–185). New York: Springer.

Morita, N. (2000). Discourse socialization through oral classroom activities in a TESL graduate program. *TESOL Quarterly, 34*, 279–310.

Morita, N. (2004). Negotiating participation and identity in second language academic communities. *TESOL Quarterly, 38*, 573–603.

Norton, B. (2000). *Identity and language learning: Gender, ethnicity, and educational change*. Harlow: Pearson Education.

Ochs, E. (1996). Linguistic resources for socializing humanity. In J. J. Gumperz & S. C. Levinson (Eds.), *Rethinking linguistic relativity* (pp. 407–437). Cambridge: Cambridge University Press.

Ochs, E., & Schieffelin, B. B. (2008). Language socialization: An historical overview. In P. A. Duff & N. H. Hornberger (Eds.), *Encyclopedia of language and education, Vol. 8: Language socialization* (pp. 3–15). New York: Springer.

Ohta, A. (1994). Socializing the expression of affect: An overview of affective particle use in the Japanese as a foreign language classroom. *Issues in Applied Linguistics, 5*, 303–325.

Ohta, A. (1999). Interactional routines and the socialization of interactional style in adult learners of Japanese. *Journal of Pragmatics, 31*, 1493–1512.

Ohta, A. (2001). *Second language acquisition process in the classroom: Learning Japanese*. Mahwah, NJ: Erlbaum.

Ortega, L. (2009). *Understanding second language acquisition*. London: Hodder Education.

Ortega, L., & Byrnes, H. (Eds.). (2008). *The longitudinal study of advanced L2 capacities*. Mahwah, NJ: Erlbaum/Taylor & Francis.

Rogoff, B. (1995). Observing sociocultural activity on three planes: Participatory appropriation, guided participation, and apprenticeship. In J. V. Wertsch, P. D. Rio, & A. Alvarez (Eds.), *Sociocultural studies of mind* (pp. 139–164). New York: Cambridge University Press.

Rogoff, B. (2003). *The cultural nature of human development*. New York: Oxford University Press.

Schecter, S. R., & Bayley, R. (2004). Language socialization in theory and practice. *International Journal of Qualitative Studies in Education, 17*, 605–625.

Schieffelin, B. B., & Ochs, E. (1986a). *Language socialization across cultures*. Cambridge: Cambridge University Press.

Schieffelin, B. B., & Ochs, E. (1986b). Language socialization. *Annual Review of Anthropology*, *15*, 163–191.

Schieffelin, B. B., & Ochs, E. (1996). The microgenesis of competence: Methodology in language socialization. In D. Slobin, J. Gerhardt, A. Kyratzis, & J. Guo (Eds.), *Social interaction, social context, and language* (pp. 251–263). Mahwah, NJ: Erlbaum.

Siegal, M. (1994). *Looking East: Learning Japanese as a second language in Japan and the interaction of race, gender and social context*. Unpublished doctoral dissertation, University of California, Berkeley.

Siegal, M. (1996). The role of learner subjectivity in second language sociolinguistic competency: Western women learning Japanese. *Applied Linguistics*, *17*, 356–382.

Talmy, S. (2008). The cultural productions of ESL student at Tradewinds High: Contingency, multidirectionality, and identity in L2 socialization. *Applied Linguistics*, *29*, 619–644.

Talmy, S. (2009). A very important lesson: Respect and the socialization of order(s) in high school ESL. *Linguistics & Education*, *20*, 235–253.

Tarone, E., & Bigelow, M. (2009). *Literacy and second language oracy*. Oxford: Oxford University Press.

Toohey, K. (1998). "Breaking them up, taking them away": Constructing ESL students in grade one. *TESOL Quarterly*, *32*, 61–84.

Vickers, C. (2007). Second language socialization through team interaction among electrical and computer engineering students. *Modern Language Journal*, *91*, 621–640.

Vygotsky, L. (1978). *Mind in society*. Cambridge, MA: Harvard University Press.

Watson-Gegeo, K. (2004). Mind, language, and epistemology: Toward a language socialization paradigm for SLA. *Modern Language Journal*, *88*, 331–350.

Watson-Gegeo, K., & Nielsen, S. (2003). Language socialization in SLA. In C. Doughty & M. Long (Eds.), *Handbook of second language acquisition* (pp. 155–177). Malden, MA: Blackwell.

Wenger, E. (1998). *Communities of practice: Learning, meaning, and identity*. Cambridge: Cambridge University Press.

Williams, G. (2008). Language socialization: A systemic functional perspective. In P. A. Duff & N. H. Hornberger (Eds.), *Encyclopedia of language and education, Vol. 8: Language socialization* (pp. 57–70). New York: Springer.

Yoshimi, D. R. (1999). L1 language socialization as a variable in the use of *ne* by L2 learners of Japanese. *Journal of Pragmatics*, *31*, 1513–1525.

5

A CONVERSATION-ANALYTIC APPROACH TO SECOND LANGUAGE ACQUISITION

Gabriele Kasper and Johannes Wagner

Overview

Conversation analysis (CA) has evolved from ethnomethodology (EM), a sociological approach that challenged sociology's standard epistemology. Whereas Durkheim, Weber, and Parsons studied social formations at the macro-societal level, EM, and hence CA, studies the methods ordinary people use to participate and make sense in their daily life. Sense-making draws on social orderliness, and social order is—at the level of interaction—achieved through participants' actions and practices. For this, language is the central though not the only resource. From EM-CA perspectives, language acquisition can be understood as learning to participate in mundane as well as institutional everyday social environments. The focus of CA as an approach to second language acquisition (SLA)—or CA-SLA for short—is therefore the social aspects of language acquisition and not the more "systemic" aspects of language. Consequently, many concepts and the methodology used in CA differ from those established in standard SLA. Since CA's specific contribution to SLA rests on CA's approach to interaction, its theory and methodology will briefly and partially be sketched in this chapter. For a deeper understanding, readers are referred to introductions to CA (e.g., Drew, 2005; Have, 2007; Hutchby & Wooffitt, 2008).

We start by sketching CA's defining research object, the interaction order and interactional competence, as well as its perspectives on language, cognition, and identity, and its stance on exogenous theory. We then describe several principles of CA methodology: the necessary data quality, the role and practice of transcription, membership knowledge as a requirement for analysis, and several standard analytic practices. Here we revisit the issue of exogenous theory, this time considering possible roles for it and its relation to data analysis. Turning to research findings in different branches of developmental CA, including learning and development in interactions among first language (L1)-acquiring and multilingual children and adults in professional settings, we offer evidence for second language (L2) learning as a social practice and development in the short and long term. Finally, we briefly outline items on CA-SLA's future agenda.

Theoretical Principles

The Interaction Order and Interactional Competence

CA's analytical object is talk-and-other-conduct in interaction. Just as standard sociology is primarily interested in the ordered arrangement of macro-level social institutions, so CA is primarily interested in the orderliness of interaction—what Goffman (1983) called the *interaction order*. Orderliness has several meanings in EM and CA. Interaction is orderly, first and foremost, for the participants themselves. Consistent with its origin in EM, CA finds the interaction order in the *methods* (procedures/practices) that social members recurrently and systematically use to achieve, maintain, and restore intersubjectivity in their practical activities. As Drew (2005, p. 75) put it: "The aim of research in CA is to discover and explicate the practices through which interactants produce and understand conduct in interaction." Garfinkel (1967) and later EM research has shown that these practices are forms in which actions are displayed and recognized by members of a society. Social practices are protected by "moral order," which describes the observable fact that violations of patterns and practices are treated as violations of moral norms. Take, for example, a simple practice such as queuing at a cash register in a supermarket. Breaking or even leaving the queue and insisting on regaining one's former position after returning is—at least where we live—treated by others in the queue as a moral issue. People lining up in queues accumulate rights and obligations: They have the right to be checked out after the person in front of them but they need to keep their place. Practices are thus accountable, and breaching them has to be accounted for.

Membership in a social group, then, is constituted by effective, morally accountable participation. The ensemble of practices through which interactants produce and understand conduct in interaction makes up members' *interactional competence*. Mehan (1979) pointed out that interactional competence is interactional in a dual sense: "One, it is the competence necessary for effective interaction. Two, it is the competence that is available in the interaction between participants" (p. 130). This description highlights that interactional competence cannot be reduced to an individual, intrapsychological property. Nor can it be separated from "performance." Mehan's comment that interactional competence is available *in* interaction has methodological consequences: Interactional competence can only be studied by observing interaction locally and in great detail but not by asking participants about it or through experiments. Interactional competence is a *procedural* competence, with the crucial difference from uses of "procedural knowledge" in cognitive science being that the procedures it encompasses—turn-taking, sequence organization, turn-construction, and repair—are interactional procedures rather than intramental ones.

In CA-SLA, interactional competence is understood to serve double duty as both a fundamental condition for and object of learning. Since L2 speakers' available interactional competence allows them to participate in interaction in the first place, it also furnishes the conditions to engage in the social activity of language learning and to participate more effectively in practices and activities over time. From an EM-CA perspective, Lee (2006) showed how, in ESL classroom interaction, repair and error correction—standardly taken as evidence of students' knowledge deficits—are enabled by students' competence in monitoring how talk is developing, locating trouble, and initiating or responding to modifications that are specifically tailored to deal with the problem at hand. Lee demonstrated how, in the details of classroom members' production of relevant next turns, their ongoing analysis and understanding of the prior sequence becomes visible. Whether in classrooms or elsewhere in social life, the interactional competence to make activities mutually intelligible moment-by-moment provides resources for participants and a topic of investigation for analysts to explicate the enabling conditions for L2 learning.

Language

A critical reservoir of resources in social members' interactional competence, and one that is directly implicated in the design of actions and understanding of sequentially organized behavior in talk, is the language(s) in which an activity is conducted. Although CA started as a sociological enterprise, its first two groundbreaking papers (Sacks, Schegloff, & Jefferson, 1974; Schegloff, Jefferson, & Sacks, 1977) appeared in a linguistics journal, *Language*. These papers already showed how sequential organization and turn construction are built on participants' understanding of linguistic resources. In most general terms, studies examining the interrelation of interaction and grammar build on the premise that "(1) grammar organizes social interaction; (2) social interaction organizes grammar; and (3) grammar is a mode of interaction" (Schegloff, Ochs, & Thompson, 1996, p. 33). This understanding of the grammar–interaction interface also gives the impetus to *interactional linguistics*, an effort to merge CA and (mostly functional) linguistics (e.g., Selting & Couper-Kuhlen, 2001). A key question for cross-linguistic CA research is how speakers solve generic interactional problems with the grammatical resources of their specific language(s). For instance, a generic property of turn construction is that the syntactic ordering of clausal elements projects how a turn is progressing, how it may be completed, and what action it is doing, all of which are crucial for turn-taking and sequence organization. However, typologically different languages may afford different onsets of projectability. For English, the rigid S-V-O pattern enables recipients to anticipate the progression of the turn from early on in the speaker's utterance. In Japanese, by contrast, projectability is limited by syntactic practices such as (turn-initially) flexible word order, post- rather than prepositions, unrealized constituents including subjects and objects, and the capacity of interactional particles to change the meaning of the preceding unit (Sidnell, 2009). The limitations of syntactic projectability in Japanese have consequences for the organization of self-initiated self-repair (Fox, Hayashi, & Jasperson, 1996) and collaborative completions (Hayashi, 2004), and can account for recipients' provision of response tokens (e.g., *un*, *ee*) after smaller bits of speech than in English (Schegloff, Ochs, & Thompson).

Studies of L2 interaction, learning, and development take from CA studies on the grammar–interaction interface the notion that grammar is a central resource in social members' interactional competence—a set of practices deployed in practical activities. Mori (2010) demonstrated that advanced L2 learners of Japanese with experience living in Japan conducted word searches using the distal demonstrative pronoun *are* as a placeholder for the missing word without disrupting the flow of their talk, while less proficient classroom learners of Japanese as a foreign language turned to their L1 lexicon to initiate word searches on gaps in their L2 lexicon. Employing a different theoretical resource to account for the changing uses of the pattern *what/how did you say* in the conversations of an L2 English speaker, Eskildsen (in press) drew on usage-based linguistics (UBL). As an emergentist approach to language acquisition, UBL holds that language emerges out of language use and strives to bridge such fundamental dichotomies of modern linguistics as syntax versus lexis and performance versus competence. UBL and CA thus share some fundamental premises and are apt to enter into a productive partnership.

Cognition

Just as interactional competence and language are visible in participants' interactional practices, CA relocates cognition from its traditional habitat in the privacy of people's minds to the arena of social interaction. Together with EM and discursive psychology (Edwards, 1997; Potter, 2003), CA reconceptualizes cognition as socially shared and grounded in interaction (Molder & Potter, 2005; Schegloff, 1991). At its most fundamental, orderly turn-taking requires that participants listen to each other's talk. That is, in order to speak, a prospective speaker has to listen to how the turn in progress is unfolding. Participation in interaction, then, comes with an "intrinsic motivation for listening" (Sacks et al., 1974, p. 727), a motivation that is not a matter of volition but a system constraint of interaction. Moreover, the listener's understanding becomes available to the co-participants once the former listener assumes speakership. As Schegloff noted:

> Built into the very organization by which opportunities to talk are allocated to participants in ordinary conversation is a related "understanding-display" device (Sacks et al., 1974). The consequence is that speakers almost necessarily reveal their understanding of that to which their talk is addressed, whether it is prior talk, other conduct, or events and occurrences "scenic" to the

interaction. When an utterance is addressed to prior talk, its speaker reveals some understanding of that prior talk.

(1991, pp. 167–168)

Revealing understanding includes showing problematic understanding. Speakers can choose to address problems in speaking, hearing, or understanding through repair, an interactional apparatus for handling such problems and restoring intersubjectivity. As the examples of turn-taking and repair indicate, the "understanding-display device" and the interactional methods through which participants manage their talk are inseparably intertwined. Just as both are at the heart of achieving intersubjectivity, they enable learning and development in interaction (e.g., Kasper, 2009; Mori & Hasegawa, 2009), as shown further below. Since socially shared cognition and learning are publicly displayed in interaction, they become available to researchers for analysis, obviating the need to construe hidden internal processes behind observable behavior.

Identity

For CA, identity is neither a stable internal trait—a state of mind, as it were—nor the intersection of macrosocial vectors such as social class, ethnicity, nationality, religion, gender, or speaker status ("native" or "nonnative"). While poststructuralist theories vary in the extent to which they emphasize the power relations in which an individual is positioned, on the one hand, and the individual's agency in conforming to, resisting, or subverting such positionings, on the other, CA makes no a priori assumptions about whether and which of "the usual macrosociological suspects" (McHoul, Rapley, & Antaki, 2008, p. 43) are relevant in any given interaction. Such "transportable" identities (Zimmerman, 1998) may be visible (through physical appearance) or hearable (through speech production) across situations and activities without having any bearing on the interaction for the participants. Much of the literature on L2 talk shows that, predominantly, participants do not treat their status as L1 or L2 speakers (e.g., Brouwer, 2003; Hosoda, 2006) or their cultural backgrounds (Mori, 2003; Ryoo, 2007) as relevant for their interaction. However, on occasion, differential language knowledge does become an issue for the participants. For instance, when one party asks another to supply a common L2 word that the speaker shows he or she does not know, the participant assumes the identity of L2 speaker through the action of self-initiating other-repair to plug a lexical gap (e.g., Brouwer, 2003). In other words, transportable identities are a resource for participants—the identities' local relevance is subject to the parties' interactional projects at any given moment in their talk. By the same token, identities tied to institutional activities are constituted through actions that implement institutional agendas, whether through complementary categories such as service person and customer, teacher and students, or same-category relations such as business partners in a meeting or members of a committee at work. Identities, then, are not assumed to reside in a person but are interactionally produced, locally occasioned, and relationally constituted (Antaki & Widdicombe, 1998; Benwell & Stokoe, 2006).

CA's view of identity contrasts with that of causal or correlational models in standard SLA, in which the categories research participants are recruited under (e.g., L2 speakers, their L1 backgrounds, age, gender) figure as independent variables and the research objective is to determine how these factors affect specified behaviors (the dependent variable). A different, poststructuralist approach to identity in SLA (Block, 2007; Norton & McKinney, this volume) rejects the deterministic and essentialist concept of identity in standard SLA research, proposing instead to view identity as multiple, fluid, fragmented, and conflicting. Data, mainly deriving from autobiographic sources such as interviews and diaries, are mined for evidence of such theory-stipulated versions of identity. Yet, despite its appeal to identity as "performed," "co-constructed," and "situated," poststructuralist identity research does not ground its analytical claims in the details of participants' observable social practices (e.g., Benwell & Stokoe, 2006). CA-SLA, in contrast, demonstrates the nexus of (transportable and situated) identities and L2 learning in specific interactional activities, as shown below.

CA's Stance on Exogenous Theory

From CA's ethnomethodological perspective, participants in interaction are competent agents who constantly produce and understand their social world together. The analyst's job is therefore not to second-guess actors' competent dealings in their social affairs by interpreting their world for them. Rather than supplanting social members' commonsense knowledge with sociological (or any other) theory, analysts describe the methods or practices—the competencies—through which social members conduct their activities in an orderly and therefore mutually recognizable fashion. This stance is behind EM's and CA's injunction against appeals to exogenous (i.e., externally imposed) theory to explain social members' actions and activities. CA's agnostic position toward sociological theorizing, borrowed from the phenomenological practice of "bracketing," has direct implications for CA as an approach to SLA. CA-SLA breaks with the standard practice of locating studies in a theoretical framework that supplies perspectives and concepts that make some aspects of the data analytically salient and render others less conspicuous. Against theory-stipulated analytical priorities, CA adheres to the policy that no aspect of the data can be dismissed as "uninteresting" a priori. CA-SLA is no different from sociological CA in its agnostic posture toward prior theorizing. Consequently, CA-SLA eschews employing exogenous theories of any sort, whether standard or alternative, in the process of data analysis.[1]

Research Methods

CA focuses mainly on the analysis of talk-in-interaction and records interactions on tape and/or video media. In talk, practices such as *turn-taking*, *turn-construction*, and *repair* are fundamental. Through them speakers organize the intersubjective meaning of any activity or practice. Since the 1960s, CA has described a large variety of specific, orderly practices in talk. Conversation-analytic studies deliver systematic, robust descriptions of social practices. A set of methodological and analytic principles follows.

Data Quality

Conversation analysis is data-driven. Data are collected in environments where participants are involved in consequential everyday activities—e.g., family life, work, or education. CA refers to these data as *naturally occurring*; that is, they are not produced for the analyst. Thus, to study doctor–patient communication, one needs to collect data from real doctor–patient interactions rather than actors and students role-playing these roles. CA does not study language as an abstract system, nor does it assume that studying the social organization of one setting (e.g., research interviews), licenses inferences to a differently organized setting (such as social scenes talked about in the interview).

Data relevant for CA are everywhere, since everyday life is everywhere. This is because, for CA, conversation is

> the primordial site of sociality, it is through activities managed in conversation that we conduct our ordinary social affairs, and the practices to be found in the highly organized structures and patterns in conversation underlie our ability to communicate meaningfully with one another—hence they are fundamental communicative competencies.
>
> (Drew, 2005, p. 76)

Data are transcribed at a level of granularity that makes visible the details of the sequential and temporal organization of the talk. CA's insistence on representing nonverbal and, increasingly, nonvocal conduct in transcripts comes from early CA work showing that nonlinguistic behavior is often interactionally consequential for the participants themselves.

To study SLA from a CA perspective means to make the L2 character of the data available in the transcript. This has proven problematic. CA-SLA has not developed generally accepted ways of indicating a speaker's foreign accent, for example. Accent could be made visible by orthographically modified transcription, but modified orthography risks stigmatizing the ongoing talk and might represent the L2 speaker in a stereotypical fashion (Roberts, 1997). The literature therefore often avoids orthographic modifications as long as they are not interactionally conse-quential (but see Carroll (2005) for L2 speakers' use of L2-specific phonological marking as an interactional resource). Instead, advanced transcription editors that allow access to the audio and video data at any point in the transcript have become a central tool for researchers.

Membership Knowledge

The analyst must share the participants' cultural knowledge as relevant for the research purpose. This requirement contrasts with ethnography in its classic form (see Duff & Talmy, this volume, for ethnographic research methods). While ethnographers start out as "professional strangers" who have to learn the culture of the group they are investigating through participant observation and other forms of fieldwork over extended periods of time, conversation analysts start out by approaching their data as cultural co-members. As Hutchby and Wooffitt (2008) noted, "it is absolutely necessary that conversation analysts are either members of, or have a sound understanding of, the culture from which their data have been drawn" (p. 106). Membership knowledge enables the analyst to understand the data in a pre-analytic fashion, a necessary first step toward examining what specific interactional methods produce the conduct that enables this understanding. Consequently, if the analyst does not have relevant membership competencies in the setting, ancillary interaction-*external* data are used by analysts and readers of the research report to attain vicarious membership knowledge (Peräkylä, 2004). Maynard (2003) offered particularly insightful perspectives on how CA and ethnography may be related.

Analytic Practices in CA

CA studies begin with the identification of an interactional practice, which is often spotted accidentally when CA researchers work through data. CA researchers therefore engage in *unmotivated looking* in *data sessions*—collective exercises where new data are subjected to sequential analysis. In the course of the analysis, new interactional phenomena may be spotted. The purpose of subsequent analysis is then to understand their systematic nature.

CA takes two approaches to analysis: single-case and collection-based analyses. In the first type, single fragments of talk are analyzed to demonstrate practices via prototypical examples. As Schegloff argued:

> An analytic machinery which is meant to come to terms with the orderliness of interaction, and especially the orderliness of conduct in interaction, and to do so by explicating the orderly practices of the participants in interaction (conversational or otherwise), should be able to deal in an illuminating manner with single episodes of talk from "the real world". There *is* a constitutive order to singular occasions of interaction, and to the organization of actions within them. This is the bedrock of social life—the primordial site of sociality.
>
> (1987, p. 102)

The analysis of single fragments makes it possible to describe a very high degree of complexity in talk, including multimodal and spatial dimensions of interaction (e.g., Goodwin, 2000).

Collection studies are built on sometimes very large collections of relevant instances. These studies deliver robust descriptions and advance the understanding of sequential structures in talk and of social order as shaped by the participants:

> In a *collection study*, the analyst generalizes the results of a cumulative series of single case analyses with respect to a specific aspect. All cases are compared with respect to some features by describing how, and the degree to which they are the same, similar, or different.
>
> (Mazeland, 2006, p. 158)

Deviant cases are crucial for collection studies. Fragments that seem to violate the practice need to be explained in terms of a general pattern.

Exogenous Theory and Data Analysis

As implied in the methodological practice of unmotivated looking, analysis in CA is not traditionally guided by exogenous theory (e.g., Have, 2007; Hutchby & Wooffitt, 2008). However, depending on the research goal, *pre-analytic* observations and possibly *post-analytic* connections to exogenous theory may be guided by the researcher's agenda. We have borrowed these two loci for permissible and, for some researchers, necessary CA-external considerations from a recent paper by Kitzinger (2008), in which she reaffirmed her proposal of a feminist CA. It coincides with Talmy's (2009) appeal to engage CA in a program of critical research in language education. In order to analyze how membership in the category of ESL student is produced in situated classroom interactions between students and the teacher, Talmy made a case for what he called, reminiscent of Duneir and Molotch (1999), "motivated looking." Similarly, CA researchers studying learning and development will start out by identifying sequences in which participants orient to learning, or in which development is evident in speakers' participation in a practice, the sequential placement and formatting of an action, or use of a semiotic resource (see next section). Once such sequences have been selected, they are analyzed with all standard CA principles and practices intact, that is, through a turn-by-turn sequential analysis. In other words, the data *analysis* remains the same, independent of the wider goals of the study. Based on the analysis, researchers may also find it helpful to connect the findings to exogenous developmental theory on a post-hoc basis (e.g., Hellermann, 2008; Ishida, 2006).

Supporting Findings

Developmental CA

In a programmatic recommendation at the turn of the millennium, Don Zimmerman (1999) proposed that CA include in its research agenda "the acquisition of conversational structures," that is, "the process and stages by which interactive talk emerges" (p. 198). Although such "developmental CA" (Wootton, 2006) is still a much smaller enterprise than CA as the study of members' stable interactional competencies, it comprises several branches: children's development of interactional competencies; learning and development of interactional competencies in professional settings; and L2 learning and development by adult L2 users. We will start by briefly noting some of the topics and findings in developmental CA with a focus on children and professional adults, and then lay out in more detail several key findings in CA-SLA.

Earlier work had examined children's turn-taking (Ervin-Tripp, 1979) and request development (Ervin-Tripp & Gordon, 1985; Wootton, 1981). Topics addressed in recent CA studies on the development of children's interactional competencies include how preverbal children use gaze as a resource to recognize and project actions (Kidwell, 2009) and the emergence of self-repair (Forrester, 2008). A growing literature investigates multilingual development from a CA perspective, laying out the range of practices through which children participate in routine activities in multilingual preschools (Björk-Willén, 2008; Cekaite, 2007). A common thread connecting EM and CA studies on child interaction and development is their interest in understanding how children produce their own local orders in their ordinary daily activities (Cromdal, 2008). Such orderliness is observable well before language emerges, and depends on children's already available skilled use of nonvocal resources. Thus, close analysis of the organization of children's interactional activities shows that their *sequential competence* (Wootton, 1997) enables their participation and furnishes the bedrock from which subsequent interactional structures and resources emerge. CA perspectives on children's social lives thus part company with commonsense and mainstream social science understandings of children as deficient versions of adults. Here we see a direct link to CA's stance on the interactional competencies of L2 speakers, which rejects the model of the L2 speaker as deficient communicator (Firth & Wagner, 1997; Wagner & Gardner, 2004).

In addition to children's development of interactional competencies, recent CA research has examined how adults who are novices in professional settings build on their available interactional competencies in their development of specialized professional competencies in a recurrent institutional activity. Where situated learning theory defines development rather loosely as changing participation in social practices or as the increasing ability to manage the problems of everyday life more effectively (e.g., Rogoff, 1999), CA furnishes the analytical apparatus for specifying "changing participation" and "effectiveness" in interactional terms (Nguyen, 2008).

CA-SLA

Studies in CA-SLA have gone in at least two different directions. A number of studies investigate language learning as accountable and recognizable social practices, as described in the following sub-section. That is, language learners seem to have a license to do things other speakers rarely do, for example produce hesitant and delayed turns, code shift, or ask for help and explanations. These behaviors are accountable for L1 speakers and reflexively create the identity of a L2 learner. In other words, identity as a learner can be made relevant—or not. When it is made relevant, language assistance is often accepted. When it is not, language assistance (e.g., corrections) may create severe social tensions (Takigawa, 2010).

A second group of studies traces the development of action formats, participation styles, and use of linguistic resources over shorter or longer spans of time, as described further below.

Language Learning as a Social Practice

According to the theoretical and analytical principles outlined previously, the first CA-SLA studies described the activities by which participants in interaction recognizably and accountably "do" learning as a social activity. The concept of "doing" in CA must not be taken as referring to a conscious decision by the participants or a psychological process but as practices that are recognizable for other participants. "Doing learning" is thus comparable to "doing queuing" (from our initial example).

Following an extended discussion of the epistemological and methodological premises of CA-SLA from the mid-1990s, research has started to deliver findings about the relation of social action and language learning. "Language learning as a social activity" refers to interactional moments where the participants make learning the focal concern of their interaction. Most of the evidence for "doing learning" in this sense comes from research on classroom interaction or out-of-class arrangements for L2 practice. The earliest studies were Markee's (1994, 2000) on student-initiated definition talk in full-class and peer interaction. Markee showed how students deploy their sequential knowledge of turn-taking, sequence organization, and repair, as well as claims and demonstrations of knowledge changes and definition-relevant actions, to figure out collaboratively the meanings of unknown lexical items in a meaning-focused pedagogical task.

Outside of classrooms, L2 learners actively set up opportunities for using their L2. Theodorsdóttír[2] (in press-a, in press-b) reports how L2 speakers set up learning/practicing situations in their everyday life and pursue these in organizing the business at hand by bringing the language of conversation back to Icelandic (the L2) after instances of code-switching into English. L2 speakers actively create situations in which they can practice their L2. Using the L2 is an activity specifically created and actively upheld by the L2 speakers.

Displaying and accounting for L2-related trouble in talk

Although interaction may become a site for language learning due to many kinds of L2-related problems, such moments frequently arise during word searches. In word searches (Goodwin & Goodwin, 1986), a current speaker indicates trouble in the production of a turn by abandoning the projected unit and producing speech perturbations (sound stretches, pauses, *uh*s or *uhm*s). In a study of ordinary conversations between L1 and L2 speakers of Danish, Brouwer (2003) observed how the L2 speakers showed through the design of the trouble-source turn whether or not their co-participant(s) were invited to participate in the word search or whether the L2 speaker produced his or her own solution, that is, whether the self-initiated repair projected self- or other-completion. Through invited participation in word searches, interlocutors oriented to differentially distributed language expertise between them, at that moment. Mori and Hasegawa (2009) showed how students in word searches during pair work in a JFL (Japanese as a foreign language) class made cognitive states mutually available through talk, bodily action, and the manipulation of activity-relevant objects such as a textbook. Further evidence of learning as a social activity is documented in a large body of publications (e.g., Hellermann, 2008; Kasper, 2004; Koshik, 2005; Markee & Seo, 2009; Mori, 2004).

Two examples from our own (unpublished) data on L2 interaction serve to illustrate how opportunities for language learning arise as L2 speakers pursue other practical activities.

In Extract 1,[3] Ilse, an L2 speaker of Danish, is at a bar buying cigarettes. The Danish-speaking bartender offers her a choice of different brands. It takes Ilse a little while to understand his question.

Extract 1: Cigarettes

```
01. Il:  ·hh jeg vil gerne ha::: ehm cigaretter.
              I would like have       cigarettes
02. Bar: ja hvad slags?
         yes what kind
03.      (0.8)
04. Bar: hvad slags?
         what  kind
05. Il:  pt a:hm det betyder hva:d (0.6) brand (.) t the brand
                  it means     what         brand
06.      (.)
07. Bar: ☺ja☺?
08.      (0.4)
09. Il:  ehm: har  du eh (.) Kings
              have you       Kings
10. Il:  the [Ki]
11. Bar: [nej]
          no
```

Looking at the structural order of these turns at talk, we get the following picture:

		Action	**Sequential position**
1	Il	order	*main sequence*
			Part A of adjacency pair[4]

2	Bar	request for specification	*first inserted sequence Part A*
3	Il	–	*noticeably missing response*
4	Bar	repeat	
5	Il	lexical clarification request	*second inserted sequence Part A*
7	Bar	answer	*second inserted sequence Part B*
9	Il	question for brand	*third inserted sequence Part A*
11	Bar	answer	*third inserted sequence Part B*

In this extract, Ilse's (the customer's) request leads to an insertion sequence about the desired brand, which leads to an additional insertion sequence about a lexical item. When that sequence is closed, yet another insertion sequence is started about the availability of the specified brand. At the end of the extract, the bartender has still not executed the order given in line 1—it is still open and relevant for later action (not shown here).

CA-SLA describes the resources that L2 speakers, jointly with their interlocutors, draw upon to keep the interaction going. In Extract 1 we see the L2 speaker, Ilse, display what troubles and prevents her from moving forward in the interaction. L2 speakers do not breach the social order by doing things their co-participants cannot make sense of. Instead they display resources for sense-making that make their talk meaningful for their co-participants. In this way they create sensible normality and orderliness in their behavior that the co-participants acknowledge (note the smile voice in the bartender's response to Ilse's lexical trouble, line 7). Actively creating opportunities for talk and actively pursuing intersubjectivity in spite of troubles in language understanding and production are practices that L1 speakers recognize as creating and upholding environments for learning. L1 speakers "play along" (as seen in Extract 1) and do their share.

In Extract 2, we show how L1 speakers provide L2 speakers with words and concepts that they may pick up for further use. This extract is taken from a business phone call between a Danish (J) and a British (T) sales representative. T will be visiting Denmark on an upcoming business trip and both speakers are planning T's arrival and airport pick-up.

Extract 2: Afternoon Tea
```
01. J:   and so w[e have ehm: (0.4) l↓unch and eh::
02. T:          [xx
03.      (0.4)
04. J:   oh that is not lunch h (.) in the afternoon that
05.      is: (.) breakfast.
06.      (0.8)
07. T:   that is,
         (0.3)
09. J:   that is not not ehv-
10. J:   you have ·hh
11. T:   tea.
```

```
12.           (0.7)
13.    J:    °*e*° tea in the [mor]
14.    T:                      [xx af]ternoon it is [tea].
15.    J:                                             [and]
16.    T:    in the [morning] it is ↓break↑fast
17.    J:           [xx xx]
18.    J:    y↓e:s,
19.           (.)
20.    T:    then:
21.    J:    then lunc[h,
22.    T:             [lunch.
23.    T:    ·hh then afternoon tea:,
24.    J:    tea: ye[s
25.    T:           [and then dinner in the evening.
26.    J:    dinner in (de ri) xx yes?
27.    T:    so [some people will have] dinner at work
28.    J:       [   hhe     hhe hhe    ]
29.    T:    we have dinner at lunch time a:nd dinner tim[e.
30.    J:                                                [hhh.
31.    T:    dinner time is also someti:mes known as lunch
32.    T:    lunch time is dinner ti[me
33.    J:                           [whats time have you normally
34.          dinner time in England?
35.           (0.5)
36.    T:    well we: we: [x
37.    J:                 [six o'clock?
38.           (.)
39.    J:    s:even?
40.    T:    we:ll we usually about half past five six o'clo[ck,
41.    J:                                                   [(ja]
42.    T:    ehm: (.) at home, but it varies, some people uh eat
43.          early some people eat ↑lat[e
44.    J:                              [yes?
45.    T:    ·hh.
46.    J:    *yes*
47.    T:    some people have main meal at lunch time? an:d eh
48.          only a- a tea a afternoon tea and nothing else.
```

In line 1, J suggests having lunch after T's arrival in the afternoon. After a short delay in which T does not respond, J initiates a repair sequence by pointing out in line 4 that he used the wrong item, *lunch*, which he repairs in line 5 to *breakfast*.

After a substantial pause, T initiates repair in line 7. Note how this is done: T repeats the beginning of J's utterance up to the point where the trouble source apparently occurred. In his next turn (line 9), J does what people do after a repair initiation of this kind—he starts to repeat his own utterance from line 4. In other words, J responds to the repair initiation as if T had not heard the previous talk. But J abandons his repeat in line 9, and indicates that he now realizes that the trouble source is located in his own previous turn (line 4). In other words, he now treats T's repair initiation not as a case of bad hearing but as indicating another type of problem.

In line 10, J abandons another formulation that is then completed by T, delivering a correction of J's line 4/5: In the afternoon, "you have tea."

After some delay, J indicates where *tea* belongs in his own understanding (*in the mor*). At this point it is evident that J has a profound deficit in the naming of British mealtimes. He himself had changed the focus of the talk from planning the arrival day to organization of mealtimes in Britain (line 4: *that is*), and now T lectures him about the sequence of mealtimes in Britain (lines 14 to 32) while J indicates understanding by acknowledgments (lines 41, 44, 46).

When T reaches what can be heard as a generic idiomatic formulation (Drew & Holt, 1998)—*dinner time is also sometimes known as lunch lunch time is dinner time*—J advances the talk further by asking about the specific time of day for "dinner time" and specifying possible candidates (*six o'clock* line 37, *seven* line 39). Thus, while his earlier repeats and acknowledgments *claimed* understanding of T's lecture, J now *shows* understanding by building his turn on the information given by T.

Extract 2 shows how a repair sequence transforms into a lecturing/instruction sequence. J's change of frame into a "generic" formulation (*that is*, line 4) might have been the catalyst for this shift. We can see that the L1 speaker gives a lexical explanation when the L2 speaker makes his troubles obvious and that the production of T's explanation is accompanied by J's indications of understanding.

In Extracts 1 and 2 we have demonstrated that L2 talk affords moments of learning. By pursuing their use of the L2, the speakers actively create possibilities for such moments to occur. In both extracts, the L1 speaker becomes a resource for the L2 speaker to practice and gather new "input." One of the major tasks for CA-SLA is to understand and describe how these at times very subtle moments of learning are systematically created by the L2 speaker. The task is to show how L2 speakers systematically—i.e., as practices—create these opportunities within interactions about other things in the world, and understanding and describing these practices will remain a central occupation for CA-SLA.

Development of Interactional Competence

Development in the short term

In contrast to language learning as a social practice, "development" is observable to analysts through comparing different moments within an activity or successive activities over a longer period (Zimmerman, 1999). Borrowing from Markee (2000), we refer to the former as "development in the short term" and the latter as "development over time."

Development in the short term is well illustrated by Ishida (2006), who traced how a JFL student's understanding and use of interactional particles such as *ne* and the verbal suffix -*yoo* developed within a dyadic decision-making activity. Over the course of the 10-minute interaction, the JFL speaker showed increasing understanding of the response trajectories of *ne*-marked assessments and of *jaa*-initiated prior turns, and began to use modal markers to move a decision-in-progress to completion. Ishida argued that the shared objective to come to a joint decision at several points in the interaction oriented the L2 speaker to the sequential contexts in which her co-participant used modal resources and thereby provided occasions for microgenesis—the emergence of higher-order cognitive functions through interaction (Wertsch & Stone, 1978). Changes in the L2 speaker's understanding and use of modal markers became analytically visible through comparison of similar sequences in the activity, yet at no time did the participants orient to the activity as *learning*. Nor did development issue from repair or correction.

An instance of lexical learning in the short term can be seen in Extracts 3A and 3B.[5] The participants are two teenage boys, Chungho and his younger brother Jinho (L2 English/L1 Korean speakers), their friend Tom (L1 English), and a cat. Tom and Chungho are talking while Jinho has gone to the restroom. Just before, while the three boys were sitting at a table chatting, the cat had snapped at Jinho's hand. Now the cat has positioned himself on top of the stairs opposite the restroom. Chungho and Tom are watching the scene.

Extract 3A: Attack 1 (Kim, 2009a)

```
01. C:   the cat is (.) waiting for my brother
02. T:   khe heh it's gonna bite his other
03.      fi(hh)ngers heh heh heh
04.      (1.5)
05. T:   it's hunting you ehh heh heh heh
06. C:   HEH HEH [heh heh      heh heh [heh
07. T:           [eh heh heh heh       [eh
08.      heh heh heh heh heh
09. T:   ((Tom mimicking cat growling))
10. C:   I think (0.3) it will be very funny (.)
11.      if (0.6) he just (0.3) comes out of
12.      the restroom, (0.8) and (0.9) standing
13.      (0.8) in front of the stairs (0.8) and uh
14.      (.) cat jumps [(0.7) into him
15. T:                 [mh heh heh ye(hh)ah
16.      atta(hh)cks heh heh heh heh heh heh
```

After Chungho formulates what he sees the cat doing in line 1, he and Tom collaboratively develop a hypothetical scenario of an adversarial encounter between the cat and Jinho (lines 2–5). Both treat the imagined scene as laughable and funny. Perhaps inspired by Tom's performance of a cat sound projecting imminent violence, Chungho launches a small hypothetical story of feline aggression against his brother (lines 10–14), prefaced as something that to him is a *funny* matter. At the moment the story's point becomes clear (*cat jumps*, line 14), Tom starts a laughter turn in overlap, in which he aligns himself with Chungho's assessment of the story as funny. Following the agreement token *yeah* (line 15), he reformulates Chungho's description *jumps into him* with *attacks* (16), a more succinct characterization of the cat's imagined action. Said under continued laughing, what might be heard as a correction is not at all oriented to as such by the participants. For them, the interactional project of the moment is "doing being friends" by imagining a funny scene together. Neither of them appears the least bit concerned with language learning. In the next turn (not shown), the talk shifts to a different topic.

Extract 3B starts less than a minute after Extract 3A.

Extract 3B: Attack 2 (Kim, 2009a)
```
01. C:   I thinked (.) that (2.5) maybe uh
02.      (0.6) m the cat (0.9) this cat can be
03.      my side
04.      (1.2)
05. T:   could be your what?
06. C:   my side
07.      (1.4)
08. T:   your side?
09.      (0.4)
10. C:   yeah
11. T:   how do you mean?
12. C:   uh when he attacks him, (0.6)
13. T:   oh::
14. C:   eh he runs to him an' (.) chew his
15.      [fingers
16. T:   [eh heh heh heh heh yeah it's like
17.      your bodyguard
```

After Chungho resumes the topic of the cat (lines 1–3), Tom indicates that he has trouble understanding the word *side* (line 5). After two unsuccessful rounds of other-initiated repair, Tom asks Chungho more explicitly to clarify what he means by *my (your) side* (line 11). In response, Chungho formulates an action sequence that shows the cat to be *my side*. After describing the cat's action in *when he attacks him* (line 12), Tom claims that he now understands (*oh::*, line 13). Chungho's next turn elaborates how the cat would attack Jingho (lines 14 & 15). Before Chungho has finished his turn, Tom aligns himself to Chungho's description through laughter, an agreement token (*yeah*), and by comparing the cat's role to that of Chungho's bodyguard. With this last action in the extract, Tom demonstrates (rather than only claims, as in line 13) that the understanding problem has been resolved.

In line 12 of Extract 3B, then, Chungho effectively uses the word *attack* to clear up Tom's difficulty. There is no way of telling whether in Extract 3A he did not know the word, or did not recall it, or knew it but did not mean to use it. The temporal structure of line 14, *(.) cat jumps (0.7) into him*, does not suggest that Chungho was searching for an alternative verb. To hold ourselves to the interactional facts, however, we can register that (1) the L2 speaker does not use a possible target word at time 1; (2) the word is delivered by a co-participant; (3) there is no immediate uptake, recognition, or other reaction; (4) the L2 speaker uses the word without delay, correctly, and without assistance or prompting at time 2. These observations allow us say that "learning in the short term" is in evidence, but no claims are possible about whether the word becomes a durable resource in the L2 speaker's lexical repertoire (cf. Firth & Wagner, 2007). From a Vygotskyan perspective (Vygotsky, 1978), we are witnessing the learner's appropriation of a cultural tool during social interaction, an important process in ontogenesis. Observations about short-term development have not only been made about lexical items—Pekarek Doehler and Steinbach (in press) show how a group of students in a language classroom achieves control over a French morphosyntactic construction.

Development over time

A fast-growing literature provides evidence for development over time. For the most part, this research adopts a longitudinal perspective, but at least one published study is based exclusively on cross-sectional data. Kim (2009b) examined how L2 speakers of Korean at different proficiency levels use the discourse markers *-nuntey* and *-kuntey* in conversations with Korean L1 speakers. Based on patterned uses of the markers in different turn positions, she described a developmental trajectory that corresponded to the diachronic grammaticalization[6] process shown for these discourse markers. Kim thus theorized the developmental process as an instance of acquisitional grammaticalization. This study is a good example of connecting CA findings to exogenous theory subsequent to analysis (see page 125).

Longitudinal studies have investigated the development of interactional competencies in a range of settings, such as business phone calls, pharmacy consultations, and study abroad. The analytical foci are highly varied, ranging from such activity-specific actions as caller identification at the beginning of telephone calls (Brouwer & Wagner, 2004) to specific (socio)linguistic resources, such as the use of *tu* and *usted* in L2 Spanish synchronic chat (González-Lloret, 2008). In a longitudinal case study—a format well known from naturalistic SLA research—Ishida (2009) examined how an L2 learner of Japanese developed his use of the interactional particle *ne* during study abroad in Japan. Over a ten-month period, the student expanded his use of *ne* to different sequential contexts and so was able to engage more actively and effectively in developing talk. This study connects with research on the development of resources for indexing epistemic and affective stance from a language socialization perspective (see Duff & Talmy, this volume). In a series of longitudinal case studies, Nguyen (2006, 2008) traced how pharmacy interns develop their interactional competencies in the professional activity of patient consultation. Nguyen's case studies document how, over time, an intern became more apt at presenting expert information to patients while establishing an affiliative relationship with them (2006), and how interns progressively organized the sequential ordering of tasks in the consultation more effectively (2008).

In a book-length CA study on L2 learning and development, Hellermann (2008) examined changes in adult ESL students' indigenous methods of accomplishing social order in their classrooms, conceptualized as communities of practice. Specifically, the study focused on the sequential organization of openings, storytellings, and disengagements in teacher-assigned dyadic tasks. Regardless of proficiency level, the students jointly oriented to the task requirements and thereby to themselves and each other as accountable members of their classroom community of practice. Beginning-level students relied more heavily on embodied action through nonverbal resources, and while their boundary actions and storytellings were recognizable as such for participants, they were composed of fewer action types and extended over brief turns. The higher-proficiency students, on the other hand, organized these sequences with expanded repertoires of social actions and linguistic practices. They also constructed affiliative relationships with their co-participants through humor and positive assessments. As shown also in Ishida (2006, 2009), social affiliation is reflexively related to the development of interactional competence: Marking affiliative stance through the resources of an L2 is a central objective for L2 development, while affiliative relations serve as the matrix for continued and future participation in social activities and thereby for further occasions for L2 learning. In one sense, by conceptualizing classrooms as communities of practice, Hellermann's study follows a well-established tradition in qualitative classroom research. The particular achievement of Hellermann's study was to demonstrate how the classroom communities of practice at his observation site were reflexively constituted through the observable local operations by which student dyads and the teacher organized their participation.

We close this section by returning to a telephone call by the same participants as in Extract 1. In Extract 4A, J is discussing his own upcoming trip to Britain with T.

Extract 4A: Washed and Pressed 1

```
01. T:   a::nd eh then you can (.)
02.      ·hhhh once you've sort of (0.3)
03.      got yourself sort of e:h (0.4)
04.      ·hhhh washed and pressed
05.      hhe hhe [hhe hhe hhe.
06. J:           [hm:↓:m.
07. T:   ·hhh e::::hm:: then we'll: we'll
08.      go out in the evening and then
09.      show you som::e (.) eh of Southampton
10.      on the following morning
```

Here, we are interested in the item *washed and pressed* (line 4), which comes up in a conversation between participants some time later, when T is planning a trip to Denmark.

Extract 4B: Washed and Pressed 2

```
01. T:  e:::hm, so one hour to (us) so we'll be at home
02.     say [by:] two::
03. J:      [mm].
04.     (0.4)
05. T:  to your house [by tw]o.
06. J:                [ye:s].
07. T:  we can perhaps talk then about wha to do.
08.     (.)
09. J:  so you can be washed and pressed
10.     (.)
11. J:  I remember your words hhhe hhe
12.     [hhe hhe] hhe hhe [hhe hhe]
13. T:  [(hhe)]           [perfect].
14. J:  ehh hh↑e hhe hh↓e hh hh.
15. T:  washed and pr↓es[sed.
16. J:                  [yeah
17. T:  hosed d↓own.
18. J:  hhe hhe hh[e hh[e hh[e hh[e.
19. T:            [ehh [hhe [hhe [hhe
```

In Extract 4B, line 9, J uses a version of a slightly unusual idiom; additionally, he accounts for it by referring to their earlier talk (Extract 4A, line 4). This is one of the few instances in our data where the participants themselves present their version of where they picked up words and phrases, regardless of whether they did so after having been exposed to the phrase once, or whether they remembered and used the item after the earlier conversation. These two extracts, then, give us the L2 speaker's own version of their learning history as part of a social conversation.

The research on learning and development that we have reviewed and illustrated in this section both offers points of contact with established SLA traditions and highlights the specific contributions that a CA perspective brings to the field at large. As we have pointed out, by bringing CA to bear on L2 talk in such different social settings as business phone calls, service encounters, and ordinary conversation, concepts and topics from sociocultural theory, language socialization, and situated learning theory can be connected with the analysis of observable interactional practices in ongoing social activities. One immediate task ahead is to further expand the existing corpus of CA-SLA studies. Further items for CA-SLA's agenda will be suggested in the final section below.

Future Directions

One topic to pursue in future research is the way in which L2 speakers' available interactional competencies in other languages, including the L1, organize their participation in L2 talk, and what developmental changes may be seen in that regard. So far, the transfer of interactional practices to L2 talk has been peripheral to the field. Golato (2002) and Taleghani-Nikazm (2002) described instances of pragmatic transfer as interactional moments that the participants orient to as problematic, but transfer as a participant concern has not yet become a major analytical problem in CA-SLA research. Such research will be necessary in order to find out (1) whether transfer, a notion with a famously controversial history in SLA, is—or can be made—compatible with CA's theoretical principles; (2) whether (if the first question is answerable in the positive) transfer is a unitary phenomenon or—more likely—a collection of diverse interactional practices and resources; and (3) whether such probable diversity still allows cases of cross-linguistic, cross-discursive, and cross-interactional influence to be treated as the same phenomenon.

As noted earlier in passing, identifying the development of interactional competencies hinges critically on comparison. Therefore CA-SLA needs to clarify what count as comparable interactional events. Such clarification is necessary for comparing actions and practices cross-culturally or cross-linguistically, or in different activity types, as well as for comparing actions and practices over time, as described above. As more findings in the different domains of developmental CA become available, it will also be possible to see how the methods of learning and the developmental trajectories in these domains compare.

Related to the issue of comparability, CA-SLA needs to develop a position on its relationship with ethnomethodology and discursive psychology. CA-SLA researchers commonly point out CA's intellectual debt to EM (which we do not dispute) and sometimes describe their brand of CA as "ethnomethodological CA." But as recent debates between EM and CA proponents indicate (e.g., Kitzinger, 2008; Wowk, 2007), there are critical differences between the two traditions that have important theoretical and methodological implications for CA-SLA. For instance, as a consequence of wider epistemological differences, ethnomethodologists and conversation analysts (understood as diverse and overlapping research communities) differ in their views on the validity of collection-based and single-case analyses. CA-SLA needs to continue this debate on its own premises as it has direct consequences for research practices.

Discursive psychology (DP) has only just begun to make a cautious entrance into CA-SLA (Kasper, 2009; Markee & Seo, 2009), but most likely we will soon see more uptake in SLA studies. Perhaps the most urgent question to ponder when DP is incorporated into CA-SLA is its position on the treatment of cognition, emotion, and other "intrapsychological" states and processes. DP is agnostic toward the ontological status of psychological phenomena and radically anti-cognitive in its methods of treating psychological topics (Edwards, 1997). CA, on the other hand, shows a more diverse treatment of cognition in interaction. Conversation analysts have therefore been taken to task by discursive psychologists and ethnomethodologists for what they see as lapses into cognitivism. As CA-SLA diversifies its research program, practitioners need to engage with these debates and develop their own stances on the issues to advance CA-SLA's program with a view to theoretical coherence, methodological accountability, and relevance for social intervention.

Appendix: Transcription Conventions

[ ]	points where overlapping talk starts and ends
(0.5)	length of silence in tenths of a second
(.)	micropause of less than two-tenths of a second
underlining	relatively high pitch
CAPS	high volume
::	lengthened syllable
–	cut-off; self-interruption
?	rising intonation contour
.	falling intonation contour
,	continuing intonation contour
↑↓	marks a sharp rise or fall in intonation
xx	unintelligible speech
(speech)	speech transcriber is unsure of
(( ))	transcriber's descriptions of events, including nonvocal conduct
hh	audible outbreath
·hh	audible inbreath
(hh)	laughter syllable within a word
° °	passage of talk quieter than the surrounding talk
☺ ☺	passage of talk in smiley voice
★ ★	passage of talk in creaky voice

Notes

1   This point will be elaborated upon and qualified in the following section.
2   Theodorsdóttír's data were collected from L2 learners of Icelandic outside of classrooms, often in service encounters.
3   See Appendix for transcription conventions.
4   An *adjacency pair* consists of two turns by two speakers such that the first pair part produced by the first speaker makes a specific type of second pair part relevant, with the second pair part routinely being produced by the second speaker, for example request/response, question/answer. Thus, Ilse here requests cigarettes, expecting the bartender to comply (but, in this case, the bartender is unable to—see below). An *insertion sequence* is a sequence of turns that is inserted after a first pair part of an adjacency pair to solve some kind of problem preventing the second pair from being produced. Thus, the bartender here needs to know the cigarette brand Ilse wants before he can comply with her request.
5   Our analysis of the extracts builds on Kim's original analysis (2009a, pp. 172–174, 177–178).
6   *Grammaticalization* is a process in language change whereby content words lose their semantic meanings and transform into function words.

References

Antaki, C., & Widdicombe, S. (Eds.) (1998). *Identities in talk*. Thousand Oaks, CA: Sage.

Benwell, B., & Stokoe, E. (2006). *Discourse and identity*. Edinburgh: Edinburgh University Press.

Björk-Willén, P. (2008). Routine trouble: How preschool children participate in multilingual instruction. *Applied Linguistics, 29*, 555–577.

Block, D. (2007). *Second language identities*. London: Continuum.

Brouwer, C. E. (2003). Word searches in NNS–NS interaction: opportunities for language learning? *Modern Language Journal, 87*, 534–545.

Brouwer, C. E., & Wagner, J. (2004). Developmental issues in second language conversation. *Journal of Applied Linguistics, 1*, 29–47.

Carroll, D. (2005). Vowel marking as an interactional resource in Japanese novice EFL conversation. In K. Richards & P. Seedhouse (Eds.), *Applying conversation analysis* (pp. 214–234). Basingstoke: Palgrave Macmillan.

Cekaite, A. (2007). A child's development of interactional competence in a Swedish L2 classroom. *Modern Language Journal, 91*, 45–62.

Cromdal, J. (2008). Childhood and social interaction in everyday life: Introduction to the special issue. *Journal of Pragmatics, 41*, 1473–1476.

Drew, P. (2005). Conversation analysis. In K. L. Fitch & R. E. Sanders (Eds.), *Handbook of language and social interaction* (pp. 71–102). Mahwah, NJ: Erlbaum.

Drew, P., & Holt, E. (1998) Figures of speech: figurative expressions and the management of topic transition in conversation. *Language in Society, 27*, 495–523.

Duneir, M., & Molotch, H. (1999). Talking city trouble: Interactional vandalism, social inequality, and the "urban interaction problem." *American Journal of Sociology, 104*, 1263–1295.

Edwards, D. (1997). *Discourse and cognition*. London: Sage.

Ervin-Tripp, S. M. (1979). Children's verbal turn-taking. In E. Ochs & B. Schieffelin (Eds.), *Developmental pragmatics* (pp. 391–414). New York: Academic Press.

Ervin-Tripp, S. M., & Gordon, D. P. (1985). The development of requests. In R. L. Schiefelbusch (Ed.), *Communicative competence: Acquisition and intervention* (pp. 61–96). Beverly Hills, CA: College Hills Press.

Eskildsen, S. W. (in press). The L2 inventory in action: Conversation analysis and usage-based linguistics in SLA. In G. Pallotti & J. Wagner (Eds.), *L2 learning as social practice: Conversation-analytic perspectives*. Honolulu, HI: University of Hawai'i, National Foreign Language Resource Center.

Firth, A., & Wagner, J. (1997). On discourse, communication and some fundamental concepts in SLA research. *Modern Language Journal, 81*, 285–300.

Firth, A., & Wagner, J. (2007). Second/foreign language learning as a social accomplishment: elaborations on a reconceptualized SLA. *Modern Language Journal, 91*, 798–817.

Forrester, M. A. (2008). The emergence of self-repair: a case study of one child during the early preschool years. *Research on Language & Social Interaction, 41*, 99–128.

Fox, B. A., Hayashi, M., & Jasperson, R. (1996). Resources and repair: a cross-linguistic study of syntax and repair. In E. Ochs, E.A. Schegloff, & S.A. Thompson (Eds.), *Interaction and grammar* (pp. 185–237). Cambridge: Cambridge University Press.

Garfinkel, H. (1967). *Studies in ethnomethodology*. Englewood Cliffs, NJ: Prentice Hall.

Goffman, E. (1983). The interaction order. *American Sociological Review, 48*, 1–17.

Golato, A. (2002). German compliment responses. *Journal of Pragmatics, 34*, 547–571.

González-Lloret, M. (2008). *"No me llames de Usted, trátame de tú": L2 address behavior development through synchronous computer-mediated communication*. Unpublished doctoral dissertation, University of Hawai'i.

Goodwin, C. (2000). Action and embodiment within situated human interaction. *Journal of Pragmatics*, *32*, 1489–1522.

Goodwin, M. H, & Goodwin, C. (1986). Gesture and coparticipation in the activity of searching for a word. *Semiotica*, *62*, 51–75.

Have, P. ten (2007). *Doing conversation analysis: A practical guide*. London: Sage.

Hayashi, M. (2004). Projection and grammar: Notes on the 'action-projecting' use of the distal demonstrative *are* in Japanese. *Journal of Pragmatics*, *36*, 1337–1374.

Hellermann, J. (2008). *Social actions for classroom language learning*. Clevedon: Multilingual Matters.

Hosoda, Y. (2006). Repair and relevance of differential language expertise in second language conversations. *Applied Linguistics*, *27*, 25–50.

Hutchby, I., & Wooffitt, R. (2008). *Conversation analysis: Principles, practices and applications*. Oxford: Polity Press.

Ishida, M. (2006). Interactional competence and the use of modal expressions in decision-making activities: CA for understanding microgenesis of pragmatic competence. In K. Bardovi-Harlig, J. C. Félix-Brasdefer, & A. Omar (Eds.), *Pragmatics and language learning, Vol. 11* (pp. 55–79). Honolulu, HI: University of Hawai'i, National Foreign Language Resource Center.

Ishida, M. (2009). Development of interactional competence: changes in the use of *ne* in L2 Japanese during study abroad. In H. thi Nguyen & G. Kasper (Eds.), *Talk-in-interaction: Multilingual perspectives* (pp. 351–387). Honolulu, HI: University of Hawai'i, National Foreign Language Resource Center.

Kasper, G. (2004). Participant orientations in German conversation-for-learning. *Modern Language Journal*, *88*, 551–567.

Kasper, G. (2009). Locating cognition in second language interaction and learning: Inside the skull or in public view? *International Review of Applied Linguistics*, *47*, 11–36.

Kidwell, M. (2009). Gaze shift as an interactional resource for very young children. *Discourse Processes*, *46*, 145–160.

Kim, Y. (2009a). *Achieving reference in talk-in-interaction: L1 and L2 English speakers' conversation*. Unpublished doctoral dissertation, University of Hawai'i.

Kim, Y. (2009b). Korean discourse markers *-nuntey* and *-kuntey* in native–nonnative conversation: An acquisitional perspective. In H. thi Nguyen & G. Kasper (Eds.), *Talk-in-interaction: Multilingual perspectives* (pp. 317–350). Honolulu, HI: University of Hawai'i, National Foreign Language Resource Center.

Kitzinger, C. (2008). Developing feminist conversation analysis: A response to Wowk. *Human Studies*, *31*, 179–208.

Koshik, I. (2005). *Beyond rhetorical questions*. Amsterdam: Benjamins.

Lee, Y.-A. (2006). Towards respecification of communicative competence: Condition of L2 instruction or its objective? *Applied Linguistics*, *27*, 349–376.

Markee, N. (1994). Towards an ethnomethodological respecification of second language acquisition studies. In E. Tarone, M. Gass, & A. Cohen (Eds.), *Research methodology in second language acquisition* (pp. 89–116). Hillsdale, NJ: Erlbaum.

Markee, N. (2000). *Conversation analysis*. Mahwah, NJ: Erlbaum.

Markee, N., & Seo, M.-S. (2009). Learning talk analysis. *International Review of Applied Linguistics in Language Teaching*, *47*, 37–63.

Maynard, D. W. (2003). *Bad news, good news. Conversational order in everyday talk and clinical settings*. Chicago, IL: Chicago University Press.

Mazeland, H. (2006). Conversation analysis. In K. Brown (Ed.), *Encyclopedia of language and linguistics, Vol. 3* (2nd ed.) (pp. 153–162). Oxford & Amsterdam: Elsevier.

McHoul, A., Rapley, M., & Antaki, C. (2008). You gotta light? On the luxury of context for understanding talk in interaction. *Journal of Pragmatics, 40,* 42–54.

Mehan H. (1979). *Learning lessons.* Cambridge, MA: Harvard University Press.

Molder, H. te, & Potter, J. (Eds.) (2005). *Conversation and cognition.* Cambridge: Cambridge University Press.

Mori, J. (2003). The construction of interculturality: A study of initial encounters between Japanese and American students. *Research on Language & Social Interaction, 36,* 143–184.

Mori, J. (2004). Negotiating sequential boundaries and learning opportunities: A case from a Japanese language classroom. *Modern Language Journal, 88,* 536–550.

Mori, J. (2010). Learning language in real time: A case study of the Japanese demonstrative pronoun *are* in word-search sequences. In G. Kasper, H. thi Nguyen, D. R. Yoshimi, & J. K. Yoshioka (Eds.), *Pragmatics & language learning, Vol. 12* (pp. 15–42). Honolulu, HI: University of Hawai'i, National Foreign Language Resource Center.

Mori, J., & Hasegawa, A. (2009). Doing being a foreign language learner in a classroom: Embodiment of cognitive states as social events. *International Review of Applied Linguistics in Language Teaching, 47,* 65–94.

Nguyen, H. thi (2006). Constructing 'expertness': A novice pharmacist's development of interactional competence in patient consultations. *Communication & Medicine, 3,* 147–160.

Nguyen, H. thi (2008). Sequential organization as local and longitudinal achievement. *Text & Talk, 28,* 501–528.

Pekarek Doehler, S., & Steinbach, F. (in press). Emergent L2 grammar: socially situated learning and the on-line elaboration of grammatical constructions. *Applied Linguistics, 31.*

Peräkylä, A. (2004). Reliability and validity in research based on naturally occurring social interaction. In D. Silverman (Ed.), *Qualitative research* (pp. 283–304). London: Sage.

Potter, J. (2003). Discursive psychology: Between method and paradigm. *Discourse & Society, 14,* 783–794.

Roberts, C. (1997). Transcribing talk: Issues of representation. *TESOL Quarterly, 31,* 167–172.

Rogoff, B. (1999). *Everyday cognition: Development in social context.* Lincoln, NE: iUniverse. com.

Ryoo, H. (2007). Interculturality serving multiple interactional goals in African American and Korean service encounters. *Pragmatics, 17,* 71–94.

Sacks, H., Schegloff, E. A., & Jefferson, G. (1974). A simplest systematics for the organization of turn taking for conversation. *Language, 50,* 696–735.

Schegloff, E. A. (1987). Analyzing single episodes of interaction: An exercise in conversation analysis. *Social Psychology Quarterly, 50,* 101–114.

Schegloff, E. A. (1991). Conversation analysis and socially shared cognition. In L. B. Resnick, J. M. Levine, & S. D. Teasley (Eds.), *Perspectives on socially shared cognition* (pp. 150–171). Washington, DC: American Psychological Association.

Schegloff, E. A., Jefferson, G., & Sacks, H. (1977). The preference for self-correction in the organization of repair in conversation. *Language, 53,* 361–382.

Schegloff, E. A., Ochs, E., & Thompson, S. (1996). Introduction. In E. Ochs, E. A. Schegloff, & S. A. Thompson (Eds.), *Interaction and grammar* (pp. 1–51). Cambridge: Cambridge University Press.

Selting, M., & Couper-Kuhlen, E. (Eds.) (2001). *Studies in interactional linguistics.* Amsterdam: Benjamins.

Sidnell, J. (2009). Comparative perspectives in conversation analysis. In J. Sidnell (Ed.), *Conversation analysis* (pp. 3–28). Cambridge: Cambridge University Press.

Takigawa, Y. (2010). *Dispute and language expertise: Analysis of bilingual couple talk in Japanese.* Saarbrücken: Lambert Academic Publishing.

Taleghani-Nikazm, C. (2002). A conversation-analytic study of telephone conversation opening between native and nonnative speakers. *Journal of Pragmatics*, *34*, 1807–1832.

Talmy, S. (2009). Resisting ESL: Categories and sequence in a critically "motivated" analysis of classroom interaction. In H. thi Nguyen & G. Kasper (Eds.), *Talk-in-interaction: Multilingual perspectives* (pp. 181–213). Honolulu, HI: University of Hawai'i, National Foreign Language Resource Center.

Theodorsdóttír, G. (in press-a). Language learning activities in real-life situations: Insisting on TCU completion in second language talk. In G. Pallotti & J. Wagner (Eds.), *L2 learning as social practice: Conversation-analytic perspectives*. Honolulu, HI: University of Hawai'i, National Foreign Language Resource Center.

Theodorsdóttír, G. (in press-b). Opening up opportunities. Second language learning outside of the classroom: the case of one service encounter. In Hall, J. K., Hellermann, J., & Pekarek Doehler, S. (Eds.). *L2 Interactional Competence and Development*. Bristol: Multilingual Matters.

Vygotsky, L. S. (1978). *Mind and society: The development of higher mental processes*. Cambridge, MA: Harvard University Press.

Wagner, J., & Gardner, R. (2004). Introduction. In R. Gardner & J. Wagner (Eds.), *Second language conversations* (pp. 1–17). London: Continuum.

Wertsch, J. V., & Stone, C. A. (1978). Microgenesis as a tool for developmental analysis. *Quarterly Newsletter of the Laboratory of Comparative Human Cognition*, *1*, 8–10.

Wootton, A. J. (1981). Two request forms of four year olds. *Journal of Pragmatics*, *5*, 511–523.

Wootton, A. J. (1997). *Interaction and the development of mind*. Cambridge: Cambridge University Press.

Wootton, A. J. (2006). Children's practices and their connections with "mind." *Discourse Studies*, *8*, 191–198.

Wowk, M. T. (2007). Kitzinger's feminist conversation analysis: Critical observations. *Human Studies*, *30*, 131–155.

Zimmerman, D. H. (1998). Identity, context and interaction. In C. Antaki & S. Widdicombe (Eds.), *Identities in talk* (pp. 87–106). London: Sage.

Zimmerman, D. H. (1999). Horizontal and vertical comparative research in language and social interaction. *Research on Language & Social Interaction*, *32*, 195–203.

6

A SOCIOCOGNITIVE APPROACH TO SECOND LANGUAGE ACQUISITION

How mind, body, and world work together in learning additional languages

Dwight Atkinson

> Mind is invisible nature, while nature is visible mind.
>
> (Schelling, in Beiser, 2000, p. 33)

Overview

The core claim of a sociocognitive approach is that mind, body, and world function integratively in second language acquisition (SLA). This does not mean that we can never speak of cognition per se when discussing SLA, but it does mean that cognition per se is a fiction. This claim, which may trouble SLA researchers, is based on the following reasoning.

Like all organisms, human beings are *ecological* organisms—they depend on their environment to survive. For this same reason, humans are *adaptive* organisms—they survive by continuously and dynamically adapting to their environment. Cognition plays a central role in this endeavor by promoting intelligent, adaptive action-in-the-world, and to do so it must be intimately aligned with its environment. Put differently, cognition is a node in an ecological network comprising mind–body–world—it is part of a *relationship*. This view contrasts sharply with the dominant understanding of cognition as "mind-in-a-vat" or "lonely cognition," i.e., *cognition per se*.

A sociocognitive approach has striking implications in several areas. The first is learning. Instead of viewing learning as a rarified activity—as occurring mostly in exotic locations (e.g., classrooms), at the behest of special people (e.g., teachers), for hazy, abstract purposes (e.g., education)—it sees learning as a default state of human affairs. If we constantly and sensitively adapt to our environments, then learning is continuous, at least insofar as durable adaptive change occurs in the learner–world system. Recent developments in cognitive science, neuroscience, anthropology, and biology support this view by re-envisioning cognition as an *open system*—as continuously and dynamically adapting to worldly conditions.

A second implication of a sociocognitive approach is that cognition is extended and distributed—it projects out into the world, often via the multitude of adaptive tools invented by humans. Maps, toothbrush holders, clocks, interlocutors, runway lights, the internet, literacy, computers, datebooks, GPS systems, teachers, cell phones, grammar exercises, and many more ecosocial creations organize and support cognition—by affording sociocognitive activities that would be difficult or impossible without them. I suggest below how such *cognitive technologies* (Clark, 2001) and *affordances* (Gibson, 1979) aid not just cognition but also learning.

Finally, a sociocognitive perspective has striking implications for SLA. It views SLA, like other forms of learning, as a natural, adaptive process of ecological alignment. This is hardly to deny that cognition is crucial in SLA, but cognitivist views ignore the profound embeddedness of language learning in the world. From a sociocognitive perspective, the best way to promote SLA is to place learners in situations where the L2 is necessary for social action—where they need it to survive and prosper. Such learning will often, if not always, take place within *situated activity systems*, as described below.

Theoretical Principles

As should now be obvious, sociocognitive perspectives are well outside the SLA mainstream. In this section, I try to sharpen the differences by redefining three concepts central to SLA from a sociocognitive perspective: cognition, language, and learning. Once this task is accomplished, the focus can shift directly to SLA itself.

Cognition

Classical/mainstream cognitive science is based on a core set of assumptions, all of which have influenced SLA studies (see Introduction, this volume; Atkinson, 2002; Boden, 2006). These include: (1) mind is a thing in itself—virtually everything needed to explain the (mature) mind's workings can be found *in* the mind; (2) abstract, logic-like thought is the fundamental type of cognition; (3) minds operate like serial computers, making cognition the logical ordering and manipulation of symbols; and (4) cognition operates in a rigidly top-down, rule-governed way.

Embodied, embedded cognitive science (e.g., Atkinson, 2010a, 2010b; Wheeler, 2005) has thrown these assumptions into doubt by arguing that human cognition is first and foremost *adaptive intelligence*—it exists primarily to help us survive and prosper in our ecosocial worlds. Instead of a serial computer, cognition is therefore an *open biological system* designed by evolution and experience to align sensitively with the ambient environment. How else could weak, vulnerable, ecologically nonspecialized creatures like ourselves have survived and prospered, evolutionarily speaking, than by being natural-born adapters and learners? Thinking *with* the ecosocial environment is paramount in adaptive human intelligence.[1]

A substantial body of work supports this position. Theoretically, such conceptualizations as *situated cognition*, *distributed cognition*, and *extended mind* trouble the mind–world dichotomy. Thus, Clark and Chalmers (1998) argued that the line between mind and world dissolves when cognition "extends" radically across it: Cognition and its supporting environment are at least sometimes functionally integrated. Consider, for example, cognition-for-driving. When traveling by car, we typically follow the preexisting road grid rather than striking out on our own across roadless country. In this sense, the road grid does much of the direction-finding for us—it encodes a map or plan that it is therefore unnecessary to have in our heads (Gee, 1992). Getting from point A to point B thus requires no detailed mental representation of the land traversed; rather, one needs to know just a few environmental cues and responses to them; for example, to get to work, I turn right at the apartment entrance, left at Walmart, bear right onto Northwestern, and soon the campus appears straight ahead. In short, the cognition needed for driving is quite modest when roads think for you!

The body is also intimately involved in cognition. Empirically, researchers have demonstrated that: bodily states, bodily orientation, and emotions affect and are affected by cognitive processes; cognitive development depends on embodied action; and neural mechanisms underlying cognition are fundamentally embodied (see Atkinson, 2010a; Barsalou, 2008; Clark, 1997; Gibbs, 2005; and Glenberg, 1997 for reviews). In the last area, a major discovery has been that of *mirror neurons* (Iacoboni, 2009; Rizzolatti & Craighero, 2004)—cerebral neurons that fire both when observing others performing specific actions and when performing those same actions oneself. This discovery has cast doubt on the mainstream view that cognition, perception, and motor action are clearly separate phenomena, as well as the notion of elaborate, decontextualized cognitive representations. Instead, it suggests that others' actions and intentions are comprehended by having an embodied "feel" for what they are doing, saying, etc., because the neural circuits for performing and perceiving real-world action overlap. Mirror neurons also provide a neurophysiological basis for: (1) *behavioral synchrony*, a pervasive aspect of human interaction, as described just below; and (2) *imitative learning*—currently receiving widespread attention as a fundamental type of human learning (Hurley & Chater, 2005).

To perform adaptive, cooperative social action, individuals' behaviors must be tightly synchronized:

> Two important functions of social cognition are the adaptive regulation of the behavior of the other . . . and adaptive co-regulation . . . For action to be efficient and adaptive, it must be closely tuned to the environment. Adaptive social action is the emergent outcome of a dynamic process of moment-by-moment interaction between conspecifics. To adapt to a

continuously changing environment, the organism must have a finely tuned mechanism in place that is responsive to the multifaceted and dynamic features of the physical and social environment.

(Semin & Cacciopo, 2008, pp. 121–122)

In order to synchronize their behaviors, then, individuals must share understandings and expectations about what they are doing. Yet cognition-for-joint-action goes beyond separate cognitive apparatuses exchanging discrete signals: Individuals *align* as sociocognitive units. Such alignment is also necessary in the species of social action known as SLA, as described below.

Language

From a sociocognitive standpoint, language is a tool for social action: selling fish, arguing, sharing stories, calming children. Ironically, mainstream linguistics' success in marginalizing linguistic performance confirms its very centrality: Chomsky's rhetorical defeat of descriptive linguistics is a paradigm case of language-in-action.

Language in use must be nimble and quick to effect social action—it must be dynamically adaptive vis-à-vis its environment. Yet mainstream language processing research favors elaborately designed and rigidly top-down mechanisms, its goal being to model as much as possible mind-internally (Nausbaum & Small, 2006). But if language is for acting in the world, internalist models of language use have the same problems as mainstream cognitive models in general:

It appears that the underlying substrate of mental activity is not a repertory of well-defined, well-structured abstract symbols, and that the workings of mind cannot be generally characterized as the computational manipulation of such symbols. Rather, the substrate in which mental activity takes place should be one that meets the following requirements: It should afford maximal sensitivity to unspecified dimensions and distinctions, it should be context-sensitive, and it should be embedded in the framework of the organism's action in the world.

(Shanon, quoted in Glenberg, 1997, p. 3)

Nonmainstream linguists have made similar proposals regarding grammar. Thus, Hopper (1988) argued that grammar is *emergent*—"a vaguely defined set of sedimented . . ., recurrent partials whose status is constantly being renegotiated" in use (p. 118). Grammar, in this view, is a reflex of discourse—the always-in-process *result* of real-time language use. Instead of static, a priori constructions with stable compositional meanings, emergent grammar is built on the fly for environmentally specific use. Apparent grammatical stabilities are the result of the sedimentation of repeated language-situation correspondences in personal and social memory. Hopper's view has radical consequences for language learning: "Children do not seem to learn sentences, but rather, . . . to adapt their behavior to increasingly complex surroundings. It is an enterprise that does not stop at the age of 6, but continues throughout a lifetime" (1998, pp. 161–162).

Ochs, Schegloff, and Thompson offered a less extreme but still far-reaching reconceptualization of grammar:

> Grammar is part of a broader range of resources . . . which underlie the organization of social life, and in particular the way in which language figures in everyday interaction and cognition . . . Matters of great moment are missed if grammar's order is explored as entirely contained within a single, self-enclosed organization. Grammar's integrity and efficacy are bound up with its place in larger schemes of organization of human conduct, and with social interaction in particular.
>
> (1996, pp. 2–3)

Ochs et al. supported their proposal by describing grammar's varied interactional functions, including structuring conversational turns, managing conversational repair, indexing social identity, and co-constructing shared attention and sense-making. These functions are explored in the individual chapters of their edited volume.

The profound integration of language-in-action with other embodied, embedded semiotic resources has been demonstrated by Goodwin (e.g., 2000, 2003a). Through microanalysis of videotaped interaction, Goodwin unraveled the intricate webs of social meaning woven from grammar, intonation, gaze, gesture, head movement, bodily orientation, and additional semiotic resources. What he found was a dense complementarity of meaning-making, such that individual semiotic resources derive their effects from participating in communicative wholes:

> None of these systems in isolation would be sufficient to construct the actions that the participants are pursuing. This suggests the importance of not focusing analysis exclusively on the properties of individual sign systems, but instead investigating the organization of the ecology of sign systems which have evolved in conjunction with each other within the primordial site for human action: multiple participants using talk to build action while attending to the distinctive properties of a relevant setting.
>
> (2003a, p. 36)

Goodwin proceeded to argue that worldly environments are also crucial to human interaction—that they too provide semiotic resources through which meaning is made. Using the analogy of a football player running, he showed how the player's behavior has meaning only in relation to the football field, and other players:

> To perform relevant action in the game, a [player's] body must use structures that are located outside itself. The runner's body is given meaning by the contextual field it is embedded within. Similarly, while the playing field

contains the semiotic and physical resources that will make possible particular kinds of actions (goals, first downs, and so on), these actions can only come into being when bodies move through the field as part of a game. Each requires the other. The runner's movements are also organized with an eye toward the movements and actions of others on the field. With these structures in place, relevant aspects of the mental life of the runner, for instance his intention to move toward a particular place on the field, such as the goal-line, are immediately visible to all present, and indeed have a public organization. In short, rather than being lodged in a single modality, such as the body, talk, or structure in the environment, many forms of human action [and meaning] are built through the juxtaposition of quite diverse materials, including the actor's body, the bodies of others, language, structure in the environment.

(2003a, pp. 21–23)

The complexity of even mundane interaction presupposes highly evolved skills of coordination for performing joint action—exactly the skills an animal with modest physical resources, no niche specialization, and a large, malleable brain would have needed, and continues to need, to survive in an unkind world.

Kinsbourne and Jordan described nonverbal activity as contributing crucially to conversation by providing contextual information:

Participants in a conversation generate a host of nonverbal anticipatory elements ([facial] expressions, gestures, postures) that foreshadow how the interaction is likely to proceed. Whereas some of these actions have conventional and seemingly arbitrary connotations, many are partial embodiments of . . . embrained thought or intention. Others can, therefore, interpret these actions without a [separate] key to their meaning . . . These structures enable participants to anticipate each other's actions and meanings. Anticipating, in turn, allows smooth transitions in turn taking, and also enables each participant to continuously confirm emerging interpretations of meanings. It assists participants in cooperating to construct the trajectory of the ongoing interaction.

(2009, p. 104)

Yu, Ballard, and Aslin (2005) referred to this phenomenon as "embodied intention" in their research on the role of gaze-following in vocabulary learning, as described on page 152. Both language comprehension and language acquisition thus involve publicly observable activities rather than being locked away in nonvisible cognitive space.

Learning

Mainstream theories of learning are classically cognitivist. Whether the primary *source* of development is input from the environment, innately pre-specified knowledge, or something in between (e.g., O'Grady, 2003), such theories regard the mind as "where the action is." In keeping with such views, mainstream SLA theory's "object of inquiry [is] in large part an internal, mental process" (Long, 1997, p. 170; cf. Atkinson, 2002).

Sociocognitive approaches to learning also give cognition a central place, but they reconceptualize it as fundamentally continuous with the world. This has at least five implications for learning: (1) learning becomes dynamic adaptivity to— or alignment with—the environment; (2) if cognition extends into the world, then so must learning; (3) learning primarily involves the *thickening* of mind–world relations rather than their progressive attenuation; (4) learning enables action in, more than (abstract) knowledge of, the world; and (5) we learn *through* environmental action. I develop these points in this section, but without treating them item by item.

A key sociocognitive claim is that we learn as we live—that learning and being are integrated processes. As we continuously adapt to our environments, something of that adaptation is retained—that is, we learn by experience. If this point seems too obvious to mention, then why does mainstream learning theory, including in SLA studies, insist on separating acquisition from use? The answer is rooted in cognitivism's internalist assumptions: If real-world performance is excluded a priori, only abstract, decontextualized, virtually other-worldly knowledge/ competence remains. As a result, "the controlling image is of an abstract, isolated individual, almost an unmotivated cognitive mechanism" (Hymes, 1972, p. 272).

The static, experience-distant nature of internalist cognitive models has spurred the growth of a powerful alternative: *connectionism*. Conceptually, at least, connectionist models of cognition are open, self-organizing systems—their structure emerges in direct response to environmental input, and continues to be tuned by it, at least to some degree. Connectionist networks thereby evince nontrivial environmental engagement, and their complexity results from *environmental* complexity rather than being pre-built into the cognitive system (Ellis, 1998).

Yet connectionism itself has been critiqued, partly for some of the same problems as symbolic processing. Thus, Reeke and Edelman (1988) argued that connectionist models are implausible because they "draw their inspiration from statistical physics and engineering, not from biology" (p. 144), and are therefore based on assumptions contrary to biological fact. More recently, even connectionism's founders have started to acknowledge its shortcomings—Elman (1998), for instance, noted that connectionist models are problematic due to: (1) their disembodied nature; (2) their environmental passivity; and (3) their modeling of cognition as a brain-bound phenomenon. While attempts have been made to address these issues, there is still a wide gap between the "learning" effected by connectionist networks and human learning. This has hastened the turn toward biological systems as more appropriate exemplars for cognition and adaptive behavior (Chiel & Beer, 1997; Nausbaum & Small, 2006). At the least, a broader "constructivist" (Ellis, 2003) account that *includes* connectionist insights is now more attractive than a purely connectionist approach. We need to move beyond models of mind that are still quasi-cognitivist and mathematical, even if they aid understanding of mind-in-the-world.

The most sociocognitively promising *noncomputational* learning research to date is anthropological. This research suggests that learning is not so much extraction of meaning *from* the environment as increasing (and increasingly meaning-*full*) participation *in* it. Ingold captured some of the spirit of this proposal in describing the apprenticeship of traditional native hunters:

> The novice hunter learns by accompanying more experienced hands in the woods. As he goes about, he is instructed in what to look out for, and his attention is drawn to subtle clues that he might otherwise fail to notice: in other words, he is led to develop a sophisticated perceptual awareness of the properties of his surroundings and of the possibilities they afford for action . . . What is involved . . . is not a transmission of representations . . . but an education of attention.
>
> (2000, p. 37)

Hutchins (1995) provided a detailed account of navigation practices on military ships as products of a complex *situated activity system* (Goffman, 1961) composed of multiple human beings, the natural environment, and a broad range of physical, social, and conceptual resources—sighting tools, nautical charts, closed-circuit telephones, compasses, standard operating procedures, expert–novice relations, language, etc. In Hutchins' description, the navigational computations produced by this system are highly distributed—across the members of the navigation team (including their brains), but also the tools, environmental features, and operating procedures that co-constitute the system. The cognition involved in navigation is therefore a property of the whole system: For navigation to be performed adequately, nothing can be separated out.

Learning is a natural product of such situated activity systems, as Hutchins describes (cf. Lave & Wenger, 1991), based on actors' increasing experience, participation, and alignment with/in the system while carrying out its work. Such development can follow quite specific trajectories of participation: In large-ship navigation, novices begin by performing the initiating and simplest activity in the system—taking a sighting of a landmark—then gradually work their way *up* and *through* the system to progressively more complicated tasks. This trajectory addresses a major problem: As tasks become more advanced and complicated, there is less room for error because fewer steps remain in the system in which mistakes can be discovered and corrected. The problem is solved by putting those who have worked their way through the whole system in charge—their expertise is grounded in skills and action-oriented knowledge developed during their inward and upward trajectories of participation.

Based on studies such as Ingold's and Hutchins', learning can be seen as growing alignment (Atkinson, Churchill, Nishino, & Okada, 2007) with a complex sociocognitive environment. The *trajectories of experience* and *repertoires of participation*

(Atkinson et al.) constituting both route and result of such learning develop largely by performing the activities (in however partial, imperfect, or scaffolded a way) one is becoming proficient in. In most cases where such learning is consequential—and the argument here is that real learning is *always* consequential since it enhances our ability to survive and prosper—it will be part of a larger activity system, a socially developed, multi-person way of acting, thinking, and being in the world. To take an extreme example, it is (just) conceivable that throwing children into deep water might be a useful first swimming lesson, especially if they can quickly be scooped out again. It is far more likely, however, that the organized, scaffolded learning experience known as swimming lessons will do the job better.

Seemingly raw, natural L2 experience is likewise mediated in nontrivial ways. These may include formal instruction, which can be seen as one type of situated activity system, although important critiques have been raised on that score.[2] My point, however, is that many if not all cases of SLA involve participation in situated activity systems—activity systems that support language growth, even if their main purpose may be otherwise. Examples include: international business transactions; extended L2 involvement with friends, host families, or significant others; frequenting bars, clubs, and other social venues in L2 contexts; participation in foreign language clubs and competitions; electronic communication with L2 speakers; attending L2 religious services; and serving L2-speaking customers. The linguistic outcomes of such experiences may not mirror those of formal learning (e.g., Schmidt, 1983), but they result from real-world learning that is maximally relevant to individuals' needs and identities, the main form of learning dealt with here.

Finally, there has been research in cognitive science, anthropology, and education showing the importance of both embodied activities—e.g., gesture, gaze, and bodily orientation—and ecosocial affordances—e.g., textbooks, maps, and patterns in the terrestrial environment—in learning and teaching. This research builds on the view that: (1) "The positioning, actions, and orientation of the body in the environment are crucial to how participants understand what is happening and build action together" (Goodwin, 2003a, p. 20); and (2) "Rather than being lodged in a single modality . . ., many forms of human action [and understanding] are built through the juxtaposition of quite diverse materials, including the actor's body, the bodies of others, language, structure in the environment, and so on" (pp. 22–23). A crucial point here is that learning/teaching/understanding takes place *in the world:* It is *publicly* enacted and *publicly* available. Far from being locked away in cognitive space, learning is effected in the hybrid, partly public forum of sociocognition.

The public nature of learning has been described in a number of studies. Goodwin (2007) reviewed five conventional social settings/activity systems in which more knowledgeable individuals work with novices to ground their learning in the local multimodal environment, and in so doing make skilled practices of seeing, acting, speaking, and understanding openly available for learning. The main part of Goodwin's study involves a father and daughter working together on her mathematics homework. In a second study, Goodwin (2003a) described the situated learning/teaching of archeological fieldwork practices as an expert archeologist showed students how to find traces of ancient settlements in the soil. In both studies, Goodwin focused on how language, gaze, bodily orientation, environmental structure, and sociocultural tools were brought into alignment in effecting learning/teaching.

Regarding language learning specifically, Yu et al. (2005) showed that both L1 and L2 speech segmentation and vocabulary learning depend partly on gaze—learners actively track a speaker's gaze to help them grasp what is being referred to. As mentioned previously, Yu et al. characterize gaze in this setting as a form of "embodied intention"—as indicating how to sociocognitively align with relevant aspects of the environment.

Research Methods

The sociocognitive study of SLA is just beginning, so any account of its research methods must be emergent and prospective. Here, I describe the research methods employed in three empirical studies that might reasonably be called sociocognitive, and then introduce seven exploratory principles to guide sociocognitive research on SLA.

Methodological Review of Three Studies

The only empirical SLA studies I know of that adopt the conceptual framework described above were conducted by myself and my colleagues. Atkinson et al. (2007) and Churchill, Nishino, Okada, and Atkinson (2010) investigated the phenomena of *alignment* and *symbiotic gesture* (defined below), respectively, in a videotaped EFL tutoring session featuring an experienced Japanese teacher/tutor and her 14-year-old tutee. *Multimodal interaction analysis* (my term) was adapted from the work of Goodwin (e.g., 2000, 2003a) to analyze the data. Alluded to above in discussing Goodwin's work, this approach focuses on the use of complementary *semiotic resources* in performing sociocognitive action-via-interaction, including learning and teaching: (1) *language*; (2) *nonlinguistic vocal behavior*; (3) *gaze*; (4) *facial expression*; (5) *gesture*; (6) *head and body movement and orientation*; (7) *tools* (e.g., computers, grammar exercises); (8) *settings* (e.g., coffee shops, religious ceremonies); (9) *roles and relations* (e.g., expert-novice and family roles and relations, which are also power relations); and (10) *arrangements and practices* (e.g., participation frameworks, situated activity systems). Inclusion of elements 7–10 is warranted by the sociocognitive tenet that cognition and learning extend into the world rather than residing solely in the individual.

Atkinson et al. (2007) investigated how *alignment*—"the means by which human actors . . . flexibly depend on, integrate with, and construct . . . the ever-changing mind–body–world environments posited by sociocognitive theory" (p. 171)—might be a necessary condition for SLA. More specifically, we looked for evidence of multimodal alignment across tutor, tutee, and their complex sociocognitive environment as they worked through a series of grammar exercises focusing on the English present perfect tense. Admittedly, this is not exactly the kind of learning emphasized in the foregoing parts of this chapter, yet neither was it ruled out. Formal education also represents adaptation to a humanly constructed environment—that of the school (but see note 2 for caveats). In any event, the EFL tutoring activity analyzed was a mixed form: It was undertaken to support school-based learning, but was not itself school-sponsored.

Extract 1 and the subsequent prose description show how Atkinson et al.'s (2007) analytic methods worked in practice. In this extract, "T," the tutor, and "A," the tutee, are co-translating the Japanese sentence, *Anata wa ima made ni eigo de tegami o kaita koto ga arimasuka?* ("Have you ever written a letter in English?"), into English, with a special focus on determining the correct form of the verb:

Extract 1[3]
```
01. A:  ((Reads first part of exercise item quickly under
        her breath))
        >°Anata wa ima made ni eigo de tegami°< (2.0)
        Ima made ni=
        [Lit: You [SUBJ] ever in English letter]
        Ever
02. T:  ((Softly shadowing A's volume, intonation, and
        bodily orientation))
        =°Un ima made° [See Figure 6.1]
          Right, ever
03.     (1.0)
04. A:  [Ne:ba:
          Never
05. T:  [>Sakki no tsukaeba iin janai?< ((Searching
        unsuccessfully for earlier item on worksheet,
        using pen as pointer))
          Why not use the one you used before?
06. A:  Ima made (.8) ne- e:va ka
          Ever.          Ne- ever?
07. T:  Have you ever toka nantoka=
          Have you ever blank
08. A:  =Have you eva writu, written=
          Have you ever write, written
09. T:  =Un.
          Right.
```

In line 1, A aligns with the exercise item by reading its first half under her breath; she then aligns specifically with (by repeating) the adverbial *ima made ni* ("ever"), probably because she has been taught to use adverbials to cue correct choice of English verb tense—a crucial part of this translation task. T then aligns with A in line 2 by: (1) "latching" her own turn onto A's without a pause; (2) uttering *Un* ("Right") to confirm A's choice of the adverbial as a good place to start; (3) repeating the adverbial—*ima made*—in shortened form; (4) mirroring A's quietness by speaking in equally low tones; (5) using the same 1-3-2 intonation pattern used by A in repeating the adverbial; and (6) adopting a bodily orientation strikingly similar to A's, as seen in Figure 6.1.

The complex, multimodal process of alignment then continues as tutor and tutee begin to translate the sentence. A takes her first stab at translating the adverbial in line 4, exactly as T (line 5) tries to align A to an earlier item on the worksheet as a model for translating. The latter represents a clear attempt to have the exercise sheet act as a kind of extended cogition for A, although T in fact fails to locate the item. Next, A restates the adverbial in the partial form used by T (line 6) and then reformulates her translation of it by shifting from *ne-* (probably a partial form of "never") to *e:va* ("ever")—the correct answer. At this point T takes A's answer and incorporates it into a larger oral fill-in-the-blank frame in line 7—*Have you ever toka nantoka* ("Have you ever blank")—thereby radically altering both the focus of their activity and the sociocognitive "problem space," that is, the translation task has been reduced to finding the correct principal part of the irregular verb. A immediately aligns by repeating the sentence frame offered by T, and then arrives at the correct answer in two steps: She produces the incorrect but close to targetlike form *writu* ("write"), perhaps using it to bootstrap her way to the correct form, *written*, which she produces next. The results of this analysis are discussed in the next section of this chapter.

FIGURE 6.1 Tutor and tutee showing physical alignment (from Atkinson et al., 2007).

Extending and focusing the research just described, Churchill et al. (2010) investigated the tutor's deployment of *symbiotic gestures* (Goodwin, 2003a)—gestures used together with talk, gaze, bodily orientation, and the material structure of the environment to reorganize the "domain of scrutiny" (Goodwin, 2003b, p. 221) of participants in an interaction—to make grammatical relations publicly visible to the tutee. That is, symbiotic gestures highlight selected features of a complex environment for (broadly speaking) educational purposes. They occur within previously established *participation frameworks* (Goodwin, 1981)—formal or informal orderings of co-participating social actors that may themselves be parts of situated activity systems. Churchill et al. described the tutor's use of a single symbiotic gesture to highlight the diagnostic potential of time adverbials for choosing appropriate verb tenses in a grammar-translation task. This paper's methodology closely resembles that exemplified just above; its findings are described later.

A third and final study that may reflect sociocognitive principles is Mori and Hayashi's (2006) treatment of the use of *embodied completions* in interactions between L1 and L2 Japanese speakers/learners. An embodied completion involves using a gesture or bodily action to complete a turn at talk, as when someone requests an object from another, who then replies, "It's right . . ." and points to the object. Mori and Hayashi investigated the organization of behavior before, during, and after embodied completions, arguing that they are finely gauged attempts to produce intersubjective understanding, and may thereby facilitate SLA.

The analytical methods employed by Mori and Hayashi (2006) are based in the sociological theory–method complex called conversation analysis (CA—see Kasper & Wagner, this volume). Conversation analysts study social behavior in terms of its local organization, particularly the sequential organization of talk-in-interaction. They do so in the belief that "the truth is in the details" of person-to-person interaction—that social behavior is primarily organized at this level. CA has therefore innovated a rigorous methodology for capturing and analyzing the interactive details of talk. Extracts 1 (above) and 2 (below) were transcribed (and to some extent analyzed) using the tools of CA.

Mori and Hayashi (2006) studied interactions between L1-speaking Japanese students and their L2-Japanese speaking/learning peers during "conversation table" speech events in the United States. The focus was on how embodied completions were the carefully calibrated result, on the L1 speakers' side, of an ongoing evaluation of the L2 speaker's communicative competence, on how those completions were enacted and received, and on how they provided "incidental, interactionally motivated opportunit[ies]" (p. 195) to introduce new linguistic material. In a speech event in which teaching was not the explicit aim, then, learning opportunities were nonetheless provided via the natural machinery of interaction. I describe this study further below.

Exploratory Principles of Sociocognitive SLA Research

I close this section with an exploratory set of methodological principles on which sociocognitively oriented SLA research might be based. In so doing, I do not intend to draw rigid boundaries between this and other approaches, but to provide guidance in designing studies that can deepen our understanding of how mind, body, and world work together in SLA.

1. *Emphasis on particularity*: SLA research has focused on generalizations more than particulars. This is due largely to assumptions of uniform competence and mechanical language learning, as well as research tools grounded in positivistic science. While not eschewing generalizations, sociocognitive research methods would foreground the principle that individual-aggregating quantification is:

> not an alternative to single case analysis, but rather is built on its back. We can be led seriously astray if we allow . . . quantitative analysis to free us from the need to demonstrate the operation of what we take to be going on in singular fragments [of language in use].
>
> (Schegloff, 1993, p. 102)

2. *Emphasis on process*: Mainstream SLA research has focused largely on the linguistic *products* of SLA, most typically as measured by "artificial, discrete-point tests . . . based upon knowledge of language as object" (Doughty, 2003, p. 274). Yet, as Doughty points out, SLA is a process. From a sociocognitive viewpoint, SLA is a continuous, complex, nonlinear process that takes place at the level of mundane interaction, including in educational institutions.

3. *Emphasis on holism, integrativeness, and relationality*: Mainstream/cognitivist SLA research views learning as the extraction and processing of environmental input, or the activation via input of universal grammar. The vision is almost one of a "solipsistic . . . organism" (Lantolf & Appel, 1994, p. 11) or mental computer, fundamentally cut off from the world. In contrast, sociocognitive methodologies would study SLA relationally and integratively, as the complex interfunctionality of organism and world. From this perspective, the concept of *input* is misleading if it steers us away from understanding the fundamentally ecological nature of human existence and activity. Sociocognitive methodologies would honor this principle.

4. *Emphasis on variation*: Individuals have different worldly experiences, and through studying such experiences richer understandings of learners as human beings can be achieved. This is not to say that common developmental trajectories do not exist, but it *is* to reject uniform, mechanical, teleological development as a necessary guiding assumption of SLA research.

5. *Emphasis on concrete experience and performance*: Sociocognitive approaches hold that one learns to do by doing—by enacting real-world goals through real-world social action. Sociocognitive methodologies would therefore put the emphasis on studying real-world L2 use.

6. *Emphasis on extended cognition*: A core sociocognitive claim is that mind extends into the world, largely via social tools and systems (Atkinson, 2010a, 2010b). Socio-cognitive methodologies would therefore look for cognition and learning in worldly artifacts and practices—especially in how they *integrate* mind, body, and world.

7. *Emphasis on action as* inter-*action*: Much if not all L2 learning takes place via interaction—or (to put it sociocognitively) *inter*-action, that is, action *with and between*. We learn languages through using them to act—to interact—with/in the world. Sociocognitive research methodologies would therefore examine language learning in interaction, but interaction broadly construed, taking into account the vast range of mind–body–world linkages.

Supporting Findings

The findings of the studies reviewed above provide preliminary support for a sociocognitive approach to SLA. Thus, Atkinson et al. (2007) found ample evidence of sociocognitive alignment across tutor, tutee, and environmental affordances in a relatively formal L2 learning/teaching event. In this sense, we took a first step toward empirically supporting our main claim: that alignment is a necessary condition for SLA. We also presented—although not in detail—four examples of apparent development in the tutee's use of the "Have you ever" construction in association with various grammar exercises she was working on.[4] Thus, compare Extract 2 below with Extract 1 above, Extract 2 having occurred some 15 minutes later during completion of the same grammar exercise.

Extract 2

```
01. T:  Ah >hai saigo no mondai hai anata wa kono hanashi
        o °su-° kore made ni, ima made ne, kiita koto
        arimasuka?<
        Ok, last item. Ok, ((Reads)) "Have you up to this
        point"—ever, right?—"heard this story?"
02. A:  Eva
        Ever
03. T:  Un
        Right
04. A:  Havu you eva:
        Have you ever
05. T:  Un
        Right
06. A:  Lis:°ten° ((turns head and gazes at T))
07. T:  ((Smacks lips)) [Listen
08. A:                  [H/i/ah ((raises both hands and points
        at T with pen in right hand))
09.                     Hear
```

```
10. T:   Un hear no ii ne hear hea:rd? ((prompting A to supply
         third principal part of verb with rhythmic downward
         cuts of hand))
         Right, hear is better. Hear, heard . . .
```

In Extract 2, A immediately produces the correct adverbial (*Eva*—"Ever," line 2), proceeds directly to the correct auxiliary verb-subject-adverbial combination (line 4), and stumbles only in determining the form of the main verb (lines 6 and 8). She therefore seems to show greater facility with the forms than previously, at least within the domain of this particular learning/teaching event. Admittedly, this iteration of cooperative translating/problem-solving is different than that represented in Extract 1. Thus, T gives an indirect hint (line 1) of the verb tense cued by the adverbial when she glosses the adverbial *kore made ni* (*lit*: "up to this point") with the *ima made ni* ("ever") featured in Extract 1. Yet such "contextual" differences are also fundamental features of sociocognitive SLA: In the instance just noted, T seems to function as a kind of extended cognition for A by establishing a link between A's current and past experience with the "Have you ever" construction. In any event, evidence from in situ language learning will rarely meet the standards of experimental research: The experimentalist's need to control for contextual effects immediately disqualifies a sociocognitive approach.

Examining the same tutor–tutee interaction from a different perspective, Churchill et al. (2010) found that T used a single symbiotic gesture repeatedly across time to "make visible" the grammatical relationship between adverbial indicators of tense choice and past-tense verbs in translating sentences from Japanese to English. More specifically, T initially inscribed a tight circle in the air above the grammar worksheet in conjunction with speech and bodily orientation in order to visibly indicate the link between the time adverbial *kyonen* ("last year") and the past-tense verb form *ikimashita* ("went") in Japanese, a link that would help A to translate the sentence accurately. T then recycled the same gesture at subsequent moments where the adverbial-past-tense relationship figured in the translation task, gradually expanding the scope of the relationship to include a range of past-tense-marking adverbials. We characterized T's action as part of an *interactional routine* (Peters & Boggs, 1986), a prepatterned interaction sequence by which two or more interactants perform social action, itself instantiating Gee's *public principle* of learning:

> The meanings of the parts of new systems, whether words, visual symbols, actions, or objects, must be initially rendered public and overt, so that the learner can see the connections between the signs and their interpretations. And this is done, in first language acquisition and other forms of learning, by the ways in which words, actions, and social interaction are integrally intertwined.
>
> (1994, p. 337)

In other words, through her use of a single symbiotic gesture, T demonstrated the visible character of learning in sociocognitive space—how learning is publicly enabled and enacted.

Finally, Mori and Hayashi (2006) presented convincing evidence of (1) highly aligned interactional behavior, which (2) while not associated with a formal learning/teaching event, nonetheless presented L2 learning opportunities. Concerning the first point, Mori and Hayashi showed how an L1 Japanese-speaking interlocutor in one data extract appeared to use the following resources to construct a "recipient-designed" (p. 201) embodied turn completion: direct feedback from an L2 Japanese speaker exhibiting comprehension difficulties; multiple assessments by an L1-speaking peer of the difficulty of the interlocutor's current utterance; a second L2 speaker's explanation in English of the part of the interlocutor's utterance the first L2 speaker didn't understand; and the L1 interlocutor's own apparent assessment that the part of the utterance he had not yet produced was "projectable"—that is, that an embodied completion could reasonably be expected to complete the turn in an easily interpretable way. This diverse combination of semiotic, largely in-the-world resources suggests a complex instance of extended cognition.

Concerning the second point, Mori and Hayashi (2006) presented a data extract in which an embodied completion by an L1 Japanese speaker prompted an L2 speaker to supply a verbal version of the completion. The L1 speaker confirmed this response, and then elaborated by describing the experience signified by his embodied completion in much more sophisticated language. While the authors characterized these learning opportunities in more or less traditional terms—as focusing cognitive attention and providing recast-like opportunities—it is fairly easy to reframe them in terms of the sociocognitive concepts of alignment and extended cognition, as indicated above.

Differences vis-à-vis Other Alternative Approaches

It is my belief that the alternative SLA approaches featured in this volume have much in common, and that the authors are engaged in the same larger endeavor—to promote intellectual diversity and stimulation in SLA studies. But the value of "letting all the flowers bloom" (Lantolf, 1996) is not just in the sheer diversity and richness it provides, but also and even more in the opportunities it affords for direct engagement and fertilization *across* approaches. Any single perspective on something as complex as SLA, no matter how revealing, can describe only a small part of the overall phenomenon, so it is crucial for different approaches to interact directly. To that end, I here outline potential similarities and especially differences between a sociocognitive approach and the other approaches featured in this volume.

The sociocultural approach to SLA (sociocultural theory—SCT) described by Jim Lantolf has been characterized as a "sociogenetic cognitive theory" (Kinginger, 2002). This seems accurate, given that SCT is concerned with explaining "higher cognitive processes," including linguistic capabilities, and does so by positing a process that begins squarely in the social world but ends (although less squarely—Vygotsky wrote of psychological processes remaining "quasi-social" (in Valsiner & van der Veer, 2005, p. 81)) in the learner's head. Vygotsky and his followers used the term *vrashchivanie*, usually translated as "internalization," to describe this developmental trajectory, and much ink has been spilled in both its defense and critique. Whatever its actual meaning—concepts, after all, are social constructions—a sociocognitive approach, in contrast, would likely steer clear of any implication that mature cognition involves the internal *re*-presentation of the world or significant aspects of it.

Likewise, SCT sees cognitive development/language learning as operating dialectically: "Higher cognitive processes" such as language develop via the transformation and incorporation of radically discontinuous elements and processes into larger synthetic wholes (Vygotsky, 1978). The approach taken in the present chapter, in contrast, adheres to a basic *continuity principle* (Dewey, 1938/1953; Johnson & Rohrer, 2007) whereby no radical discontinuities occur in the development of sociocognitive capabilities. All mind-involved processes are seen equally as forms of ecological adaptation.

The differences mentioned here have implications not just for how mind–body–world relations are theorized in these two approaches, but also for how empirical studies are conducted. In a sociocognitive approach, "analytic dualism" (Lantolf & Thorne, 2006, p. 165) permitting the methodological separation of mind from world would be impossible.

Diane Larsen-Freeman's complexity theory approach to SLA has much in common with a sociocognitive approach—indeed, it has partly inspired it (Atkinson, 2002). The two approaches have grown even closer since Larsen-Freeman (e.g., Larsen-Freeman & Cameron, 2008) took the sociocognitive concept—already implicit in her work—directly on board. Because the main purpose of this section is to highlight differences, however, I will note two apparent ones. The first concerns the divergent origins of complexity theory and the sociocognitive approach. Complexity theory originated in statistical physics and systems theory—mathematical approaches to describing natural processes. A sociocognitive approach as I conceptualize it would be wary of mathematically inspired explanations of human behavior, given the origins of cognitivism in a mathematized and mechanistic worldview. For the same reasons that Reeke and Edelman (1988, p. 144) critiqued connectionism as a product of mathematical physics that therefore "looked sideways to biology," I have reservations regarding mathematically inspired approaches to SLA.

Second, as described by Larsen-Freeman (this volume), complexity theory depends on "retrodiction"—a retrospective or post hoc approach to studying natural processes, including SLA. In the sociocognitive approach I espouse here, however, processes have been studied "in-process." That is, attempts are made—so far through microanalyzing videotapes of learning situations—to study learning processes as they unfold, rather than after they have happened. This is not to argue that retrodictive approaches should automatically be forbidden in sociocognitive research on SLA (but see Principle 2 in the "Exploratory Principles of Sociocognitive SLA Research" subsection above); they have not yet, however, become part of its practice, to the extent that any standard practice has been established at all.

The identity approach to SLA described in this volume by Bonny Norton and Carolyn McKinney is a self-professed "social" approach to SLA—in this sense, it accepts the standard social–cognitive divide in SLA studies (Zuengler & Miller, 2006). In this it is fundamentally different from the sociocognitive approach. At the same time, however, identity clearly affects SLA in many ways, including its cognitive—or sociocognitive—processes. In the EFL tutoring session featured in Extracts 1 and 2 above, for instance, the sociocognitive behavior of T and A was likely mediated by their educational identities as tutor and tutee, family identities as aunt and niece, gender identities as women, age-related identities as middle-aged person and teenager, etc.

Patsy Duff and Steven Talmy's language socialization approach to SLA also falls on the social side of the standard social–cognitive division. At the same time, conceptualizing by one of the founders of language socialization studies, Elinor Ochs, directly inspired the sociocognitive approach to SLA—I was first exposed to the sociocognitive concept in Ochs' classes at the University of Southern California in the late 1980s. Other language socialization researchers, however, especially Karen Watson-Gegeo (2004), have gone farthest in conceptualizing language socialization sociocognitively, although it is still a minor interest in that area.

The CA-SLA approach described by Gabi Kasper and Johannes Wagner has also influenced the sociocognitive perspective, particularly in its focus on fine-grained, process-oriented analysis of interaction and its methods for doing so. It may differ somewhat, however, in its views on cognition. CA seeks to understand the sense-making practices of individuals in interaction—the interactive procedures through which intersubjectivity is arrived at and maintained. CA thus generally studies the publicly available aspects of interaction and eschews consideration of inner states. According to Kasper and Wagner (this volume), "socially shared cognition and learning are publicly displayed in interaction, [and so] they become available to researchers for analysis, obviating the need to construe hidden internal processes behind observable behavior" (p. 121).

Both the CA approach to cognition and the one adopted here share the view that cognition is "in the world"—that it occurs *between* people and is therefore a public process, at least in part. The sociocognitive approach, however, draws no hard boundary between "inner" and "outer" processes, preferring to envision them as occurring in an integrated sociocognitive space. That is, cognitive processes are partly visible and partly invisible—they reach across the traditional boundaries of skin and skull. If cognition is primarily adaptive—if its raison d'être is to help us to respond to/align with the environment, including other human beings, this is as it must be. Cognition's environmentally distributed nature is described throughout this chapter, but one of its (distributed) locations is certainly the head.

Future Directions

To be frank, I hesitate to speculate on future directions for a sociocognitive approach to SLA. It is so new and undeveloped that it seems open to the full range of possibilities, which of course includes no further development at all. I would nonetheless note the increasing popularity of ecological thinking in the social sciences and humanities: Much of what I have presented here is based broadly on the position that, at some level or other, "everything is connected to everything" (Gee, personal communication). While such views wreak havoc with the current-traditional scientific approach of breaking reality down into components and linear cause-and-effect relationships, they are powerfully represented in movements and concepts such as human ecology, globalization, autopoiesis, complexity theory, the Gaia Hypothesis, deep ecology, world systems theory, and ecocriticism. As human existence seems to be nearing an environmental tipping point, ecological approaches take on a significance and urgency far outweighing their adequacy as explanations (partial or full) for mundane human activities such as SLA. Yet the latter can draw value and meaning from their participation in a larger endeavor (see Kramsch, 2002 and van Lier, 2004 for other ecological approaches to SLA).

Conclusion

In this chapter, I have tried to present the case for a sociocognitive approach to second language acquisition. The term *sociocognitive* signifies a perspective that emphasizes functional unities *across* "interactants," both human and nonhuman, in a complex ecological system, and by so doing tries to blur the conventional boundaries separating them. Cognition—the guiding concept and preeminent location of second language learning for the first four decades of its systematic study—should be reconceived from this perspective as a process projecting well beyond the boundary of the skull, and rather directly into the everyday worlds of social activity and practice. This is hardly to diminish cognition's importance, however. As a thoroughly in-the-world endeavor, SLA is in fact *eminently* cognitive—if the primary purpose of cognition is to help its users adapt to and function in the world. While I wholeheartedly believe that no single approach to SLA can adequately account for its vast complexity, a sociocognitive approach can add a much-needed dimensionality to this still conceptually limited field.

Acknowledgments

I would like to thank Paul Bruthiaux, Eton Churchill, Kent Hill, Robert Nelson, Jr., Takako Nishino, Jinju Nishino, and Hanako Okada for their generous sociocognitive participation in the writing of this chapter.

Notes

1   This characterization may seem to disregard "offline cognition"—the all-important (and typically conscious) use of the mind to reflect, reason, imagine, recall, plan, and project

future courses of action. There is evidence, however, that off-line cognition has been built (evolutionarily speaking) on the back of on-line cognition, and even in its purest state maintains strong traces of its phylogenetic development (e.g., Clark, 1997; Millikan, 1995). This was the basic thesis of John Dewey (e.g., 1938/1953) and the American Pragmatist movement. It has been updated and empirically developed in recent psychology and neuroscience (e.g., Johnson & Rohrer, 2007).

2   The critique of schooling as a "form of life" is strongest in the work of Jean Lave (e.g., 1996; Lave & Wenger, 1991). The basic argument is that schools often teach practices and tools that do not transfer to real-world situations, but that rather have value only or largely within the school itself.

3   Data extracts in this chapter are transcribed using the conventions of conversation analysis (Ochs et al., 1996, pp. 461–465). The following is a basic list:

,	Nonfinal/continuing intonation followed by short pause
.	Final/falling intonation followed by pause
?	Final/rising intonation followed by pause
:	Phoneme lengthening
(( ))	Nonlinguistic event descriptions
( )	Transcriber doubt (parentheses can be filled or unfilled)
(0.6)	Pauses timed in tenths of a second
(.)	Short untimed pauses
=	"Latching," i.e., the second speaker's turn begins without pause after the first speaker's
[	Overlapping of one speaker's talk by another's
>No<	Diamond brackets enclose talk that is faster than surrounding talk
°No°	Degree signs enclose talk that is quieter than surrounding talk
No	Underlining marks various kinds of "voice quality," such as emphasis and stress
CAPITAL LETTERS	Notably high volume

4   Two of these examples were apparent cases of "microgenetic" growth (e.g., Lantolf, 2000, p. 3)—development over very short timescales—as they took place while the tutor and tutee were completing the same set of grammar exercises as described previously over a period of about 15 minutes. The other two cases occurred approximately one year later, about a month apart. It should be added that microgenetic development is often nonlinear (Churchill, 2008; Larsen-Freeman, 2006)—one should not expect the "leading edge" of development to translate directly into a stable, linear trajectory of SLA.

References

Atkinson, D. (2002). Toward a sociocognitive approach to second language acquisition. *Modern Language Journal, 86,* 525–545.

Atkinson, D. (2010a). Extended, embodied cognition and second language acquisition. *Applied Linguistics, 31,* 599–622.

Atkinson, D. (2010b). Sociocognition: What it can mean for second language acquisition. In R. Batstone (Ed.), *Sociocognitive perspectives on language use and language learning* (pp. 24–39). Oxford: Oxford University Press.

Atkinson, D., Churchill, E., Nishino, T., & Okada, H. (2007). Alignment and interaction in a sociocognitive approach to second language acquisition. *Modern Language Journal, 91,* 169–188.

Barsalou, L. (2008). Grounded cognition. *Annual Review of Psychology, 59,* 617–645.

Beiser, T. (2000). The Enlightenment and idealism. In K. Ameriks (Ed.), *Cambridge companion to German idealism* (pp. 18–36). Cambridge: Cambridge University Press.

Boden, M. (2006). *Mind as machine: A history of cognitive science.* Oxford: Clarendon Press.

Chiel, H., & Beer, R. (1997). The brain has a body: Adaptive behavior emerges from interactions of nervous system, body and environment. *Trends in Neuroscience, 20,* 553–557.

Churchill, E. (2008). A dynamic systems account of learning a word: From ecology to form-relations. *Applied Linguistics, 29,* 339–358.

Churchill, E., Nishino, T., Okada, H., & Atkinson, D. (2010). Symbiotic gesture and the sociocognitive visibility of grammar. *Modern Language Journal, 94,* 234–253.

Clark, A. (1997). *Being there: Putting brain, body, and world together again.* Cambridge, MA: MIT Press.

Clark, A. (2001). *Mindware: An introduction to the philosophy of cognitive science.* Oxford: Oxford University Press.

Clark, A., & Chalmers, D. (1998). The extended mind. *Analysis, 58,* 7–19.

Dewey, J. (1938/1953). Logic: The theory of inquiry. In J. Boydston (Ed.), *John Dewey, the later works, 1925–1953, Vol. 12* (pp. 128–150). Carbondale, IL: Southern Illinois University Press.

Doughty, C. (2003). Instructed SLA: Constraints, compensation, and enhancement. In C. Doughty & M. Long (Eds.), *Handbook of second language acquisition* (pp. 256–310). Malden, MA: Blackwell.

Ellis, N. (1998). Emergence, connectionism, and language learning. *Language Learning, 48,* 631–664.

Ellis, N. (2003). Constructionism, chunking, and connectionism: The emergence of second language structure. In C. Doughty & M. Long (Eds.), *Handbook of second language acquisition* (pp. 63–103). Malden, MA: Blackwell.

Elman, J. (1998). Connectionism, artificial life, and dynamical systems. In W. Bechtel & G. Graham (Eds.), *A companion to cognitive science* (pp. 488–505). London: Blackwell.

Gee, J. P. (1992). *The social mind.* London: Bergin & Garvey.

Gee, J. P. (1994). First language acquisition as a guide for theories of learning and pedagogy. *Linguistics & Education, 6,* 331–354.

Gibbs, R. (2005). *Embodiment and cognitive science.* Cambridge: Cambridge University Press.

Gibson, J. J. (1979). *The ecological approach to visual perception.* Boston, MA: Houghton Mifflin.

Glenberg, A. (1997). What memory is for. *Behavioral & Brain Sciences, 20,* 1–55.

Goffman, E. (1961). *Encounters: Two studies in the sociology of interaction.* Indianapolis, IN: Bobbs-Merrill.

Goodwin, C. (1981). *Conversational organization: Interaction between speakers and hearers.* New York: Academic Press.

Goodwin, C. (2000). Action and embodiment within situated human interaction. *Journal of Pragmatics, 32,* 1489–1522.

Goodwin, C. (2003a). The body in action. In J. Coupland & R. Gwin (Eds.), *Discourse, the body, and identity* (pp. 19–42). New York: Palgrave Macmillan.

Goodwin, C. (2003b). Pointing as situated practice. In S. Kita (Ed.), *Pointing: Where language, culture, and cognition meet* (pp. 217–241). Hillsdale, NJ: Erlbaum.

Goodwin, C. (2007). Participation, stance and affect in the organization of activities. *Discourse & Society, 18,* 53–73.

Hopper, P. (1988). Emergent grammar and the a priori grammatical postulate. In D. Tannen (Ed.), *Linguistics in context: Connecting observation and understanding. Advances in discourse processes, Vol. 29* (pp. 117–134). Norwood, NJ: Ablex.

Hopper, P. (1998). Emergent grammar. In M. Tomasello (Ed.) *New psychology of language* (pp. 155–175). Mahwah, NJ: Erlbaum.

Hurley, S., & Chater, N. (Eds.) (2005). *Perspectives on imitation.* Cambridge, MA: MIT Press.

Hutchins, E. (1995). *Cognition in the wild*. Cambridge, MA: MIT Press.

Hymes, D. (1972). On communicative competence. In J. Pride & J. Holmes (Eds.), *Sociolinguistics: Selected readings* (pp. 269–293). Harmondsworth: Penguin.

Iacoboni, M. (2009). Imitation, empathy, and mirror neurons. *Annual Review of Psychology, 60*, 653–670.

Ingold, T. (2000). *The perception of the environment: Essays on livelihood, dwelling and skill*. London: Routledge.

Johnson, M., & Rohrer, T. (2007). We are live creatures: Embodiment, American Pragmatism, and the cognitive organism. In T. Ziemke, J. Zlatev, & R. Frank (Eds.), *Body, language and mind, Vol. 1: Embodiment.* (pp. 17–54). Amsterdam: Mouton de Gruyter.

Kinginger, C. (2002). Defining the zone of proximal development in U.S. foreign language education. *Applied Linguistics, 23*, 240–261.

Kinsbourne, M., & Jordan, J. S. (2009). Embodied anticipation: A neurodevelopmental interpretation. *Discourse Processes, 46*, 103–126.

Kramsch, C. (Ed.) (2002). *Language acquisition and language socialization: Ecological perspectives.* London: Continuum.

Lantolf, J. (1996). SLA theory building: Letting all the flowers bloom! *Language Learning, 46*, 713–749.

Lantolf, J. (2000). Introducing sociocultural theory. In J. Lantolf (Ed.), *Sociocultural theory and second language learning* (pp. 1–26). Oxford: Oxford University Press.

Lantolf, J., & Appel, G. (Eds.) (1994). *Vygotskian approaches to second language acquisition.* Norwood, NJ: Ablex.

Lantolf, J., & Thorne, S. (2006). *Sociocultural theory and the genesis of second language development.* London: Oxford University Press.

Larsen-Freeman, D. (2006). The emergence of complexity, fluency, and accuracy in the oral and written production of five Chinese learners of English. *Applied Linguistics, 27*, 590–619.

Larsen-Freeman, D., & Cameron, L. (2008). *Complex systems and applied linguistics*. Oxford: Oxford University Press.

Lave, J. (1996). Teaching, as learning, in practice. *Mind, Culture, & Activity, 3*, 149–164.

Lave, J. & Wenger, E. (1991). *Situated learning: Legitimate peripheral participation.* Cambridge: Cambridge University Press.

Long, M. (1997). Construct validity in SLA research: A response to Firth and Wagner. *Modern Language Journal, 81*, 318–323.

Millikan, R. (1995). Pushmi-pullyu representations. *Philosophical Perspectives, 9*, 185–200.

Mori, J., & Hayashi, M. (2006). The achievement of interculturality through embodied completion: A study of interactions between first and second language speakers. *Applied Linguistics, 27*, 195–219.

Nausbaum, H., & Small, S. (2006). Investigating cortical mechanisms of language processing in social context. In J. Cacioppo, P. Visser, & C. Pickett (Eds.), *Social neuroscience: People thinking about thinking people* (pp. 131–152). Cambridge, MA: Cambridge University Press.

Ochs, E., Schegloff, E., & Thompson, S. (Eds.) (1996). *Interaction and grammar.* Cambridge: Cambridge University Press.

O'Grady, W. (2003). The radical middle: Nativism without universal grammar. In C. Doughty & M. Long (Eds.), *Handbook of second language acquisition* (pp. 43–62). Malden, MA: Blackwell.

Peters, A., & Boggs, S. (1986). Interactional routines as cultural influences upon language acquisition. In B. Schieffelin & E. Ochs (Eds.), *Language socialization across cultures* (pp. 80–96). Cambridge: Cambridge University Press.

Reeke, G., & Edelman, G. (1988). Real brains and artificial intelligence. In S. Graubard (Ed.), *The artificial intelligence debate: False starts, real foundations* (pp. 144–173). Cambridge, MA: MIT Press.

Rizzolatti, G., & Craighero, L. (2004). The mirror-neuron system. *Annual Review of Neuroscience, 27,* 169–192.

Schegloff, E. (1993). Reflections on quantification in the study of conversation. *Research on Language & Social Interaction, 26,* 99–128.

Semin, G., & Cacioppo, J. (2008). Grounding social cognition: Synchronization, coordination, and co-regulation. In G. Semin & E. Smith (Eds.), *Embodied grounding* (pp. 119–147). Cambridge: Cambridge University Press.

Schmidt, R. (1983). Interaction, acculturation, and the acquisition of communicative competence: A case study of an adult. In N. Wolfson & E. Judd (Eds.), *Sociolinguistics & second language acquisition* (pp. 137–174). Rowley, MA: Newbury House.

Valsiner, J., & van der Veer, R. (2005). On the social nature of human cognition: An analysis of the shared intellectual roots of George Herbert Mead and Lev Vygotsky. In H. Daniels (Ed.), *An introduction to Vygotsky* (2nd ed.) (pp. 81–100). New York: Routledge.

van Lier, L. (2004). *The ecology and semiotics of language learning: A sociocultural perspective.* Dordrecht: Kluwer.

Vygotsky, L. (1978). *Mind in society: The development of higher psychological processes.* Cambridge, MA: Harvard University Press.

Watson-Gegeo, K. (2004). Mind, language, and epistemology: Toward a language socialization paradigm for SLA. *Modern Language Journal, 88,* 331–350.

Wheeler, M. (2005). *Reconstructing the cognitive world: The next step.* Cambridge, MA: MIT Press.

Yu, C. Ballard, D., & Aslin, R. (2005). The role of embodied intention in early lexical acquisition. *Cognitive Science, 29,* 961–1005.

Zuengler, J., & Miller, E. (2006). Cognitive and sociocultural perspectives in SLA: Two parallel worlds? *TESOL Quarterly, 40,* 35–58.

7

SLA AFTER THE SOCIAL TURN

Where cognitivism and its alternatives stand

Lourdes Ortega

The field of second language acquisition (SLA) has been transformed by a process since the mid-1990s of profound critique against the cognitive foundations of the discipline and by the long-ranging deployment of socially oriented reconceptualizations of second/additional language (L2) learning. The changes have been intense and important enough to have been characterized as constituting a social turn in SLA (Block, 2003). The present collection gathers six theoretical alternatives that show we may already be standing in a transformed field of SLA after the social turn.

What can we make of differences between cognitivism and its alternatives in SLA? And how can our knowledge about difference as well as similarity between the two extremes of the cognitive–alternative polarity, as well as among the alternatives themselves, help advance our understanding of the various theories from which SLA researchers can draw? I explore these two questions in this chapter. I argue that SLA is stronger and better after the social turn in two ways. First, unique insights have been gained with the addition of socially oriented theoretical alternatives that the existing cognitive theories could not help us unpack prior to the social turn. Second, the epistemological diversity we find in SLA—both across and within social, sociocognitive, and cognitive theories alike—fosters multiple and improved understandings of SLA.

Three Dimensions of Difference between Cognitivism and its Alternatives

I see three broad dimensions along which traditional SLA approaches and alternative ones can be thought to differ. They are sketched below. I am in part inspired by the analysis that educational researcher Anna Sfard (1998) developed, although in her case it was for the purpose of characterizing the clustering of educational theories around the two metaphors of acquisition and participation.

First, the most obvious difference between cognitivism and its alternatives in SLA is that the former draws from *psychological* and the latter from *socially oriented explanations* for L2 learning and associated constructs. Traditional psychologically oriented theories construe knowledge as residing in the mind, assume that learning is an individual accomplishment, and posit that mind achieves learning through environmental stimuli. By contrast, the SLA theories featured in this book, as well as others, view learning as a social accomplishment and posit that knowledge and learning are socially distributed, have social histories, and are only possible through sociality. Perhaps the theoretically most elaborate incarnations of this position can be found in the sociocultural theory (SCT—Lantolf, this volume) and the language socialization (LS—Duff & Talmy, this volume) approaches, because both have developed unique and highly specific definitions of "language learning." Thus, in SCT, language learning is learning to engage in cognitive mediation in the L2. This is done by progressing along a continuum from reliance on collaborative scaffolded L2 activity toward increasingly more independent forms of regulation. In LS theory, on the other hand, language learning is learning to enculturate, that is, learning to become—via participation in language use—an insider who can perform the social meanings and practices of a new L2 community.

But cognitivist SLA and its alternatives also differ along a second dimension, resulting from their position as to whether knowledge exists separate from its context, leading to divergent goals of *abstractness* versus *situatedness*. Cognitive SLA theorists pursue abstractness as a value because they assume that knowledge can stand alone, available in and transferable across bounded minds and contexts. By contrast, socially oriented SLA theorists pursue situatedness, sharing a deliberate choice to emphasize knowledge and learning as parts enmeshed in greater wholes. They thus capitalize on epistemological insights from contextuality, mutuality, contingency, cultural embeddedness, and embodiment. This preference for situatedness is reflected in particular theoretical/analytical principles seen in each alternative, of which I can name here: the microgenetic method in SCT (Lantolf, this volume), retrodiction instead of prediction in complexity theory (CT—Larsen-Freeman, this volume), the poststructuralist definition of identity as hybrid, ambivalent, relational, and fluid across space and time in the identity approach (Norton & McKinney, this volume), the multidirectional contingency of enculturation processes in LS (Duff & Talmy, this volume), unmotivated looking in search of the radical emic perspective in conversation analysis for SLA (CA-SLA—Kasper & Wagner, this volume), and the construct of alignment in the sociocognitive approach (Atkinson, this volume).

A third dimension of difference between cognitive approaches and the alternatives presented in this volume is whether they focus on *entities and objects* versus *actions and processes*. Cognitivist SLA adheres to the former view and relies strongly on taxonomies and categories: "language," "learner," "native speaker," "communicative competence," and so on. By contrast, alternative perspectives capitalize on actions and processes that imply being in action and emergent being. In their constructs and explanations, they invoke images and metaphors of constant flux, relations and practices, and dynamism. As a result, the six alternatives have helped reconceptualize key entity-like constructs as processual ones, which can be listed as follows from more circumscribed to broader in scope:

- *The language faculty* is reconceptualized as the emergent, social co-adaptation of open complex systems by CT (Larsen-Freeman, this volume).
- *Cognition* is reconceptualized as thinking mediated by objects, concepts, others, and self by SCT (Lantolf, this volume); and as adaptive being and acting with(in) the world by the sociocognitive approach (Atkinson, this volume).
- *Interaction* is reconstituted as achieving, maintaining, and repairing intersubjectivity by CA-SLA (Kasper & Wagner, this volume), and the quality of intersubjectivity itself emerges contingently in the unfolding turns of interactants and is thus sequentially and temporally co-produced.
- *Learning* is recast as participating (marginally, peripherally, or legitimately) in recognizably recurrent situated language use, and otherwise observing and performing social values and practices, by LS (Duff & Talmy, this volume) and the sociocognitive approach (Atkinson, this volume).
- And, finally, *sense of self* is reconceptualized as the emergent and ever-changing positioning and repositioning of human agentivity vis-à-vis the power-laden and power-structured social world by identity theory (Norton & McKinney, this volume).

The deployment of socially oriented theories that seek to explain SLA and the three dimensions of difference that have emerged from it have yielded, I believe, uniquely useful insights. Why would such insights be unique and useful? In an article published in a special issue on epistemic diversity and dissent, feminist bioethics philosopher Rebecca Kukla (2006) argued that certain individuals and communities, because of their contingent experiences, perspectival stances, and shared interests, develop an epistemic attunement in certain domains that affords them special acuity and better epistemic warrants in that domain. Kukla's proposal is a recapitulation of feminist standpoint epistemology (e.g., Harding, 1986). She seeks to transcend relativism in "not claiming that truth is relative to a perspective, but rather that different perspectives can yield different forms of rational access to the independent truth" (p. 87). Similarly, I contend that the social outlook on SLA as a whole, and the research communities behind each of the alternatives in this book, have developed stances and acuteness that uniquely add to the field's capacities to investigate additional language learning. Other SLA communities need and can benefit from these alternative perspectives.

The Collective Contribution of Alternative SLA Theories: Beyond Dichotomous Thinking

An important contribution has been made to SLA studies by the collective move of the alternative theories to recast as *actions and processes* the same phenomena that cognitive theories historically portrayed exclusively as *entities and objects* (the third dimension of difference identified in the previous section). The contribution is bold, if subtle, and in my opinion should not be underestimated. Namely, with this process-oriented reconceptualization effort, the SLA alternatives have offered new theoretical and analytical tools that can help overcome dichotomous thinking in future work on additional language learning.

This is no small feat. Rational theories since the Enlightenment have made progress by analytical thinking organized into discrete categories and taxonomies. But a disadvantage of this practice is that it easily creates a straitjacket of dichotomous thinking. Alternative, in-between understandings are impossible when things and phenomena must belong to either–or categories: mind–body, cognition–sociality, langue–parole, competence–performance, acquisition–use, creation–imitation, rule–rote, native–nonnative, and so on. The explanatory value of dichotomous categories and dichotomous thinking has greatly eroded in our contemporary world. Our societies and citizens routinely face non-dichotomous, ambivalent experiences. These experiences of "in-betweenness" (Bhabha, 1994/2004) are afforded by four interrelated phenomena. Globalization has blurred the meaning of geographical distances and national borders (Scholte, 2000); new technologies have rendered obsolete the conceptualization of objective time as a binary of here-and-now versus there-and-then (Ess, 2009); postcolonialism has created a new world order that complicates the conquered–conqueror dialectic of past colonial world orders (Sharp, 2009); and new ethnicities, which emerged out of the sociological realities of immigration and diaspora, have brought (visible and invisible) cultural, linguistic, religious, racial, and ethnic hybridity (Hall, 1991). Why would the value of dichotomous thinking be preserved intact in matters of explaining language and language acquisition, when the world—and with it the research worlds of the social sciences, humanities, and natural sciences (e.g., Oreskes, 2003)—has experienced a shift toward hybrid and fuzzy categories and interpretive, probabilistic, and stochastic logics?

Indeed, the rejection of dichotomies is a shared theme across the chapters of this book, particularly the dichotomies of competence–performance and acquisition–use that have held sway for so long in modern formal linguistics as well as cognitively oriented SLA studies. Rejecting dichotomies and dualisms is easier said than done, however, and the strength in engineering theoretical and analytical tools around activities and processes is that it makes it possible to move forward empirically. An excellent illustration of this point is the ways in which processual understandings of identity have been deployed and are now available for inclusion in actual investigations thanks to alternative theories of SLA, such as portable, situated, and performed identities in CA-SLA (Kasper & Wagner, this volume) and dynamic, hybrid, and relational identities in identity theory (Norton & McKinney, this volume). A more concrete example, and one closer to the traditional concerns of cognitive SLA studies, is the development by Aljaafreh and Lantolf (1994) of a framework for analyzing negative feedback episodes along a 13-point continuum of graduated and contingent other-regulation. This proposal offers a possible analytical solution to cognitive researchers' increasingly felt realization that explicitness and implicitness are not inherent, dichotomous properties of phenomena like recasts or prompts, but contingent upon the contextual details of delivery (Ellis & Sheen, 2006).

Unique Contributions of Specific Alternative Approaches

The unique contributions made by each alternative approach in this book are of no less importance. Admittedly, there is much subjectivity in choosing to highlight only one novel insight stemming from each alternative. I nevertheless try to do just that here.

The two socially oriented SLA theories that have seen the largest research growth thus far are SCT (Lantolf, this volume) and CA-SLA (Kasper & Wagner, this volume). SCT's singular contribution may have been to mount a full research program around the contention that L2 learning is not something that happens to people (in opposition to the Chomskyan view of first language acquisition) but something people make happen through intentional social interaction and co-construction of reflected-upon knowledge. Constructs such as mediation attuned to the Zone of Proximal Development, concept-based instructional praxis, and languaging are tools that articulate this argument for intentional, conscious/explicit language learning at the needed levels of specificity to be researchable. The most powerful and forward-looking insight that CA-SLA has established empirically and theoretically is, in my opinion, that L2 users are not deficient users. The non-deficit view of L2 learning is shared by many in applied linguistics at an intuitive level, but letting it shape research programs has proven more difficult (Seidlhofer, 2001). The CA-SLA antidote for the deficit approach is the view of "doing" communication as a social accomplishment, and the sharp tools that have helped lodge the anti-deficit lens in the empirical realm are CA's radical emic perspective and the construct of intersubjectivity. No phenomenon and no deficit category (e.g., "nativeness," "error") have any reality or content in CA-SLA unless co-oriented to by interactants. In this way, the contention that deficit is not a necessary part of additional language learning need not remain at a theoretical level and instead can be brought into the empirical arena.

Two other alternative perspectives in this book are newer and have just begun to bloom in SLA studies: CT and the sociocognitive approach. Each offers, nevertheless, some unique and useful insights that cannot be found in cognitivism or the other alternatives. CT researchers help tackle a long-lasting theme in SLA—variability—in a truly novel way (Larsen-Freeman, this volume). They teach us that individual variability and change are the two central phenomena to be explained in SLA. Co-adaptation, soft-assembly, and the unknowableness of open complex systems are constructs that move variability to SLA's explanatory center. For its part, the unique insight of the sociocognitive approach is to redirect SLA researchers' imagination to the powerful construct of embodiment and its associated empirical evidence in other fields (Atkinson, this volume), thus extending useful bridges between social approaches and the latest trends in cognitive science that SLA cognitivists may increasingly be willing to cross in the future.

Finally, LS theory and SLA identity approaches are the two alternatives motivated by the broadest social scope among those in this book, as both accommodate substantially more of the macro-realities of L2 learning than the other approaches. Like SCT and CA-SLA, they have now grown into burgeoning and well-established research traditions, although they might be located as easily in the wider landscape of applied linguistics as the narrower field of SLA. What may be the unique contributions to SLA studies made by each? In my opinion, like no other alternative, the LS perspective has been able to carve out a fundamentally transformed and expanded understanding of the "what" of L2 acquisition (Duff & Talmy, this volume). In investigating enculturation into not only new grammars and discourses but also new repertoires of social practices, values, and indexicality, the LS perspective has shown empirically that SLA researchers must account for the fact that learners' goals in learning another language are more realistically grounded in the social world and indexicality, and more complex and subtle, than cognitivism ever allowed for. In a nutshell, LS theory uniquely aids in the recognition that the content of "language" in "language learning" must be radically rethought. SLA identity theory, in turn, takes us even further along this path (Norton & McKinney, this volume). It makes the convincing case that additional language learning is much more than just learning language, even under the widest understandings of what language is. It is about power and social transformation. The irrevocable centrality of power in language learning, which surfaces only optionally in studies conducted under the purview of other alternative theories, becomes the most unique contribution of identity theory to SLA studies after the social turn.

SLA: Stronger and Better after the Social Turn

In sum, cognitive SLA in the 21st century cannot remain unchanged due to the following compelling insights brought about by the deployment of alternative theories:

- Dichotomies are ill-fitted to help us investigate language learning in our contemporary world.
- Second language learning is in important ways intentional, conscious, and explicit.
- Language learning and language learners are not defined by deficit.
- Individual variability is a central construct for studying language development.
- Language learning is supported by embodied experiences (with)in the physical and social world.
- Language learning encompasses not only new grammars and discourses but also social practices, values, and indexicality.
- Additional language learning is always about power as much as about language.

How different cognitive theories and their ongoing research programs will act upon this rich awareness of social, sociocognitive, and sociocultural dimensions of additional language learning remains to be seen. But the intellectual content of cognitivism in SLA will not be untouched by the unprecedented understandings brought about by the arrival and development of these alternative theories.

Diversity among Alternatives

Extending the comparative insight to what might then be common or different among the theories in this book is an informative exercise, because it shows clear signs of intellectual diversity across approaches, rather than simply between alternative and traditional ones. It is striking, indeed, how otherwise clear dimensions of difference between cognitive and socially oriented understandings of SLA do not lead to homogeneous or deterministic choices about ways of doing and valuing research within those alternatives.

In fact, the cognitive–social polarity aligns only partially with the kinds of research methods and standards favored by the cognitive versus alternative SLA theories. Cognitive theories pursue abstractness and therefore often prioritize generalizability of research knowledge. By contrast, the alternatives pursue situatedness and thus often value a different research goal: illuminating the particular via contextualization. However, SCT, CA-SLA, and CT do appear to hold that generalizations can be built on the shoulders of highly contextualized and situated evidence. A second interlocking choice, that of quantitative versus qualitative research methods, is even less useful in trying to map out differences between cognitive and alternative SLA theories, instead highlighting differences among the latter. While the majority of the alternative theories in this book are decidedly qualitative, SCT and CT appear to allow quantitative (as well as qualitative) methods in order to understand situated data and perhaps even to bring about situated interpretations.

The nature of the data counted as most relevant, as well, creates further commonalities and differences that cluster differently across different alternatives. All six approaches invoke the need for longitudinal data, or data that allow for time-scaling and trajectory-tracking, from the turn-by-turn sequentiality of CA-SLA and the sociocognitive approach, to the emergence of learning in SCT's microgenetic method, to the dense longitudinal corpus evidence of CT, all the way to the ethnographic or narrative data collected over long periods of time in the field of LS and identity theory. But other differences in the data types prevalent in each approach are notable.

Thus, naturally occurring oral discourse is the main data source for CA-SLA and the sociocognitive approach, as readers will instantly appreciate by eyeballing the data illustrations given in Kasper and Wagner's and Atkinson's chapters. CT (Larsen-Freeman, this volume) stands alone as an approach that examines diverse product-oriented data types (oral and written, naturally occurring and elicited), but that must be structured as dense longitudinal corpora wherein linguistic variability can be inspected along timescales and the emergence of learning can thus be reconstructed by retrodiction. In this, CT probably stands the closest of all six approaches to interests pursued from traditional cognitive perspectives. It points at new directions for quantitative analyses of learner language capable of handling variability (Larsen-Freeman & Cameron, 2008; Verspoor, de Bot, & Lowie, in press), and in doing so holds great potential for positively impacting cognitive SLA researchers' use of quantification and statistics. Identity theory (Norton & McKinney, this volume) privileges retrospective and self-report data of an ecological kind (e.g., ethnographic interviews; diaries written for both pedagogic and research purposes; fieldnotes crafted during prolonged engagement with research contexts). It has also historically paid more attention to content analysis of such data than to their discursive construction, although this is rapidly changing (see Pavlenko, 2008). SCT (Lantolf, this volume) and LS (Duff & Talmy, this volume) are perhaps the two approaches that accommodate the greatest diversity of data types, as they look for relevant evidence in a free mixture of discourse as well as introspections, retrospections, and self-reports. A difference between these latter two approaches is that the contrived elicitation of data by researchers is widely employed in SCT but sparse in LS, where more naturalistic evidence, often derived via thicker ethnographic engagement, is preferred.

In the end, then, the alternative SLA theories presented here share ontological and epistemological perspectives about the nature of reality, knowledge, language, and learning, but their basic research methodologies are complex and reveal much more diversity than perhaps seems evident at first blush.

Diversity within Cognitivism

The diversity within the SLA alternatives featured in this book also has its counterpart within cognitive SLA approaches. This is often downplayed when framing and explicating SLA alternatives, but should not be forgotten.

In fact, there are at least two noticeably different kinds of cognitivism in SLA. One arises from within formal linguistic frameworks that investigate the possibility that the language faculty is supported by innate knowledge and language-specific mechanisms and relatively independent from other cognitive capacities (e.g., Hawkins, 2001; White, 2003). In these theories, which one could describe as *linguistic cognitivism*, the human language faculty is construed in the most reduced psychological sense of housing core syntax and its morpho-phonological and morpho-semantic interfaces, and environmental influences are defined as outside the scope of research programs. By contrast, the second kind of cognitivism encompasses SLA work by scholars who do not necessarily commit to linguistic nativism and instead place an explanatory premium on interactions between clearly bounded learner-internal and learner-external variables. The term *interactionism* is commonly employed to refer to this family of theories by first language acquisition scholars (Bohannon & Bonvillian, 2009). Interactionist cognitivism encompasses much varied work, including not only the interaction approach (Gass & Mackey, 2007), but also general cognitive theories that often offer conflicting explanations for L2 learning, such as skills acquisition (DeKeyser, 2007) versus input processing (VanPatten, 2007). It has also provided the thrust for work in other SLA domains, such as individual differences (Dörnyei, 2005), cross-linguistic influences (Jarvis & Pavlenko, 2008), task-based language learning (Samuda & Bygate, 2008), and age effects (Muñoz, 2006).

It is as alternatives to interactionist cognitivism, and not so much to linguistic cognitivism, that the approaches in this book can best be understood. True, socially oriented SLA researchers reject Chomskyan positions, such as the compartmentalization of knowledge into the competence–performance dichotomy, and they harshly oppose native competence as a fictive ideal focusing on deficit and core syntax—an impoverished, narrow notion of what is learned. In the end, however, these are broad-brush, philosophical prolegomena that do not find their way into specific parts of alternative approach research programs. Quite simply, socially oriented SLA theories do not aspire to settle theoretical issues of nativism versus empiricism empirically, they just take empiricism as the starting point and then get on with their research.

Struggles over Diversity in SLA

Interactionist cognitivism and the alternative SLA theories presented in this book focus on similar phenomena related to learning agents and their learning environments, but each proposes radically different ways to do so. I believe it is precisely because much is shared between interactionist cognitivism and these alternatives that so much is at stake when it comes to formulating and strategically using difference to advance alternatives in the field or to protect traditional cognitive achievements. There would be no clash, only indifference or mild neglect, if psychologically oriented interactionist cognitivism and socially oriented alternatives shared less in terms of their research investments.

A good example of shared research investments can be found in studying how learners and others handle so-called "errors," or unrecognized/dispreferred linguistic choices, during oral communication. Some 10 years ago, this issue was studied only as "negative feedback" or "oral error correction" through the lens of cognitive-interactionist SLA (see Lyster, in press). At present, the same phenomenon has been the object of sustained attention from alternative theoretical perspectives. In SCT, (Lantolf, this volume) it can be investigated as "graded and contingent other-regulation," building on Aljaafreh and Lantolf's (1994) pioneering study. In CA-SLA (Kasper & Wagner, this volume) it has attracted much empirical attention under the construct of "repair." Working within systemic functional linguistic theory, Mohan and Beckett (2001) also put forth a proposal to approach "error correction" from the viewpoint of negotiation of meaning-making and "editing of discourse," although this interesting new line has not yet been taken up by other researchers. In the future we may witness even more vigor in deploying the full variety of alternative lenses available to SLA researchers on this phenomenon, as indicated in recent publications on "error correction" from the additional theoretical perspectives of LS theory (Friedman, 2009), and CT and usage-based emergentism (Hartshorn et al., 2010). Once again, we do not witness the same degree of shared research interest within linguistic cognitivism. In this family of cognitive theories, the construct is known as "negative evidence," and researchers investigating it as a primary focus (e.g., White, 1991) are the exception rather than the rule. Instead, it is typically examined as a straw man, only then to be discarded as irrelevant to theory building (e.g., Schwartz, 1993).

On Behalf of Epistemological Diversity

In-depth comparative analysis of cognitivism and its alternatives is beyond the scope of this chapter. But even the sketchy notes I have offered so far reveal unheeded and unprecedented theoretical diversity in SLA. We might treat such diversity in three ways. First, we might see it as an impediment to progress toward definitive knowledge-building. In this case, we would reject it and protect ourselves against it. Second, we might see diversity as proof that different research worlds, even within the same discipline, are so isolated and turned inwards that communication across epistemological lines is impossible. In this scenario, we might disparage dissenting views as utterly incomprehensible and would eventually let each research world go about their business without further concern for one another. Third, we might treat diversity as providing epistemic resources that can benefit each of the available research programs. Here we would want to find ways to cultivate mutual, deep engagement across these differences. In other words, we have a choice in SLA studies among entrenchment, incommensurability, and epistemological diversity. Entrenchment is likely to be a temperamental reaction that is unsustainable in the long run. Incommensurability is an option that some may find merit in at this juncture in the history of SLA studies. I want to argue that the third option, epistemological diversity, is the best choice (Ortega, 2005).

The construct of incommensurability, which was developed most notably by Kuhn (1962/1996), posits that implicit theoretical assumptions determine scientific knowledge, its evaluation, and its disciplinary and public communication, and that when different research communities live with different implicit assumptions, they basically create their own language and worldview, making evaluation and communication across epistemologies impossible. Other philosophers of science and education, however, have worked hard to make space for some form of communication across paradigms despite apparent incommensurability. For example, in their discussion of theoretical (in)commensurability in SLA studies, Dunn and Lantolf (1998) identified "dialogic engagement" as a viable alternative to the conflictive spirit that entrenchment and some forms of incommensurability engender. Citing work in philosophical pragmatism, they envisioned researchers engaged in "contesting and defending validity claims in communicative action" and in the process "com[ing] to reflect upon, and potentially reinterpret, their own view of things" (p. 430). Sfard (1998) imagined a similar possibility when she declared the desirability of letting competing metaphors about learning (in her case, acquisition versus participation) thrive because "when two metaphors compete for attention and incessantly screen each other for possible weaknesses, there is a much better chance for producing a critical theory of learning" (p. 11). Critical pragmatism and critical realism have been identified by other applied linguists as attractive alternatives to incommensurability because they promote rational engagement across epistemological lines (e.g., Corson, 1997). The proposed arguments for choosing epistemological diversity over incommensurability are always both moral and epistemic: Acceptance of diversity and engagement with dissent are viewed as desirable normative values related to democracy and liberal ideals of the good life as well as choices that lead to improved knowledge and understanding of the phenomena researchers care about.

Another way to think about dialogic engagement, and a way that appeals less to the rational-logical, critical-liberal bases of pragmatism and critical realism, is via feminist standpoint epistemologies, which seek to challenge received views of what count as knowledge and scientific warrants but also to transcend relativism (see Harding, 1986; Keller & Longino, 1996; Kukla, 2006). I find one such proposal particularly illuminating of the transformative potential of epistemological diversity: the idea of *"world"-traveling* developed by U.S.-based Argentinian poststructuralist feminist María Lugones.

Lugones (2003) wants to nurture the possibility of harvesting resistance from experiences of domination, much like Bhabha (1994/2004) described in-betweenness as a liminal achievement of moments or processes when cultural differences are felt and articulated in nonbinary ways. As with Bhabha, Lugones' main tool is the imagination, and she employs quotation marks to indicate that she asks us to travel to imagined "worlds" rather than physical or temporal ones. "World"-traveling requires exercising our imagination, first, in order to remember experiencing ourselves "being another person in another reality" or "being more than one" (p. 57) and, second, in order to identify with others from their own subject positions by deeply (and in her terms, playfully and lovingly) "understand[ing] *what it is to be them and what it is to be ourselves in their eyes*" (p. 97, italics in original). These two ways of accessing other "worlds" enable us to recognize our plurality as well as that of others. This understanding is transformative because it makes us "fully subjects to each other" (p. 97) and also teaches us to imagine the possibility that people are neither only oppressed nor only oppressors, but both (note the achievement of non-dichotomous knowing here). As Lugones described it:

> By traveling to other people's "worlds," we discover that there are "worlds" in which those who are the victims of arrogant perception are really subjects, lively beings, resisters, constructors of visions even though in the mainstream construction they are animated only by the arrogant perceiver and are pliable, foldable, file-away-able, classifiable.
>
> (p. 97)

From traveling to others' "worlds" emerges the possibility of not only agentive resistance from within accommodation but also empathic understanding of difference, instead of conflictive and hopeless feelings of entrenchment and incommensurability. If we can experience ourselves as more than one and others as they experience both themselves and us, then perhaps we can also understand how other people understand and judge their own knowledge and theories and how they understand and judge ours. This, in turn, makes it possible to imagine ourselves and others as less epistemologically unitary and impermeable than we may be otherwise inclined to assume. If so, then we may be in a better position to engage in genuine dialogue and to cultivate a sense of pluralism of knowledge and values—epistemological diversity—that is very much based on moments and processes where the crossing of our disciplinary "world" boundaries is enabled. It is not important to actually share worldviews, standpoints, knowledge, and epistemic or normative values. As Kukla (2006) noted, this ideal may be unattainable. What is important is to preserve the ideal as a normative value and thus to invest in the possibility that we may end up sharing understandings, even if partially and imperfectly:

> Simply consigning oneself or others to a partial and inaccessible standpoint has to count as a failure of responsibility. Through mutual education and attention we can strive to cultivate a maximally inclusive shared perspective in which all warrants that could be available to anyone are available to everyone.
>
> (p. 92)

For some cognitivists and socially minded SLA researchers alike, no doubt, the existence of shared-but-discordant interests between cognitive theories and their alternatives will be lived as an epistemic disaster leading SLA studies to failure or as a hopeless and even conflictive kind of incommensurability. But it helps to remember that it is precisely because cognitive and alternative theories in SLA often seek to explain overlapping, mutually valued phenomena surrounding additional language learning, but from different ontological and epistemological standpoints, that the feelings of tension, clash, and incommensurability arise. For me, the crisis caused by the social turn in SLA has led the field into the kind of fruitful epistemological diversity that affords unique opportunities to enrich our multilayered understanding of additional language learning. I hope the diverse, alternative SLA theories gathered in this volume will help readers invest in this project of epistemological diversity, leading in the long run to a fuller and ultimately better understanding of the learning of additional languages.

References

Aljaafreh, A., & Lantolf, J. P. (1994). Negative feedback as regulation and second language learning in the zone of proximal development. *Modern Language Journal, 78*, 465–483.

Bhabha, H. (1994/2004). *The location of culture* (Rev. ed.). New York: Routledge.

Block, D. (2003). *The social turn in second language acquisition*. Washington, DC: Georgetown University Press.

Bohannon, J. N. I., & Bonvillian, J. D. (2009). Theoretical approaches to language development. In J. B. Gleason & N. B. Ratner (Eds.), *The development of language* (7th ed.) (pp. 227–284). Boston, MA: Allyn & Bacon.

Corson, D. (1997). Critical realism: An emancipatory philosophy for applied linguistics? *Applied Linguistics, 18*, 166–188.

DeKeyser, R. (2007). Skill acquisition theory. In B. VanPatten & J. Williams (Eds.), *Theories in second language acquisition: An introduction* (pp. 97–112). Mahwah, NJ: Erlbaum.

Dörnyei, Z. (2005). *The psychology of the language learner: Individual differences in second language acquisition.* Mahwah, NJ: Erlbaum.

Dunn, W. E., & Lantolf, J. P. (1998). Vygotsky's zone of proximal development and Krashen's "i + 1": Incommensurable constructs, incommensurable theories. *Language Learning, 48*, 411–442.

Ellis, R., & Sheen, Y. (2006). Reexamining the role of recasts in second language acquisition. *Studies in Second Language Acquisition, 28*, 575–600.

Ess, C. (2009). *Digital media ethics.* Malden, MA: Polity.

Friedman, D. A. (2009). Speaking correctly: Error correction as a language socialization practice in a Ukrainian classroom. *Applied Linguistics, 31*, 346–367.

Gass, S. M., & Mackey, A. (2007). Input, interaction, and output in second language acquisition. In B. VanPatten & J. Williams (Eds.), *Theories in second language acquisition: An introduction* (pp. 173–196). Mahwah, NJ: Erlbaum.

Hall, S. (1991). Old and new identities, old and new ethnicities. In A. D. King (Ed.), *Culture, globalization and the world system* (pp. 41–68). London: Macmillan.

Harding, S. (1986). *The science question in feminism.* Ithaca, NY: Cornell University Press.

Hartshorn, K. J., Evans, N. W., Merrill, P. F., Sudweeks, R. R., Strong-Krause, D., & Anderson, N. J. (2010). Effects of dynamic corrective feedback on ESL writing accuracy. *TESOL Quarterly, 44*, 84–109.

Hawkins, R. (2001). *Second language syntax: A generative introduction.* Malden, MA: Blackwell.

Jarvis, S., & Pavlenko, A. (2008). *Crosslinguistic influence in language and cognition.* Mahwah, NJ: Erlbaum.

Keller, E. F., & Longino, H. (Eds.). (1996). *Feminism and science.* New York: Oxford University Press.

Kuhn, T. S. (1962/1996). *The structure of scientific revolutions* (3rd ed.). Chicago, IL: University of Chicago Press.

Kukla, R. (2006). Objectivity and perspective in empirical knowledge. *Episteme, 3*, 80–95.

Larsen-Freeman, D., & Cameron, L. (2008). *Complex systems in applied linguistics.* New York: Oxford University Press.

Lugones, M. (2003). *Pilgrimages/Peregrinajes: Theorizing coalition against multiple oppressions.* New York: Rowman & Littlefield.

Lyster, R. (in press). Roles for error correction in second language instruction. In C. Chapelle (Ed.), *Encyclopedia of applied linguistics.* Malden, MA: Wiley-Blackwell.

Mohan, B., & Beckett, G. H. (2001). A functional approach to research on content-based language learning: Recasts in causal explanations. *Canadian Modern Language Review, 58*, 133–155.

Muñoz, C. (Ed.). (2006). *Age and the rate of foreign language learning.* Clevedon: Multilingual Matters.

Oreskes, N. (2003). The role of quantitative models in science. In C. D. Canham, J. J. Cole, & W. K. Lauenroth (Eds.), *Models in ecosystem science* (pp. 13–31). Princeton, NJ: Princeton University Press.

Ortega, L. (2005). For what and for whom is our research? The ethical as transformative lens in instructed SLA. *Modern Language Journal, 89*, 427–443.

Pavlenko, A. (2008). Narrative analysis in the study of bi- and multilingualism. In M. Moyer & Li Wei (Eds.), *The Blackwell guide to research methods in bilingualism* (pp. 311–325). Malden, MA: Wiley-Blackwell.

Samuda, V., & Bygate, M. (2008). *Tasks in second language learning.* New York: Palgrave Macmillan.

Scholte, J. A. (2000). *Globalization: A critical introduction.* New York: St. Martin's.

Schwartz, B. D. (1993). On explicit and negative data effecting and affecting competence and linguistic behavior. *Studies in Second Language Acquisition, 15,* 147–163.

Seidlhofer, B. (2001). Closing a conceptual gap: The case for a description of English as a lingua franca. *International Journal of Applied Linguistics, 1,* 133–158.

Sfard, A. (1998). On two metaphors for learning and the dangers of choosing just one. *Educational Researcher, 27*(2), 4–13.

Sharp, J. P. (2009). *Geographies of postcolonialism: Spaces and power of representation.* Thousand Oaks, CA: Sage.

VanPatten, B. (2007). Input processing in adult second language acquisition. In B. VanPatten & J. Williams (Eds.), *Theories in second language acquisition* (pp. 115–136). Mahwah, NJ: Erlbaum.

Verspoor, M., de Bot, K., & Lowie, W. (Eds.). (in press). *A dynamic approach to second language development: Methods and techniques.* Amsterdam: Benjamins.

White, L. (1991). Adverb placement in second language acquisition: Some effects of positive and negative evidence in the classroom. *Second Language Research, 7,* 133–161.

White, L. (2003). *Second language acquisition and Universal Grammar.* New York: Cambridge University Press.

INDEX

ALTERNATIVE APPROACHES TO SECOND LANGUAGE ACQUISITION

This volume presents six alternative approaches to studying second language acquisition—"alternative" in the sense that they contrast with and/or complement the cognitivism pervading the field. All six approaches—sociocultural, complexity theory, conversation-analytic, identity, language socialization, and sociocognitive—are described according to the same set of six headings, allowing for direct comparison across approaches.

Each chapter is authored by leading advocates for the approach described: James Lantolf for the sociocultural approach; Diane Larsen-Freeman for the complexity theory approach; Bonny Norton and Carolyn McKinney for the identity approach; Patricia Duff and Steven Talmy for the language socialization approach; Gabriele Kasper and Johannes Wagner for the conversation-analytic approach; and Dwight Atkinson for the sociocognitive approach.

Introductory and commentary chapters round out this volume. The editor's introduction describes the nature of the cognitivism pervading the field, setting the stage for discussion of alternative approaches. Lourdes Ortega's commentary considers the six approaches from an "enlightened traditional" perspective on SLA studies—a viewpoint that is cognitivist in orientation but broad enough to give serious and balanced consideration to alternative approaches.

This volume is essential reading in the field of second language acquisition.

Dwight Atkinson is Associate Professor at Purdue University, specializing in second language acquisition, second language writing, and qualitative research approaches. He is author of *Scientific Discourse in Sociohistorical Context: The Philosophical Transactions of the Royal Society of London, 1675–1975* (1999) and co-editor of *Directions in Applied Linguistics* (2005).